ESSENTIAL CARE FOR DOGS

Jackie Drakeford
and
Mark Elliott
BVSc. VetMFHom. MRCVS. MIPsiMed. PCH

ESSENTIAL CARE FOR DOGS

A Holistic Way of Life

SWAN·HILL
PRESS

This book is dedicated to all vets who
work within the spirit of holism

The photographs used in this book are mainly copyright of the author and a few
others are reproduced by permission of Camilla Beaton, P. Blackman, E. Dearden and
B. Hurley.

First published in the UK in 2005
by Swan Hill Press, an imprint of Quiller Publishing Ltd

British Library Cataloguing-in-Publication Data
    A catalogue record for this book
    is available from the British Library

ISBN 1 904057 45 4

The information in this book is true and complete to the best of our
knowledge. All recommendations are made without any guarantee on the part
of the Publisher, who also disclaims any liability incurred in connection with
the use of this data or specific details.

Printed in China

Swan Hill Press

An imprint of Quiller Publishing Ltd.
Wykey House, Wykey, Shrewsbury, SY4 1JA
Tel: 01939 261616 Fax: 01939 261606
E-mail: info@quillerbooks.com
Website: www.swanhillbooks.com

Contents

A contented group of Italian Greyhounds

1 Ahead of the Game

Choosing the right dog and preparing your home

Whether you have had dogs all your life or are about to get your first one, choosing the right dog for your lifestyle is an important decision. You will be asking yourself exactly what you want from the dog, what you do not want, and of course what you can offer the dog in return for the lifetime of love and companionship that she will offer you. Do you want a pedigree or a crossbreed, a large, small or medium dog, a high or low maintenance type? How much time and effort do you want to put into training her, what sort of family is she expected to fit in with, what other pets and commitments do you have? And of course, what sort of dog do you like looking at? Choosing a dog purely for her looks has the same disaster potential as choosing a spouse that way, but even so, you will be looking at that dog for a long time, longer than a lot of marriages last, so it is unfair to both you and the dog if you choose one that you do not find pleasing to the eye. Equally, it is a bad idea to choose a dog because you feel sorry for her. The best reason for choosing a particular dog is because, having set eyes on her, you feel that your life would be impoverished without her. If, however, she is already here, and you have to make the best of someone who is perhaps not what you would have chosen (and she of course is having to make the best of you) then keeping her happy and in the best of health will go a long way towards smoothing your relationship. Ideally, you will be able to choose your dog, and a little homework before you go out to find her will be time very well spent.

UNDERSTANDING

Dog care has changed radically over the last few decades, mostly for the better, with more people willing to invest time and money in their dogs' welfare, and valuing them as family members. Understanding of the dog as a dog, however, has correspondingly been lost. Fewer people grow up with dogs – work commitments often preclude owning a pet that needs so much care and company – and even fewer have any experience of the dog as a working animal. Consequently, when the working instinct shows itself, or the dog does something that is quite normal for a dog to do but not perhaps the right side of human social behaviour, people are startled and confused and have no previous experience upon which to draw. Modern dog behaviourists sometimes add to the problem by seeing issues such as aggression, dominance or hypersexuality where they don't really exist, because they too are unfamiliar with the natural dog.

For many new owners, keeping a dog is something not so much of an uncharted voyage as an overcharted one, with lots of 'experts' adding their two penn'orth and giving conflicting advice. Our attitude towards dogs has changed tremendously, and there is considerable social and sometimes legal pressure on what is essentially normal, unremarkable dog behaviour. This book seeks to reintroduce the dog, not as a fluffy toy or child substitute, but as the wonderful, vibrant and above all different beast that she is. In order to care for her properly, and to get the most out of her company, we who are supposedly more intelligent must rediscover her needs and motives, and instead of trying to suppress the natural dog in her, learn to enjoy it. People who are at ease with their dogs enjoy them so much more than those who are frequently at loggerheads with them. The roots of this comfortable situation lie in knowing what to expect, and gently adapting it to suit both of you. A dog has to be a dog, has no other choice than to be a dog, and should be permitted to be a dog.

The fact that she has a will, needs and desires of her own can come as a shock to people who have never had much to do with dogs previously, especially when she demonstrates that she enjoys fulfilling her own needs more than she does yours. Because many of us lead lives that are totally divorced from other species, we do not realise that a puppy will behave like a toddler, complete with tantrums, that the adolescent dog will challenge your authority, the mature dog will not be in her prime for ever, and that the elderly dog needs extra care, that her senses will become dulled, and she may suffer from senility. The dog does not realise the extent of her dependence on us, nor that human fickleness can betray her for simply behaving like a dog. Because we are so far from the raw natural world, we often do not perceive that our dog is still very much a part of it, and it a part of her. We have buried our own natures so deeply that we demand far too much of our dogs sometimes, expecting them to treat our houses and gardens as objects of value, to tailor their feeding and exercise requirements to our own commitments and convenience, to 'understand every word we say' when we don't bother to show them what we want, but only scold them for doing what we don't want. If we are ignorant, loving them is not enough. We can innocently condemn them to all manner of loneliness, frustration and boredom, then be annoyed when they find ways of alleviating their tedium that don't suit us. There are issues of dog behaviour that never seem to be explained, and the result is disharmony between dog and owner. We can only be human: they can only be dog. Sometimes we have to meet halfway.

PEDIGREE OR CROSSBREED?

If you choose a pedigree dog, you will have a very good idea of what the finished article will be in terms of size, colour, and so on. With a mongrel, there is always a question mark over how she will turn out, though you will be able to make an educated guess by looking at the size of her paws and limbs relative to her age, and she may well look distinctly like the mixture that is in her. Black, black and white and black and tan dogs hold their colour, spotted or flecked breeds start white and develop their markings later, but pure white dogs are born white. With other colours, a general rule of thumb is that they are born dark and the coat lightens as the pup grows. In terms of health, almost every pure breed of dog has a tendency to this or that problem, and it is important to research the breed that you have chosen to see what these are.

Some breeds are very unhealthy indeed, some have the potential to be so but good rearing and general care can avoid these conditions developing, and some are very healthy, with only the occasional problem. Responsible breeders will have both parents tested before they breed from them, and will make the results available to you. Beware, however, of the breeder who says that the dogs are (for instance) 'hip and eye scored' but does not have the results to show you. I vividly remember one such who bred from a dog with an appalling hip score. Yes the dog had been scored all right, and the pups were duly advertised as having had both parents scored, but the breeder conveniently never had the score results to hand.

It is always worth a chat with your vet to see what he or she sees most of, and within which breeds, plus an average cost of treatment. Some breeds are such health timebombs that canine insurance companies load the premium against them – again worth a check before you ever commit yourself to one breed. If there is a breed with known health issues but which has stolen your heart, then choose your breeder carefully and ask for advice before you buy. Most breeders are extremely knowledgeable about their particular breed, and can give you useful information, which you should heed. If they say do not exercise the dog very much before it is two years old, and do not let her run up and down stairs or jump out of the car, then be prepared for trouble if you ignore this. Look at the older dogs that the breeder has, and see what condition they are in. Ask yourself if you can cope with what you see. Can they walk freely? Would it break your heart if the breed had an average lifespan of six to eight years? Could you cope with a dog that had to have heart medicine when still relatively young? If you are after a breed with known respiratory difficulties, can you handle the gasping, wheezing and snoring that is natural for that breed? Are you willing to go 'the extra mile' in coping with distressing skin conditions? Would a dog with a strong natural body odour, or one that drooled sheets of saliva, repel you? Better to find all this out before you part with several hundred pounds for starters and pay the vet's mortgage for years afterwards.

The crossbred litter – anybody's guess

Would a dog that drools be a problem?

Most breeders would rather you 'wasted their time' by asking and seeing, than place a puppy in the wrong home. In fact, you are likely to find that a good breeder will grill you about the kind of home you can offer, too.

Crossbreeds and mongrels rarely have anything like the health problems displayed by purebred dogs because of a condition known as 'hybrid vigour' where the health of the offspring of the first cross of any two pure breeds is far better than the health of either parent breed. Although hybrid vigour supposedly only exists in the offspring of two pure breeds, observation teaches that the vast majority of mongrel dogs have far less in the way of inherited health problems than the majority of pedigree dogs. They are tough, usually free from physical exaggeration, and lead long, trouble-free lives, often only needing veterinary care as the result of injury, or in extreme old age. Humans have altered the shape of the dog, sometimes unforgivably so, in breeding for this or that characteristic, but it seems that once the pedigree is left behind, the crossbred dog reverts as quickly as possible to a healthier animal in every way. Observations of street dogs around the world indicate that there is an optimum shape, size and colour to which the dog species will regress within a few generations.

COAT

Some breeds have such a profuse coat that they need professional grooming. This might hold no fears for you: you can learn how to turn your dog out exquisitely, and

A high-maintenance coat

What about moulting?

be justifiably proud in doing so. Or you can have the money and commitment to take your dog to a groomer at frequent intervals. However, if you cannot fulfil either of these requirements, then it is unwise to think that you can get by with the kitchen scissors, or horse clippers. Think carefully before you choose a breed whose coat needs to be sculpted.

Would a dog that moulted be of concern to you? Some short-coated dogs can moult just as much as long-coated dogs, and the hairs will find their way everywhere. Some dogs have double coats, with a soft underfluff and long guard hairs on top. Will it be a chore or a pleasure to keep the coat clean and free from dead hair? Some coats pick up mud, twigs and other outdoor detritus, to scatter lavishly around the house. Are you likely to resent this? If you have the heating on high throughout the colder months, and keep your dog indoors, there is going to be a corresponding long-term moult for your dog. For some people, this is merely a matter of getting a more appropriate vacuum cleaner, but for others it can take on the mantle of a tragedy. Equally, you can get a thin-coated dog, or even a hairless or partly hairless one, which will minimise moulting and coat care, but mean that your dog will have to wear a coat when she goes outside in cold weather instead. And of course, you will have to have the heating on indoors. Is an increase in the heating bill preferable to an hour of grooming four times a week? Only you can answer that.

TEMPERAMENT AND BEHAVIOUR

Like any other animals, including people, different dogs within a litter will have different temperaments, and different breeds will display breed-specific behaviour patterns. With a mongrel, you will be able to take an educated guess if some of the ingredients are obvious, or failing that, will have to wait and see. It is extremely important to get a dog whose temperament is sympathetic to yours, and to your lifestyle. For instance, if you have a lot of small pets such as rabbits and guinea pigs, a dog with a highly developed prey drive is not for you. If yours is a rowdy household full of loud music, television on in every room, children shouting and doors slamming, you should not consider a gentle, introverted breed. If you have retired neighbours who like quiet, or shift workers who need to sleep during the day, a dog that likes to hear its own voice will cause misery. Do you intend to take your dog for miles of walks every day, rain or shine, or do you need one with more modest exercise requirements? Are you willing to commit to some training each day, are you competent to take on one of the more independent breeds and put in sufficient work to make her socially acceptable? Better to find out now.

It is a curious fact that breeders who will give you every help with the physical characteristics of their particular breed can be remarkably coy when asked about behaviour. Sometimes they simply don't know: show dogs in particular tend to be kept in a very artificial environment, often never exercised outside the home paddock, nor socialised away from the breeder's other dogs. Though few pet dogs receive much obedience training, the majority of show dogs get none at all, though a great deal of effort will be spent on 'ringcraft' which is, after all, their job. The consequence is that some show people will accept as normal what a pet owner would not tolerate, especially in matters of house-training or excessive noise. This is worth remembering when many pedigree pets are originally from a litter bred for the show ring: the best are kept for show, and the rest are homed as pets. The behaviour that might drive you to drink is either unknown by or irrelevant to the show dog breeder. He or she has raised a bouncing, healthy litter with the objective of meeting the breed criteria exactly, and these are physical criteria only. I would also add that, to succeed in the show ring and not break down under the pressure, a show dog does not need intelligence. Working dogs and mongrels knock spots off show dogs when it comes to grey matter, and this is not always such a good thing. The smarter the dog, the more challenging she can be as a companion. Working dogs tend to be more reactive, quicker on the uptake, and quicker to respond. They are demanding to train because they are so smart, whereas show dogs are demanding to train because they are less clever. Choose what suits your temperament.

There are some lovely euphemisms with regard to behaviour. As with estate agents' jargon, it can be amusing to read between the lines.

Independent	Train it if you can; we couldn't
Good House Dog	Barks incessantly
Full of Life	Hyperactive
Good Guard	Stands over anything, growling
Family Dog	Messy personal habits
Hound	Deaf once on a scent
Forward Going	Disappears like snow in summer
Gundog	Retrieves things you'd rather not touch
Sighthound	Often need binoculars to see it
Sheepdog	Rounds anything up
Sporty	Lamentable tendency to vanish down holes

Hound types – deaf once on a scent

PUPPIES

Having established what sort of dog you would like, the most usual practice is to find a list of breeders of that particular breed if you are after a pedigree dog. This can be obtained by contacting the Kennel Club (see: Useful Addresses), but be warned – Kennel Club (KC) registration is only that – it does not guarantee anything other than that the dogs are pure bred. It is for you to establish whether the pups seem healthy and well-reared. Healthy pups are round and active, don't have runny eyes, noses or bums, and don't smell of anything except puppy – a curious, slightly peppery smell. Well-socialised pups are eager to meet you, running up to you in a bunch, and, having satisfied their curiosity, toddling off again to play or sleep. Check with the breeder when feeding time is, and ask to visit around then, because you can't pick your puppy from a sleeping heap half as well as you can when the whole bunch of them is dancing about. Puppies that are reared in the house, with all its attendant noise and comings and goings, are likely to be more forward than pups reared in kennels or sheds, but don't shy away from the outdoor litter.

With large litters and large breeds, out of doors is often the only way to survive rearing them! An outside litter that has had plenty of human contact will be nearly as good as the indoor one; beware, however, of shy, cringing pups who have probably only had human contact when someone comes in to feed and clean them. However far you have come, don't buy puppies that tug your heartstrings, perhaps because they look sickly and dirty, because they seem frightened, have big sad eyes, or because if you take one, there is just one more left (how convenient) so the breeder will do you a special price for the pair. Don't buy from the breeder who won't let you see the litter or the mother, and comes to the door with one pup, which is thrust into your arms if you are alone, or those of the nearest child if you come en famille. This is quite different from the breeder who genuinely does only have one puppy left, and tells you which one it is, but lets you see the pup with its siblings and mother. Above all,

Puppies reared in the house

please do not buy from a pet shop, or from a puppy dealer. Beware those advertisements in your local paper that start with something like 'adorable' or 'cuddly' and then continues with a list of breeds eg 'Loveable Westies, Golden Retrievers, King Charles Spaniels....'. Good wine needs no bush, and good breeders don't need to advertise in the small ads or use words like 'fluffy' and 'cute' to sell their pups. Few breeders breed a whole list of different breeds, either. Pups from pet shops and dealers, while they might be well fed, may not have been carefully bred from health-screened parents, and may have missed out on vital socialisation. It really is not worth the gamble: substandard puppies turn into substandard dogs. At best, you will have significant health problems to deal with; more worryingly, there might be bad temperaments. Never buy a puppy for which you feel 'sorry', for it just gives the dealers and bad breeders more money to carry on breeding. It sounds hard, but you are far better to put all that love and hard work into an animal that will bring you joy, rather than one which will cost you a fortune and break your heart at the end of it. Rubbish puppies and good ones are not very different in price, but you will pay handsomely for the bad ones all their lives.

Also beware of the litter that is advertised as having been 'reared with children'. Children and puppies are made for each other, but 'reared with children' can also mean mauled and terrified by children. Very young children are hard work, and so are very young puppies: unless this is a professional arrangement where kennel staff are employed, it is a racing certainty that the puppy care will have come a long way behind the demands of the children. While some breeders make a fine job of rearing both, and both will benefit enormously from being brought up together, there are too many parents who allow children to pull puppies about. I saw a litter raised by a woman whose toddler took to carrying the puppies around by their heads. She made no attempt to correct this, and all of the puppies grew up to be cripples, though of course it was the new owners who discovered this. I still know the woman (who has given up breeding, thank goodness) and she still refers to the litter as having been 'an unlucky one' without the slightest idea of the cause of their bad luck. So, 'reared with children' does not necessarily mean that the puppies will adore children – if you follow up an advertisement like this, take time to see how the children interact with them, and if the pups are being treated like toys, take your money elsewhere. If, however, the children are respectful of the puppies and play nicely with them, those puppies are likely to be very good family dogs.

Suppose you have decided on a crossbreed: these will be advertised in the small ads. and it is up to you to decide if they are what you want. See them with their mother, and if possible find out about the father – most will have been bred to a local dog and you should be able to at least see a photograph. Sometimes the bitch owners have no idea of what the father was, or there could be several to choose from, but if they know, then you can have a good idea of how the pups will turn out. Price is always interesting with this sort of litter: rearing puppies properly is not cheap, and also it is a sad fact that people value what they pay for, so do expect to pay a reasonable price. However, some people do rather take the mickey, and I have seen crossbreds advertised at several hundred pounds – for which you could buy a pedigree dog. Unless a dog has been crossbred for a particular purpose, the way some working dogs are, it is not worth the price of a pedigree dog.

The dog rescue centres are good places to look for pups, but these really are a lottery, for there will be little idea of parentage unless the mother was brought in with them. Some staff are very astute at working out a dog's breeding, and some won't have a clue but will make something up to please the punters: it is a very individual issue. I know a twenty-nine inch greyhound/saluki cross that, when she was homed as a pup, was said to be a Jack Russell terrier cross whippet. Pups can be much of a muchness to begin with, but you should have an idea of how big they will grow by looking at the growth plates, which are the 'lumps' on the wrist and hock joints, and by the size of the puppy's feet. If of course you aren't at all worried by size or breeding, and confident to take the pup that catches your eye – a perfectly good way of choosing one – then the rescued litter at the dogs' home is a good place to start.

ADOPTION RESTRICTIONS

Dog rescues charge an 'adoption fee' for every dog they re-home, and at time of writing, this is usually in the region of £100. Pay up with good grace, for this is little enough compared to the costs of rescuing a dog and giving her basic care for the duration of her stay. Some dog rescues offer professional 'aftercare' in the form of approved dog trainers and behaviourists, and if you take a dog with an ongoing medical condition, some will pay the veterinary bills too. Some will give you a potted history of the dog, her likes and dislikes, and her background, which is immensely helpful, but with other places, you are on your own once you have taken the dog. I

Homed as 'Jack Russell terrier/whippet cross'!

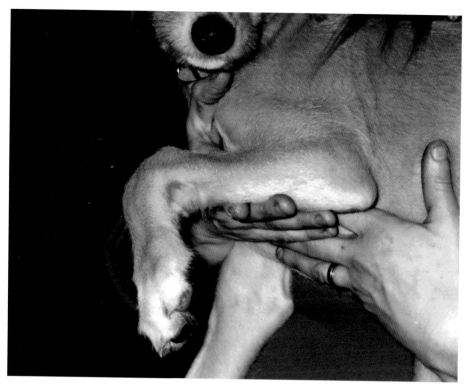

Growth plates on wrist

have found many dog rescues to be rather economical with a dog's age; either they genuinely do not know, or they routinely knock off a few years because they find younger dogs are easier to place. The name that the dog has at the rescue may well have only been hers since she came in: if you don't like it, feel free to change it.

With some places, a professional assessment is made, which is invaluable but expensive; with others, you find out the hard way, or else take the dog with sweeping generalisations (never let her off the lead/unsuitable with cats/keep her muzzled) but no mention of how to train out any contentious behaviour, or even that it is possible. Expect to have a 'home check' from a member of staff, who will want to see that your garden is adequately fenced, and that the dog is not going to be left alone for long spells (how long is too long varies with each rescue centre). They may also do an interim check to see that the dog has settled in. These checks are undertaken in the dog's best interests, so be good-humoured about them, and if changes are recommended, they are proposed for the dog's benefit and to help you to live happily together. A few people don't realise, for instance, that a dog must be properly fenced in, or that if you can't afford to fence the whole garden, a part of it made into a pen, or preferably a kennel and run, will suffice. However, a few rescue centres go further. Most insist that the dog is castrated or spayed, some will not allow the dog to be worked, and a few will not even let the dog be kept in a kennel – which is odd considering that is how most of them are kept when in rescue.

Some of these restrictions are unreasonable: working-bred dogs love to work, and there is nothing wrong with keeping a dog entire as long as you are responsible about it. A warm, dry kennel can be a haven for a dog, and it is useful to have somewhere that she regards as her territory where she can be left safely away from unsuitable visitors, even if she lives mostly in the house. The rescues say that, technically, the dog remains their property, even though money has changed hands, and that the 'adoption' can be cancelled by them at any time, and they can take the dog back. I don't know whether this is legally enforceable, but it must put a lot of people off taking a rescue dog, which is a pity.

OLDER DOGS

You might choose to bypass all this puppy business, and get an adult dog. There are many advantages to this, and a few disadvantages as well. Many dogs come into rescue as 'teenagers', and if you have teenage children, you might sometimes wish that you could do the same with yours. It takes a great deal of love and commitment to ride out the storm of a stroppy adolescent, and to remind yourself of the lovely person/dog that lurks underneath all the raging hormones and attitude. Some people can't be bothered, so when the cute puppy phase ends, they get rid of the dog. What you will get is a teenage hooligan, probably completely untrained, but if so, also unspoilt. It takes a little time and a lot of patience to set one of these on the right road again, and your reward is immense, for the result can be a marvellous dog. One of mine came to me that way: I was her third home, and she was under a year old. She was one of the easiest dogs I have ever had, and a delight to own.

Adult dogs often come up for rehoming, usually through no fault of their own. Marriage breakup, work commitments, a transfer abroad, ill health, a new baby, having to take on an elderly parent or an invalid – suddenly the dog has to go. Dogs cannot follow their owners into most types of sheltered housing or nursing homes, and of course sometimes the dog outlives the owner and there is no-one willing to take her on. These dogs can be depressed, even traumatised, by their change in circumstance, and often the right holistic remedy will be of great value for helping them to survive their grief and bewilderment (See Chapter Eight). Possibly the greatest tragedy is when an elderly dog is cast off because she has become expensive in health terms, or to make room for a new puppy. These older dogs have so much to offer the right person: puppy behaviour and adolescent tantrums are long past, the dog is usually clean in the house and may well have been properly trained at some point, she will be used to being left for a reasonable time, happy to go for car rides, and she won't want as much exercise as she did in her youth. Drawbacks can be an increase in age-related health problems, ingrained bad habits (but these can be trained out) and perhaps some simple care and maintenance issues such as dirty teeth or obesity. Obviously, you will consider what lifespan an older dog has left, and only you can decide whether the ease of having her at that age is worth the inevitable decline and death coming sooner. I'd say go for it: with proper care, they can last much longer than the average, and they have so much to offer.

GRATITUDE

Please don't expect a rescued dog to be 'grateful'. Some that have been through bad times can be immensely appreciative of simple pleasures like proper food, care and exercise, but others can be depressed and mistrustful. It takes time for them to come round, especially if they have had several homes. They may have deep-rooted terrors which they can never overcome, sometimes quite obscure ones like the smell of diesel, men in hats, or public houses. They are not being 'silly' and should not be forced to face up to their fears. Time is a great healer but cannot heal all things. Sometimes changes come about over such a long period that you hardly notice them: some two years after I took on my rescue dog, one of my friends said to me that she had finally lost 'that haunted look'.

BREED RESCUES

If you are set on a particular breed, you would do well to contact the breed rescue. Dealing only in their breed, these rescues are extremely knowledgeable, do a thorough assessment on each dog that comes in and each person who wants one, and do their considerable best to place each dog as an individual. The breed rescues don't pull their punches either, and will warn you if there are any character or physical attributes that you need to know about. They usually offer professional aftercare if there are health or behaviour hiccups, too. I cannot understand why the big dog rescue charities do not make more use of this expertise. You can find out individual breed rescues from the Kennel Club, or by doing a Search on the Internet.

WARNING

Because each breed has its peculiarities, and because what is unsuitable for one home is no problem to another, I have – mostly – not mentioned breeds by name. However, I am going to make a single exception as a warning to the first-time dog owner. Avoid the cross between a border collie and a labrador. For some reason, this cross usually embodies the worst traits of each breed, and a great many dogs of this cross are euthanased for aggression. In experienced hands, a dog of this breeding will be a good companion, for they are intelligent, and eager for occupation, but they can easily go the other way. Should you wonder at this, I can recommend the following two tests: go to all your local rescue centres and see how many dogs of this type are in their kennels. Buy all the glossy dog magazines for two months: read their problem pages and note how many letters refer to this cross or to 'crossbred collies' or 'labrador cross'.

While there will always be exceptions, this is most usually a dog for the expert, and not for a family home. Leave well alone.

PREPARING YOUR HOME

It is really exciting to be looking forward to your new dog. You may have a bit of a wait, perhaps while a litter is born, or a puppy becomes old enough to leave home, or maybe the dog rescues don't have quite what you want available just yet. Use the time wisely to dog-proof your home and garden – if you don't want it stress-tested to destruction, then hide it, move it or fence it off – and browse through some information about the type of dog that you have chosen. Indulge yourself with a trip to a pet accessories emporium, and choose a few toys and a food and water bowl for your new family member, some Vet-bed and maybe a dog bed. Remember the dog bed will be chewed, so don't push the boat out. Time enough for a fancy bed when she has outgrown the need to gnaw everything. Charity shops can be good sources of suitable bedding, as well as soft toys, but don't buy anything with bits like glass eyes that can be pulled out and swallowed. If buying pet shop toys, pick ones that will feel good in her mouth – shiny nylon in bright colours has great people appeal but is not as nice to mouth as canvas or cotton. One of my puppies treasured an old leather wallet – no dangerous metal bits – but of course if you do this, you must keep leather goods that are not puppy toys well out of reach.

You will need a soft brush and a flea comb, and some nail clippers. It will be a while before puppy is big enough to wear an ID tag, but you might as well order it now. If you are taking on a grown dog, then a collar and lead will be needed too. Now is the time to visit a few different dog training classes and see which one will suit you. I have to say that, while this would be a good time to train the family as well, experience shows that you might as well whistle Dixie for all the co-operation you are likely to get. The sudden tidiness which is the only way to save possessions from puppy modification tends not to happen until the risk is actual, and a few important items have been destroyed. However, a certain amount of shutting doors and gates training would not come amiss, and it is useful to affix bolts to gates and organise the odd padlock. Don't forget that no matter how you drill people, there is always some oaf who will leave a gate open, and many dogs are lost this way. Make sure that yours cannot escape if this happens.

SLEEPING

Caring owners are aware that the right food and sufficient exercise are important considerations, but relatively few give sufficient thought to sleeping arrangements. Yet sleep deprivation leads straight into illness for humans, and it is much the same with dogs. Ever been 'put up' by friends with the most uncomfortable of beds, or worse, being deemed sufficient for the guest room? Remember how quickly you became short-tempered, and the sheer bliss of going home and sleeping in your own bed? Comfortable beds are not a sin, but an essential part of maintaining good health, and as far as dogs are concerned, 'where' is just as important as 'what'.

Dogs spend the larger part of their day asleep: this sleep is light, easily disturbed, and full of dreaming. The dog will awaken at the slightest thing, especially if it is the sort of noise or sequence of events that lead up to something that might concern a dog. Little puppies and old dogs sleep deeply and can be frightened and disoriented if awakened suddenly. 'Let sleeping dogs lie' goes the old saying, and we should. Furthermore, they should have somewhere to sleep that is not a busy human thoroughfare, that is safe from 'invasion' from other animals or visitors, and that they do not feel they have to defend. Beds should be raised off the floor: a blanket on a concrete surface is not enough, and even a proper bed will take the chill if directly in contact with the ground. Dogs like dark, covered places to sleep, and humans like to be able to get at beds and bedding to clean it, so find an arrangement that caters for both requirements. When you wash dog bedding, take care to use a non-allergenic detergent, and keep away from fabric softener – it smells as bad to your dog as the 'doggy' bed smelled to you. Also be careful what you use to wash floors in dog areas, and rinse them well – dogs can develop allergies from lying in floor-cleaner.

Kennelled dogs can have a choice of bedding: hay is softer than straw, but both

A bed to grow into

can be dusty and harbour parasites. Shavings are clean and absorbent, but not very warm, and bits of all of these can sneak into eyes and ears. Paper bedding is warm and hygienic, but beware the sort made from strong fibres, which can wind around legs and tails and pull tight. Blankets, Vet-bed, duvets if your dog is past the chewing stage, are all warm, clean and safe, and equally appropriate in kennel or house. Dogs are great snugglers, and appreciate the sort of bedding that can be raked up into a pile and then wriggled into. A smart fabric bed might look great to you, but it doesn't have a high snuggle factor – put a blanket on top and see how much more your dog enjoys it. Beds stuffed with polystyrene beads are lovely for dogs to scrunch down into (very noisily – don't have one in your bedroom) but if the dog decides to dismember it, you will be finding bits of polystyrene for years afterwards. Does this sound like the voice of experience? Beads even sneaked into the freezer, I can tell you.

HOUSE RULES

Decide where house demarcation lines are before you ever bring the dog home. Dogs don't always feel secure if they have access to too much house, and it is sensible to restrict them to a few areas, at least until house rules are established. Upstairs is better out of bounds to puppies, who should not be taxing their growing limbs by pelting up and down stairs, and who are still learning house-training. Newly rescued dogs, too, are better where you can keep an eye on them, until you find out all about their little

A toy that feels good in the mouth

Sleeping arrangements – informal

Sleeping arrangements – luxurious

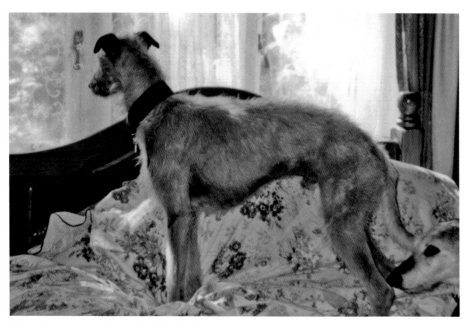

If you don't want the dog on the bed, shut the door

foibles – remembering that a behaviour problem to one person is a sign of character to another. Family members who don't want a dog in their room should learn to shut the relevant door. However, it is unhelpful and bewildering to the dog if you want her to stay downstairs, and the children keep smuggling her into their rooms. Dogs prefer order to subterfuge. If you have furnishings that you wish to keep smart, deny the dog access to those areas unless you are there too. Don't expect her to 'know' she should keep off the furniture in one room if you allow her on it in others. The two best dog training aids in the world are the door and the lead: shut the door indoors and put the dog on the lead outdoors whenever you need to establish control.

LIFESTYLE

Finally, be ready to enjoy the companionship of a naturally healthy dog. Your life will never be quite the same again, your house and garden never quite as pristine, but then neither will they be quite as important. You will be going out in the kind of weather and at the sorts of times that you would not previously have considered, and you will do so gladly. Your wardrobe will change: walking boots, coats and hats will dominate, while your smart clothes will be in a smaller size because of the good effects of all that exercise you are taking. Dry-cleaning will be a thing of the past: if it doesn't wash, you won't be buying it. Because of the positive effects that natural feeding has on your dog, you may well change your own eating habits for the better.

Your garden will never be quite the same

Because of the gentleness and effectiveness of natural therapies on your dog, you might try these yourself, and discover the benefits of working with your immune system for better health. Through your dog, you will read the pleasure from a dip in an icy pond, running along the beach, or following an exciting scent. If you are not ready or willing for these changes, then turn back now, while you still can.

NATURAL HEALTH

Even with breeds that are notorious for inherited illnesses, dogs have an inborn potential for natural good health, which we can enhance by proper feeding, housing, exercise and, yes, training, because a trained dog is much happier and more secure than an untrained dog, and happiness is healthier than unhappiness. Dogs like to be secure in their position within their human family; contrary to what old-fashioned behaviour therapists preach, most dogs are not a seething mass of dominance seeking an outlet, and are quite content with their place in your family. Dogs do become stressed, though, when they perceive themselves in charge or needing to take charge because the human owner seems weak and indecisive, so proper training is necessary.

While the following pages introduce you to the best ways of keeping a natural dog, we do mention several methods of enhancing health holistically. This does not mean that we are opposed to the use of drugs or surgery, just that it is preferable to work within the dog's own framework of natural health for as long as possible.

Orthodox medicine is really only concerned with treating the physical symptoms of disease and is reluctant to accept those therapies that do not fit in with its dogma. The cynic would say that drugs which cannot be patented and therefore be hugely income-earning, and which cure rather than create dependency, are of little interest to the pharmaceutical industry. Consider all we read about development of vaccines for this and that minor illness: the ultimate way to make money is to create a need in the 'healthy' population (not that I am against vaccines, because for life threatening diseases they are essential), and some would also consider neutering in the same capacity. Holistic medicine on the other hand, be it for humans or animals, concerns itself not only with the physical aspects of disease, but also the mental and emotional world of the patient, exploring aspects of lifestyle, environment and diet that all add up to achieving a healthy state with a balanced lifestyle that is sustainable long term. A short list of these natural therapies follows; there are others we do not mention, which does not mean that they are less good or should be disregarded, but simply that some are easier to find than others.

THE LAW

It is illegal for anyone who is not a qualified veterinary surgeon to treat anyone else's animal without first obtaining veterinary referral, no matter how highly qualified they are in their particular discipline. You can, however, legally treat your own animal without this, provided you do not cause 'unnecessary suffering'. If you choose to use holistic therapies on your own animals, be aware that some of these therapies are strong medicines in their own right, and can cause harm if misapplied. It is always preferable to take the advice of a practitioner who is suitably qualified in the particular discipline that you are using. Equally, be aware that, as in every other area, some professionals are very much better than others. Word of mouth is a strong recommendation. Holistic practitioners are especially well placed to recommend others in adjacent professions whose skills might be of use to you in a particular situation.

TREATMENTS

Many treatments are non-invasive, and in the main they are safe to use in that if you do use the wrong treatment or too much of it, you will do no harm. Most harm comes when one does not seek professional help quickly enough when things are not going well. Some treatments work well with orthodox medicine (hence often being known as 'complementary') and some work so closely with the existing immune system that immune-suppressant medication, e.g. steroids, makes their use difficult or inappropriate. Some treatments are straightforward enough that studying a few textbooks will be sufficient to give the pet owner sufficient knowledge to use them, and some types require years of dedicated study. Even the simpler disciplines, however, go far deeper than mere first-aid use, and are the more rewarding for further learning.

A particular therapy may draw your interest at once, or instead might repel you. This does not mean that this therapy is better or worse than that, but that you empathise more with one sort or another. If that is the case, then go with your feelings: we don't all like or work well within exactly the same framework.

Acupuncture

Acupuncture forms part of Traditional Chinese Medicine (TCM), which was first developed by the Chinese over 3000 years ago and is still practised today. This alone gives it the credibility it deserves, but additionally modern research is now beginning to create understanding of how it works. Acupuncture is based on a principle of the flow of energy, or Qi (pronounced chee), around the body through non-anatomical channels known as meridians. If the flow of Qi passing through any of the channels is disturbed, the health of the body will be impaired, which leads to disease. Treatment is by the stimulation of precise anatomical points on the meridians to restore the healthy flow of Qi and thus facilitate the healing or pain-relieving abilities of the body. The knowledge of these points is based on results recorded over thousands of years. The body's energy flow increases and decreases in each meridian in a fixed cycle each day, and as each meridian is linked to the organs of the body, distortions in those meridians can affect, or reflect, that organ's function. Correction of this is the basis for acupuncture being able to assist with many functional health problems. However, acupuncture is probably best known for its ability to alleviate the pain of diseases such as hip dysplasia, spinal arthritis (spondylitis) and many other locomotor problems. Although not a cure, it is a very useful way to avoid the use of painkillers with their associated side effects, and should be considered for all early cases of arthritis.

An acupuncture treatment involves the insertion of fine surgical steel needles into a selection of acupuncture points appropriate to the problem to be treated. Not all dogs allow this, and so the use of high quality laser therapy is becoming more common, often with as good, if not better effect. By law, only qualified vets are allowed to use acupuncture needles on animals. However, if you wish to provide back-up care for your dog, simple training from a qualified practitioner will allow you to perform finger pressure, or acupressure, at home in support of any conventional treatments your dog may be having. Like acupuncture, acupressure is based on the theory of Qi, and is said to reduce pain by relaxing the muscles. It is applied with very light fingertip or finger-nail pressure on the acupuncture points; some styles of acupressure also involve rubbing, kneading and rolling. As with any therapy, do not continue if your dog appears to resent the treatment.

Aromatherapy

Aromatherapy is the use of volatile aromatic plant oils to cause physiological and psychological changes in the patient. The molecules of these essential oils enter the body and the bloodstream by absorption either through the lining of the nose and lungs, or through the skin, thus imparting an effect on the body and mind. Due to their concentration, essential oils used for aromatherapy should always be handled with care and given the same respect as any other medicinal substance. Fragrant essential oils have been used medicinally in Egypt and the Middle East for thousands of years, although their use is not taught in medical or veterinary schools at the present time. Several parts of the plant are used as a source of essential oil. Flowers, leaves, twigs, roots, seeds, bark and heartwood may all be used, depending on the plant. There are several methods of extracting the oils, the commonest being steam-distillation or else solvent extraction. The finest quality oils, which are extracted by carbon dioxide distillation, are very expensive. Cheaper synthetic oils are also produced for the mass market. These are unlikely to contain as many healing components as the natural oil, and this is likely to reduce their therapeutic effect. Whichever type of essential oil you choose, always buy from a reputable supplier; regard cheap oils with suspicion, and seek organic oils for preference.

Dogs have a very highly developed sense of smell. Dogs use the secretions of their glands, saliva, urine and faeces, as a means of communication and to mark their territory. Because their sense of smell is so refined, most dogs will respond almost too well to aromatherapy, and oils should be used in much more dilute form than for humans. Remember too that a dog will always try to clean the oil off by licking and may ingest toxic amounts by doing so, so be careful to prevent this. If in doubt, use a diffuser, or add a few drops to a glass of hot water to allow the aroma to colour the environment of the patient rather than applying the oil direct. The oils often work just as well this way.

Aromatherapy can be used to support any other therapy, although some feel that they can affect homoeopathic remedies adversely as these can be destroyed by strong smells. It is always worth storing aromatherapy oils and homoeopathy in different parts of a building.

Crystal Therapy

Crystals are delightful to use, non-invasive and safe: you cannot overdose with crystals, and they have an astonishing natural healing energy. Crystals have been used for healing purposes for thousands of years.

It has been demonstrated that if a human holds a crystal in the hand for more than thirty minutes, the brain waves change from alert beta waves to the more relaxed alpha waves. This effect increases the longer the crystal is held.

Crystal healing

Although it is not understood fully how crystals work on the body, they obviously emanate healing vibrations. They are said also to be able to absorb negative and pain vibrations from the patient.

As with Bach Flower Remedies, the mental state of the patient is the major factor in choosing which crystals to use. Some crystals have an affinity for certain body systems or symptoms. The factors quoted for crystal selection for humans can be applied to dogs and other animals. Once the appropriate crystals have been selected, they are placed on or around the body. Crystals can be taped to a dog's collar, or commonly they are just placed in the drinking bowl so that the patients get a dose of the essence at each drink, similar in a way to Bach Flower Remedies. It is also possible to use liquefied crystal essences, and light shone through coloured crystal filters. Colours have long been known to affect the human mind and this phenomenon is used when choosing colour schemes for high-stress areas such as hospitals and police cells. It may be that animals are similarly affected by colour. Years ago it was thought that animals could not see colours; nowadays we understand that they do have colour perception, though probably not the same as ours.

Crystal healing is helpful for dogs whose illness is due to mental and emotional problems, and it can be used to support all physical and medical therapies. I keep crystals where the dogs sleep as well.

To maintain the healing potential of crystals it is necessary to cleanse them regularly. They can be left outside where it is said that the dual action of sunlight and moonlight will cleanse the crystal. Alternatively, the crystal can be soaked, washed in salt or spring water (unless a porous type), or even better, placed for a while in a stream if you have one.

To me, the only drawback to crystals is that they are rather addictive, and it is very hard to leave a crystal shop without adding to your collection.

Flower Remedies

The Bach Flower Remedies, prepared from the stalks, petals and leaves of plants, can be used to treat mental and emotional states in both humans and all animals, and are a wonderful facilitator to aid correcting what we today describe as behavioural disorders. However, like homoeopathy, the obstacles to cure must be considered and resolved (see homoeopathy).

Bach Flower Remedies were the brainchild of Dr Edward Bach. His experience as a homoeopathic doctor had convinced him that physical disease was the body's reaction to a non-material cause. Changes in the body's fundamental vibrational energy resulted in a disturbance of mental state that could eventually lead to physical disease. Dr Bach set out to seek a means of healing that used non-toxic materials rather than potentised poisons. He noted that his own moods could be strongly influenced by the plants he came into contact with, and so he theorised that these natural vibrations of certain plants could match the vibrations associated with certain mental states.

Bach discovered a range of thirty-seven plants, and Rock Water, which assisted his patients with mental and emotional problems. He also discovered that a combination of five remedies, in a preparation he called Rescue Remedy, could be used in emergency situations as a calming treatment for all types of panic, shock and hysteria. With its successes, Rescue Remedy probably converts more people to alternative medicine annually than anything else.

Stock solutions of single Bach Flower Remedies are now sold ready-prepared, in health food stores and chemists. These remedies may be given alone or combined with up to five other essences at a time to make a medicine. To prepare a medicine, add two drops of each essence to 30ml (2 tbsp) of spring water.

There are various guides to the Bach Flower Remedies written, but I prefer the original works of Dr Bach. Select the Remedies according to the dog's mental state, using human emotions as a guide. The better you know your dog, the more you will see the remedies needed. The simplest way to dose your dog is to add three or four drops of essence to its drinking water, or you can give them direct into the mouth.

Since the work of Dr Bach, other series of flower essences have been developed, such as Californian, Alaskan and Australian Bush Flower Remedies. These have been developed with modern life in mind, and offer treatments for such factors as the ill effects of pollution and stress. These remedies are prepared and used in the same way as the Bach Flowers, and can also be used successfully on dogs.

Herbs

The use of plants to heal – herbalism – is probably the oldest form of healing still in use today. Herbal medicines play an essential part in both Traditional Chinese Medicine (TCM) and in the Indian Ayurvedic system. Today some eighty per cent of the world's population still relies on herbal medicine for the treatment of disease, and even in 'developed' nations, many drugs derive originally from herbs. Interestingly, few active agents have only one effect: they also tend to have other unwanted actions or side effects. Herbalists believe that the active ingredients of herbal medicines work together to counteract harmful side effects, and as these ingredients are purified into ever-stronger drugs those side effects become more of a problem. As we understand more of this medical system, this idea is showing to be more and more accurate, and hence there is a modern resurgence of interest in this field. With this interest has come problems, as we have been indoctrinated in the idea that bigger is better, and high doses of some herbs can be toxic. Just enough to heal is needed, and so consulting a qualified practitioner is always a good idea for anything other than first aid.

The fact that dogs and other animals actively seek out and eat plants that are known to have medical properties also supports the view that herbalism should have an established and widespread place in orthodox veterinary medicine today.

Herbal medicines can be administered in many ways. The traditional method is in the form of herbal infusions or teas, which are made from fresh or dried herbs. Good-tasting herbs can be fed directly to the dog if mixed with its food. Commercial herbal extracts in the form of tinctures are also available, and these can be given directly into the mouth, if your dog will tolerate it. Herbal capsules and tablets are available from some suppliers and herbs can also be used to make poultices and compresses.

Herbalism is best used to support conventional care. If ever the dog's condition appears to deteriorate at all, stop the treatment and consult your vet.

Homoeopathy

Homoeopathy was the first holistic system of Western medicine to be developed, some two hundred years ago. It is growing rapidly in popularity today as the failures of the drug culture in medicine are exposed, and homoeopathy is the system that offers the most realistic chance of cure when drugs fail. Homoeopathy acknowledges that the body has a natural healing force: minor cuts and grazes heal on their own, and we quickly recover from mild coughs and colds. Science calls this healing force homoeostasis; and homoeopathy stimulates this.

Samuel Hahnemann, an eighteenth century German doctor and the inventor of homoeopathy, called the body's self-healing principle the Vital Force. He saw it as an energetically active, living force, which is essential to life. His observations led him to discover that a non-lethal quantity of a toxic substance, or in fact anything that can affect the body, can stimulate healing where the symptoms of disease are similar to the effects of that poison. He created the saying 'Similia Similibus Curantor' – let likes be treated by likes. The idea that like cures like dates back to the fifth century, but had never before been used as the foundation of an entire medical therapy.

Hahnemann tested many substances on himself and his friends, and recorded the results in a volume he called the *Materia Medica*. This effectively is a book of symptoms, evolved from the original testing of a remedy, and amended by the detailed recording of cured symptoms and cases. This work has continued over some two hundred years of patient and detailed observations by clinicians, and is expanding more rapidly now with the advent of computers and the collaboration of homoeopaths worldwide such that there are now literally many thousands of remedies available.

Part of the history of homoeopathy led to the discovery of the concept of 'potentisation', and the fact that increasing dilutions of the original medicine that have been through this process have greater effect. This use of highly diluted medicines has led to misconceptions which are exploited by the orthodox practitioners and the global drug industry. First, that the essence of homoeopathy is the use of a tiny dose rather than the use of a 'similar'. Second, that because science, as currently understood, says that there are no molecules left in the highly-diluted dose, the medicine could not possibly work. Thirdly, that because the treatment is specific to the individual, therapies cannot be tested like drugs, and the regulatory powers will only look at the drug system so homoeopathy is denied research funds and opportunity as is it not 'accepted' by the corporate-controlled world. This suppression has been going on throughout the history of homoeopathy. However, the results over two hundred years speak for themselves, the public is not fooled, and to spend time working with a homoeopathic practitioner is a huge voyage of discovery and wonder that no-one, in my experience, has ever been able to question.

The aim of a homoeopath in selecting a treatment is to find the most similar remedy, or ideally the 'similimum'. A similar is the medical agent which produces symptoms closely resembling those of the sick animal, when given to a healthy volunteer; if the symptoms match completely, it is a similimum. When a dog is treated, its physical, mental and emotional reactions to the world are analysed to identify the disease and its treatment. The totality of the animal and its condition is treated, and the more you know about your dog when it is healthy, the more you can help when it is ill. The smallest dose of the similimum that will stimulate the healing process is given. In acute cases, doses are repeated until benefits are seen. In chronic cases, each dose is left to have its full effect before it is repeated.

The second law of homoeopathy is the removal of obstructions to a cure. This relates to the holistic idea that unless there are suitable nutrition and lifestyle changes, a permanent cure cannot result. How true when you think about it, and exactly what this book is about.

Massage
Massage has many beneficial effects on the physical body. By stimulating the circulation, it relaxes the muscles, helps to balance joint action and muscle function, and speeds the dispersal of diseased tissue. Massage also increases the production of the body's natural painkillers (endorphins), which optimise a feeling of well-being.

Dogs, in general, like to be rubbed, stroked and massaged, and will often seek out their owners for this kind of attention. A dog will convey its pleasure by little noises and stretching out. Massage is one of the oldest and simplest therapies of all. When a child hurts itself, a parent's instinctive reaction is to 'rub it better'. In the womb, the skin develops from the same cell layer as the nervous system and the two are closely connected. When you massage your dog, you are establishing a non-verbal communication that strengthens the bond existing between you and your pet, and increases trust. The act of giving a massage is also extremely therapeutic for owners, and studies have shown that it can help reduce the stress and blood pressure levels of the masseur, in addition to the effect on the patient.

Physiotherapy

In a similar way to massage, physiotherapy aims to restore the strength and full range of movement of an injured area by manual manipulation or by a series of controlled exercises. It can help to control pain, speed up healing, and preserve the function of injured tissue. It is of especial use after surgery, but can be used alongside all other therapies as well. Veterinary physiotherapy is slowly becoming more widely used in general veterinary practice, although its benefits have been recognised for years in the horse and greyhound racing industries.

Owners can use simple massage, the use of ice packs and gentle warmth as first aid at home. Local dog swimming pools are also of great help in arthritic and post-surgical cases and your vet will have a list of recommended ones. However, the more specialist physiotherapy techniques and equipment can inflict further injury if misapplied, and only a qualified physiotherapist should ever use these.

Qualified physiotherapists are registered and legally recognised and will only work following referral from your vet. Always ask your vet if there are any therapies or techniques that can help your pet that he/she can refer you to.

Osteopathy

This is a form of treatment based on the manipulation of the body's bony skeleton. The theory is that if the skeleton is out of alignment, the body it supports and protects cannot maintain a state of good health. The basis of osteopathy is that structure governs function.

Osteopaths treat each patient as a complete structure, paying close attention to the relationship between the musculoskeletal system and the function of the body. A thorough physical examination enables them to observe the ease and range of movement in the limbs and spine. By feeling the muscles and bones, the osteopath can locate painful areas and identify any misalignments of the skeleton. Osteopathic treatment of dogs uses soft-tissue massage techniques and joint manipulations to make adjustments to the damaged neuro-musculoskeletal structure. The techniques used on dogs and humans are very similar. Manipulation techniques make corrections which repair the damage and allow healing to occur, in a similar way to acupuncture restoring flow of Qi. After the initial treatment, the osteopath will monitor improvements by the changes that occur in the diseased area and in the body.

Osteopathy is now recognised as a valid treatment for animals, and, like the physiotherapists, trained osteopaths work strictly by referral from your vet.

Chiropractic

Like osteopathy, chiropractic concentrates on the anatomy and physiology of the dog's musculoskeletal and nervous systems, and on the safe manipulation of the spine. The difference between the two therapies lies in the basic philosophy of disease. Chiropractic theory says that if vertebral segments of the spine are misaligned, there will be undue pressure on the spinal cord or spinal nerves. This can cause interference with nerve transmissions, which may result in abnormal function and disease. If the malfunctioning vertebral segment can be repositioned by manipulation, the pressure on the spinal nerve roots is relieved and normal nerve function is restored. Chiropractic adjustment involves applying a high-velocity, short-amplitude thrust to the appropriate small facet joints of the vertebrae. It is the aim of the adjustment to correct the mechanical function of the joint and restore normal nerve function in the area. Chiropractic is a non-invasive therapy, and while the hand movements are fast, they are subtle and extremely gentle.

In the United Kingdom, the McTimoney Chiropractic Association oversees chiropractic work on animals. The qualified practitioners again only treat animals referred to them by a vet.

Reiki

Reiki is a hands-on therapy that bridges the gap between the physical therapies and the energy therapies. A practitioner's hand-placements and movements over the surface of the body are designed to direct healing energy to an injured area and to strengthen the spirit, rather than to stimulate the skin and underlying tissues themselves.

The name Reiki is thought to originate from two Japanese symbols, 'rei' meaning universal and 'ki', the non-physical life-force. Ki is basically the same as the concept of Qi in acupuncture, and the vital force in homoeopathy. Ki is available to anyone who can learn how to use it, but modern life means that most of us are disconnected

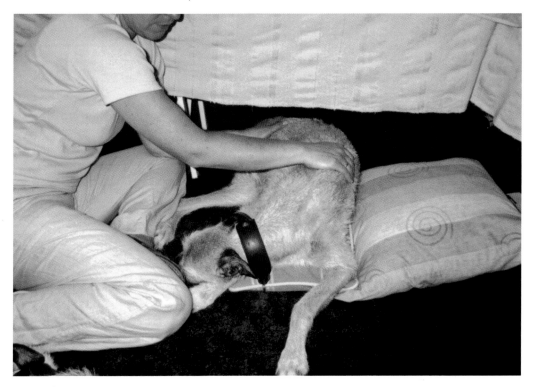

Reiki

from it. Learning Reiki reconnects people to this universal life-force, giving them the ability to assist healing of both themselves and other humans, as well as their pets.

Reiki, as well as assisting physical healing, can also be used to reassure a dog that is emotionally upset. When treating an injured dog, even if you have never tried Reiki, place your hands parallel to and above the wound. A warmth will soon be felt: this is the ki energy, and your dog will mostly relax and enjoy the sensation, but will move away or will appear restless when she has had enough. Wash your hands in a bowl of water (pre-prepared) afterwards, or shake them well, as it is amazing how many people will get a static electric shock if they touch metal afterwards. This is the build-up of the energies that has been caused by the healing. It is worth removing watches first as well, as they can be interfered with.

It is not recommended to use Reiki as the only method of treating a sick animal. If your dog is injured or appears to be ill, consult your vet as normal. However, regular use of Reiki can be very successful in supporting older dogs through the restrictions of age, and as an aid to convalescence.

PREPARATION

Time spent in preparation is never wasted, and soon you will be ready to collect your dog. If very young, she may be car-sick, so either have an indoor kennel in the car, or a large cardboard box, suitably lined with newspaper and old towels. Carry some water and a bin-liner for soiled items, and hope that you won't need them. If you are intending to have the dog on your lap while someone else drives, wear old clothes and fold a towel on your lap. You will find old clothes very useful in the next few weeks.

2 Puppy Matters

Eight weeks to eighteen months – the truth!

I really wish that puppies were not so cute, so appealing, so utterly irresistible. I wish that puppies were ugly and repellent. Maybe then only people who really want a dog would get a puppy. Have you ever seen a baby pigeon? It looks like its name – squab. It's hideous. Only its mother could love it. That's what puppies should be like. I mean, you don't often hear of unwanted pigeons, do you? Sadly, puppies are so gorgeous that people get them without really considering what is involved, and so the dog rescues fill up with puppies and young dogs whose only crime is acting like dogs. I am not going to lecture you for being unable to resist that puppy – I find them hard to resist myself – but I do want to help you through the obstacles of puppy ownership so that you emerge from the far end of the experience with a dog to be proud of, and your nerves intact. I am not going to tell you how to train that puppy, except with a few suggestions here and there, because that would be a separate book in itself. But I am going to alter your perceptions about puppies, and help the pair of you to live with each other, and know what to expect of each other.

ONE OR TWO?

It is tempting for people to get two puppies together. Maybe they have found it difficult to choose between two puppies in the litter, or there were only two left and the other one looked lonely. Sometimes breeders of the accidental litter, or one where the pups have hung around for too long before finding homes, offer to throw in the last one at a bargain price. There is the feeling that two puppies will play together and keep each other occupied. But keeping the puppy occupied is your job – let me tell you what two puppies together means:

It means more than twice the aggravation of having one puppy.
It means that the puppies will bond with each other rather than with you – which will make them the devil to train.
It means that, as they mature, they may have battles, real, live, blood-soaked battles, to determine which is the top-ranking dog.
It means never knowing which one made the puddle or ripped up the sofa cushions.
It means very stressful dog walks – or never letting them off the lead together.

It certainly is possible to raise two puppies together and make a good job of it, but it does mean a lot of work. One puppy is a lot of work anyway: you really do not need more. With two puppies, you should exercise and train them separately for the first year, until you have each one behaving itself as you would want. That's a big commitment, although after you have made it, you can put your feet up for the next

If only they weren't so appealing

ten years. Then they get old together, and you have all the elderly dog considerations doubled, until one dies and the other is either desolate without her companion, or else blossoms to such an extent that it is only then you realise how the other old biddy was keeping her down. Treat yourself to a guilt trip.

If you really want two dogs, the way to achieve harmony in the household is to get one, settle her in for the first one and a half to two years, and then get the other. That way, you are only doing intensive training with one dog at a time, and only enduring the adolescence of one at a time, too. It is much easier for each dog to bond with you, though you will have to ensure that the second dog gets 'quality time' with you on her own, especially if the first one tries to mother her. Why do I keep mentioning bonding? Well, you see, what you have is not a baby human, though she shares many characteristics. That warm, cute, immensely cuddly being is a baby wolf. Her needs and desires, hard-wired into her, are those of a predator. Overlaid with that is the fact that, as a domestic animal, she is programmed to be friendly towards people, but she is not programmed to act as people want. She is programmed to act as a wolf would. You, as her owner, will be training her not to do many things that she wants to do. Why should she please you, when with a great deal less effort, she can please herself? The answer is bonding. You can train dogs many different ways, but they will ultimately only obey you if they are bonded to you. Fear will bond, but love gets better results. If, however, the dogs bond with each other, you haven't a chance of anything other than sheer anarchy. Bonding your dog to you makes both of your lives easier, for the sake of some work at the beginning.

GENDER

If, despite this warning, you are set on having two dogs now, do you get two of the same sex, or a dog and a bitch? This is not as straightforward as it may seem. As a rule of thumb, opposite sexes get on better, but of course it does mean that either one or both will have to be neutered, or else you will have extra work at season time – or extra puppies! Don't ever believe that dogs have an incest taboo – most dogs will happily couple with their parents, siblings or other close relatives with the same cheerful abandon that they will bring to a mating of strangers. Their programming is to spread their genes over as wide an area as possible. Individual dogs will have a higher or lower sex drive, and some breeds are notorious for being reluctant to mate, but for the most part, assume that they will be at it like knives, given the opportunity. If you do go for neutering, it is nevertheless better for the dog's health if you wait until he or she is physically mature before the operation. Most bitches have a first season between six and twelve months, though certain breeds will take longer, and some bitches only come into oestrus once a year or even once every few years – sighthounds are notorious for this. Once past her first season, the bitch will be much more grown-up; if you want her spayed, after the first season is currently reckoned to be best practice. Bitches are very individual about the spacing of their seasons as well as the intensity of them. A first season can be messy and dramatic, but subsequent

The perils of having two together

ones normal and easy. A bitch may need several seasons in order to set the pattern – I have one who cycles at ten months, followed by seven months, then ten months again. I will discuss seasons and neutering in more detail shortly.

If you have two pups of the same sex, especially from the same litter, there may be fighting as they go through adolescence (do you have teenage children?) and as they mature, the fighting can become very serious, to the point that you will have to part with one of them or else keep them apart when you are not with them. Some breeds are very much worse than others for this. As a guide, look at what the breed or breeds involved were originally created to do. Feisty terrier types are much more likely to cross swords than laid-back whippets – but any dog can disagree with any other dog, and it can take the smallest of incidents to set off a ruckus.

As a rule of thumb, male dogs bond (that word again) better with female humans, and vice versa. This also applies to other domestic animals. If, however, the dog of your choice is the same sex as you are, it is no bar to ownership – but the relationship will be slightly different. People tend to say that this sex is more independent than that one, but it isn't really so: if you have set your heart on one particular pup, then get that one, and don't worry whether it is a dog or a bitch. The most important issue is that you like each other.

FIRST DAYS

Some time between eight and (usually) twelve weeks, your puppy will leave the litter and come home with you. Precisely when she does can be significant, in obvious matters such as house-training (you will not be expecting a very young puppy to last all night without emptying herself) but also in less obvious matters such as socialisation. In the four to twelve weeks period, puppies are bold and outgoing: new experiences are of great interest to them, and the breeder will feel as if he or she has been overrun by Visigoths as they eat and pillage their way through their known world. After twelve weeks, however, pups go through a timid phase. This might be a relic of pre-domestication, and meant to keep them from venturing too far from the den, eating unsuitable objects and running up to dangerous animals. In practical terms, it means that a pre-timid-phase pup will change homes more easily than a later one. However, the breeder may not want the pups to leave so early, especially if that period of their lives coincides with Christmas or a similar big festival, or the new owner would rather have a pup that is further down the road to house-training. Some people prefer to take on the pups after they have been vaccinated. Later in life, the age at which you took your pup home will be of little consequence, so take her when it suits you and the breeder, but be aware of and patient with the timid-phase pup. She will grow out of her fears soon enough; you, older and wiser, must be sure not to overwhelm her with new experiences. 'Hasten Slowly' as the German proverb goes (*Eile mit Weile*).

SMOOTHING THE WAY

There is a number of ways you can make the changeover easier. Visiting the pup and interacting with her before you finally collect her will accustom her to your smell, and so when she is in a world of strangeness, she has one point of stability. Keep an old cotton cloth in your bed for a week so that it is saturated with your smell, and leave it with the litter for a few days before you collect your puppy. She can familiarise herself with your scent during those days, and then have the cloth with her in her new home, and so find comfort in the smell of puppy-nest and the scents of her siblings. Of course, if the litter is a long way from where you live, this will not be possible, but there is still plenty that can be done.

There is a device called the Dog Appeasement Pheromone (DAP) which is obtainable from vets. It plugs into an electrical source and emits a scent said to mimic the smell of a lactating bitch. This exerts a calming effect on dogs and especially puppies. Each DAP lasts for approximately one month, which is plenty of time for settling in a puppy.

Bach Flower Remedy Walnut helps to deal with changing circumstances. Four drops either in the drinking water every time you change it, or on food, will be helpful: expect to use it for about two weeks unless puppy settles earlier. If you have other animals, especially dogs and cats, Walnut in the water for a week before the puppy comes will help with their side of the change. Even the easiest puppy is a major disruption, and staid older animals will have mixed reactions. Most will just glare at you and keep out of the puppy's way (even if it means climbing onto the worktop in the kitchen) some will growl or snap at the pup, and a very few will mother her. Dogs and even cats of either sex can do this. Occasionally, an older dog will be so stressed and jealous that she will try to injure the puppy. Don't believe that she won't – keep them supervised or separated until either the puppy is big enough to keep out of trouble, or the older dog calms down. This can occasionally take months. I recently had a letter from a man whose eighteen month old terrier had killed his ten week old puppy. They had seemed all right together. Whether indeed they had, or he had missed the warning signs, he now had a tragedy. Don't risk it. Similarly, a cat can damage a small puppy, even blind her: if there is antagonism, keep them apart unless supervised.

A well-wrapped safe hot-water-bottle will make her bed more appealing. You can get microwavable ones, or maybe you are lucky and have a stone hot water bottle from days gone by. If the latter, check the rubber seal and replace it if it has perished.

Stone hot water bottles

Stone hot water bottle well wrapped with litter of puppies

Keeping puppies and older dogs separate

I do wish someone would make these again – they are so useful. Avoid anything that has a flex which might be chewed; similarly rubber hot water bottles, however well wrapped, are not a good idea for puppies, as injury could be caused by chewing them. A radio left on low will provide a comfortable hum of sound and a fleecy blanket to snuggle into will be welcomed. Careful again with the rest of the 'family' as older dogs and especially cats will home in on the sources of warmth as well. Taking on a very young pup in a household of other pets means either constant vigilance or a secure system of shutting potential sources of trouble away from each other. Fortunately, this time passes fairly quickly.

GENERAL

Very young puppies do everything at a run, and their brakes aren't too good. They alternate periods of sleeping with spells of thundering about, getting underfoot in imaginative ways, and chewing everything they can get their mouths round. Like baby humans, baby puppies sleep like the dead, and while they sleep, they should not be disturbed. The pup needs sleep as much as food, and allowing children or visitors to wake her so that they can have the fun of her is selfish, and will ultimately result in a fractious, bad-tempered animal. Puppies also don't read manuals. Not all of them want to be fed four times a day, or the same number of times each day, or the same amount every day. I have at time of writing a six-week-old pup who eats like a timber wolf every second or third day, and snacks lightly for the other days. Don't panic if puppy doesn't seem to eat much, as long as she is bright and active. Puppies are also prone to hiccups, which they grow out of, so don't be concerned about that. Avoiding

Sleeping

jealousy from your other dogs because you are feeding puppy more often is important, and a generous supply of treats should be on hand for these times. Cut down on quantity with adult meals accordingly, or before you know it, you will have a household full of fat pets.

The great thing about puppies is that they grow out of the behaviours that drive you mad. At first, when you are only getting two hours' sleep at a time because that's how long the puppy sleeps, alternating sleep-eat-play to her individual pattern over twenty-four hours, you wonder if you are going to survive, but in a very short time, she will sleep for longer, eat more but less frequently, and be less hectic in her waking hours. Mountaineering and hurling herself off furniture should be discouraged – she could hurt herself – and you wonder whether you should encase the whole interior of the house in steel, or if a padded cell would be more appropriate, but this all passes. And puppies are wonderful for teaching the rest of the household to be tidy, as if you don't want it chewed or taken for a run around the garden – put it away!

CHEWING

Puppies chew. Some breeds are notorious for it, but all puppies chew. They chew to ease their gums when the needle-like milk teeth come through, they chew because part of discovering their world is to gnaw everything they can get their mouths around, they chew when they are shedding their milk teeth and growing their adult set at between four and six months old, and they chew to settle these teeth in their

If you don't want it chewed . . .

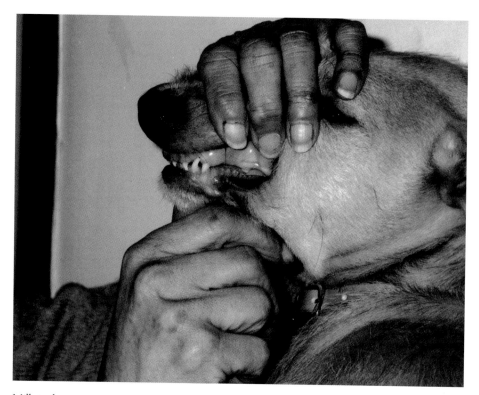

Milk teeth

Chewing

heads. And they chew to release endorphins when lonely or upset, chew to ease stomach ache, and chew just for the hell of it. Chewing is nice. You won't stop a pup from chewing, and nor should you try. What you should do is supply lots of safe items for her to chew: a dog only has so much chewing in her, and as long as she can chew enough for her needs, your house should not suffer too much. Never leave a dog alone near things that you don't want chewed, though – you cannot expect her to know which of your household items is precious to you. Don't give her a shoe to chew if you don't want her to chew other shoes – she can't tell a discarded shoe from your favourites.

Adult dogs will chew as well, though rarely with as much commitment as a puppy. The need remains, however, and can flare up at any time. Items given to a dog to chew should be checked for safety (don't take the pet shop's word for it: they want to sell the stuff) and there are no safety regulations for pet toys. Therefore, use your own common sense. Never give a dog a toy that can be chewed into pieces that might be swallowed, or that might catch a tooth and break it. Puppy teeth can come out several at a time when they are teething – most unnerving to find on the doormat – usually with little blood or signs of discomfort, unlike our teething. But apart from that, you want your dog's teeth to stay in good condition, so don't let her chew wooden or plastic toys, or carry stones. Some of the 'treats' marketed as dog chews are decidedly unsafe: many have been bleached with chemicals, and some can cause blockages if a lump is gnawed off and swallowed. Nothing beats a good raw bone, or set of them, for chewing, though be careful if you are a multi-dog household. Bones really are a matter 'of contention' and some dogs will fight when bones are present. Others will not: mine happily eat bones within a few inches of each other, and have been known to share opposite ends of the same bone. This is, however, unusual, and I suggest that you separate your dogs when you give them bones, and let them savour these in privacy. Puppies enjoy chicken wings to chew and eat, and will often stalk and 'kill' them before eating. Thus our beloved companions remind us that the wolf is within all the time.

MOUTHING

All the while your puppy is going through the chewing stage, she will attempt to mouth you, other dogs, and sometimes herself. This is her personal voyage of discovery. Mouthing will allow other dogs to teach her how much is too much, and is the beginning of teaching 'bite inhibition', which is vital in a canine or canine/human social relationship. She needs to know how hard she is allowed to close her jaws, and she will learn that dog skins are tougher than humans'.

Mouthing is sometimes mistaken for biting, but it is not. Though the needle teeth are sharp and the tiny jaws can exert a surprising amount of power, the mouthing pup is not trying to hurt you. She will be disciplined by her siblings, who will refuse to play with her if she mouths too hard, by other dogs which will growl and snap at her, and by us. Above all, she must learn not to mouth holes in people or their clothing. She is testing, and we must react appropriately, otherwise she will not know what to do. This does not mean slapping her or flicking her on the nose. The correct approach to mouthing is just what her fellow dogs do – squeal and turn away from her. The implication is: 'That hurt. I'm having no more to do with you.' She will

Mouthing

immediately offer placatory behaviour, flattening her ears and squirming. Resume interaction, and she will mouth again. Show her again that if she mouths, you do not play. Substitute a toy or a piece of vegetable for whatever part of you she has her jaws around, in exactly the same way as you would distract a toddler whose behaviour is inappropriate. Individual puppies can mouth very hard, and should not be made excited by vigorous play – you cannot expect to 'wind her up' and then have her stop when you don't like what she is doing. Keep your interaction calm, and gently but persistently discourage the mouthing. Given the right responses, the pup should grow out of mouthing behaviour in a few weeks, but as in all things, some will take longer than others.

THE INDOOR KENNEL

It looks like a cage to us, but to your puppy, it is safe haven. The indoor kennel is such a boon, especially in the multi-pet household. Line the tray with newspaper and have a cardboard box with bedding in at one end, put a blanket over the top so that it is dark and den-like, and there you have the perfect puppy home. When you need to go out, you can shut the door, and otherwise you should leave it open so that it doesn't become a prison. Toss the odd treat in there so that there is always something nice to find when pup goes in. Though you should plan your time so that a very new puppy is not left alone for long spells, there will be times when you have to be out of the house, and a little puppy should never be left where she can run into danger. She should not be loose to chew electric flex or torment older pets. Jealousy is a terrible emotion: people can't handle it, so don't expect your resident pets to. Where cats will probably move out temporarily – most cats have several homes anyway, did their owners but know it – some dogs may attack the puppy. Even if your other pets seem very tolerant, don't take risks. Puppy is safer shut apart from them when unsupervised. It is only for a few weeks, and it may save her life.

NAMING

Choosing a name for your puppy is important for both of you. For the pup, the name should be unlike the name of any other household member, and unlike any command. It might sound cute to have dogs with similar names – Popsy, Topsy and Mopsy – but the dogs won't know which one you are talking to. Likewise, the dog called Mo isn't sure if you said 'No' and Donna might be perpetually expecting dinner. Make life easy – choose a name that is unmistakable. For yourself, you should pick a name that trips easily off the tongue, and that doesn't have more than two syllables, else the dog will be in the next county by the time you have finished calling her. Don't pick a name that shortens to something that you will find embarrassing or others will consider politically incorrect. The name you choose will, on occasion, be shared at volume with the public at large – but at least dogs don't have to worry about their initials making them blush.

It is a strange fact that, after you have chosen the dog's name with care, she acquires at least two more names. What is more, she will answer to them. Like the child whose full name is only used when a parent is irate, the dog will know which nicknames are used with gentle affection ('You useless old fleabag') and which command instant response and no argument. If you intend to train your dog to a high standard, you may well wish to keep one of these monikers specifically for competition. Each one of my dogs has a name which is only used in obedience trials, and no-one appears to have noticed yet.

A dog's name should always be associated with pleasure. Don't call her by name to scold her (you will find plenty of other names appropriate for this purpose) or do something she dislikes, such as putting in eyedrops: each time you do this, you weaken her response to recall. Children love to know a dog's name, but then will shout it over and over, hoping to get a reaction from the dog. The reaction that you will get is – weakened recall. Tell the children a different name. This is, of course, not possible with your own children: I can only suggest you become a stern and unreasonable parent if they misuse the given name.

Once you have chosen a name, stick to it. Don't expect the dog to be anything other than thoroughly confused if she is Maddy one day and Bella the next. Despite the temptation of nicknames, keep to the one name until your pup's response is sound – which comes surprisingly quickly. Greet your dog by name when you return from being out, call her by name for nice experiences, repeat her name as you make a fuss of her. If your dog has come to you with a name that you dislike, change it. It will only take a couple of days of using the new name with the old one – 'Peggy-Susie' and then dropping the old name. Dogs, you will find, learn their names a great deal faster than humans, as long as you start them off clearly.

HOUSE TRAINING

The puppy should not be left to empty herself in her kennel. It is her instinct to keep her immediate environs clean, but once this taboo is broken, it can be the very devil to housetrain her. So take her out very frequently, and stay with her while she empties herself, praising her after she has done so. Pups are easily distracted, so praising her just as she starts to perform may put her off. Avoid eye contact until she has finished what she is doing. Never just 'put' her out, because she will be upset at being outside on her own, and she does not know that you expect her to empty. She will want to come in, and once she is in, she will recollect that she needs to void bladder and/or bowels, and will do so indoors. This is not being 'naughty' – she is a baby and not given to guessing what you are thinking. You have to make it easy for her to do what you want. So, immediately you get up – no you don't have time to attend to your own ablutions or put the kettle on – take her out, wait for her to empty herself, praise and reward her (this is a good time for a small edible treat) then go back indoors with her. If you only want her to use certain parts of the garden, take her to these and temporarily fence off the others. Puppies like short grass and newly dug areas to empty on, so make life easy and provide her with one or both of these. Encourage her by using the same word or phrase, so that soon she will associate the words with the action. This is a boon in adult life, when you want your dog to empty herself and she knows what you have in mind. Be careful, though, not to use a phrase which crops up frequently in conversation (very risky) or that is an embarrassment in polite company.

Winter housetraining is slightly harder than in summer: puppies are reluctant to go out in pouring rain, and chill easily if they get soaked (rub dry, wrap her in a towel, and put her next to her hot water bottle). A covered area is a good idea, and it needn't be large – ours all find under the garden table is quite adequate shelter from the rain! Keep your house on the cool side and then it won't be such a penance for her to go from a warm house to the bitter outdoors. You can always put on another pullover.

After she has eaten, after she has woken up, she must be taken straight outside. If she starts to sniff and circle, take her out. Carry her if she is very small, because all babies leave it until the last minute, and there may not be time! Don't expect her to hang on until it's convenient for you. Properly done, housetraining is very inconvenient for you, but it doesn't take long in terms of the lifetime of a dog, and it is good to have an adult pooch that you can trust to be clean whatever the circumstances. Remember how long it takes to housetrain humans if you start to get impatient.

ACCIDENTS

Every puppy has accidents. Don't comment on these, but still take puppy out if you just failed to catch her in time. If it happened some time ago, just clean up using a non-ammonia agent. Ammonia to a dog smells like a good place to pee, and she may return to the same spot and use it again. Biological detergent is good to use and discourages repeat performances. Please don't 'rub her nose in it'; this is old-fashioned and teaches the dog nothing except to hide her accident better, and keep away from you because you can be dangerous. If a puppy eliminates indoors, that is your fault for not watching her better.

OTHER DOGS

It is usual for the pup to find the presence of other dogs intimidating when she needs to empty, and she is better taken outside on her own. Sometimes, even the smell of where other dogs have eliminated will inhibit her. You can't fight this, so take her to a part of the garden where the others have not marked. She will quickly find her preferred area. If you have time for forward planning before you get your pup, keep a part of the garden free for this purpose, and fence your other dogs away from it.

OVERNIGHT

Some people sleep like the dead, others awaken at the slightest noise, and more than a few have to get up in the night for a pee. Dogs are just the same. Very young puppies cannot last all night, so set your alarm and take them out after every three hours, having made sure that they emptied themselves last thing before bed. If their paper is wet or soiled, then every two hours should be tried, gradually extending the time until – halleluja! You can sleep all night. I have found it useful to have the puppy beside the bed, in a large cardboard box lined with plenty of newspaper. When the puppy stirs and maybe starts to squeak because she is full, that is enough to wake me, and she is then carried outside. It can be wonderfully bracing out there in your night attire, waiting for a pup to find exactly the right place to empty herself. If you are a sounder sleeper than I am, the alarm clock method is better. Contrary to old-fashioned dog-keeping theories, the puppy does not become 'spoilt' by sleeping beside you. Indeed, she finds it a great comfort. While some pups settle at night right from the first, others cry, and a crying pup is loud out of all proportion to her size. She is not crying because she is naughty or trying to wind you up. She is crying because she is a baby on her own away from all that is familiar and comforting, and she is frightened. Beside your bed, she can smell and hear you, and does not feel so alone. Within a very short time, she will be sleeping through the night, and you can then move her, in stages, out of the bedroom to where you would like her to sleep. Some people like to leave a radio on low, or have a clock with a loud tick, as 'company' when the pup is in a room on her own, and this is another good time for the DAP.

FREEDOM

During the day, keep the puppy in the same room as yourself, and then you are on hand if she decides to chew on the electric flex or get too close to the fire. Treat her as you would a human toddler – never left alone or unsupervised. She should not be confined to her kennel for long spells, but needs the freedom to explore her surroundings. Puppies follow spells of hectic play with sleep, and should be left in peace when they sleep, as this is just as important for their development as proper feeding. Encourage her to sleep in the right place – if she falls asleep where she drops, carry her to her proper bed. In the garden, she should be watched to see she does not eat anything poisonous or otherwise harmful. See that she has no access to slug pellets or garden chemicals, rodent poison and the like, and don't use coconut fibre on your flowerbeds, because it is very toxic to dogs. Make sure that she cannot gain access to sharp garden implements, car maintenance or DIY equipment. Even string is dangerous to a puppy. Precious or dangerous areas should be fenced off – it is only for a short time, and she is not to know that a pond will drown her, or that you paid a fortune for your rare golden Himalayan doodah that is now strewn to the four winds.

OUTDOOR KENNEL

There is nothing wrong with keeping a pup in a secure outdoor kennel and run. If there is another dog kennelled within sight, so much the better. It is, however, unwise to kennel a pup with an adult dog, or even an older pup. Puppies can be annoying, and if the other dog has not the space to get away, it may resort to attacking the pup. This does not mean that the adult dog is vicious, cannot be trusted, or that irritating phrase 'It could have been a child'. These are dog matters, and dealt with quite differently from human mores. Wild canid pups are often injured by adults. Don't put yours at risk. While we are talking risks, make sure that rats do not have access to the kennel – not only does that put the pup at risk of contracting disease, but a small pup can be killed by rats.

NOISE IN KENNELS

A pup on her own in an outdoor kennel can do a fair bit of singing: it is not the ideal choice if you have close neighbours. Stopping a pup being noisy in kennels is difficult: spraying with water is often suggested, but this results in a wet pup with wet bedding and more work for you. You can get a collar which sprays citronella when the pup makes a noise – citronella is very unpleasant to dogs – but this, while it may stop some dogs, is not tackling the cause of the problem. The pup is lonely. If you can only have one dog, she should spend more, not less, time with you. When she is good and tired, she will be pleased to curl up in her bed, maybe with a bone to chew. And again, this is a good time to try the DAP, and some Bach Rescue Remedy in her water.

Gardening the puppy way

A few dogs are always noisy in kennels, no matter what you do, and if this is giving you issues with other people, you may have to keep the dog indoors instead. Sadly, while we are all expected to put up with any amount of human noise, the smallest amount of noise from a dog can have the neighbourhood on your back, with the weight of the local council behind it. You can even have a Noise Abatement Order served, and have to part with your dog. While constant dog noise can certainly be very irritating, it does seem a pity that the same tolerance cannot be extended to a crying puppy that there is for crying children.

Also, beware becoming a scapegoat. I know of a lady with an elderly dog who began to receive complaints of her dog howling when she was out. This howling coincided with another neighbour getting a dog and leaving it shut out all day while she coped with her children (why on earth did she get a dog?) and indeed it was this dog that was doing the howling. However, the first dog was large and the noisy dog was small and cute, so the large uncute dog attracted the complaints. The lady dealt imaginatively with the problem by arranging for a relative to take the dog home at random times, at the same time asking those who complained to give her precise details of when and for how long her dog was supposed to be howling. It will come as no surprise to you that her dog could apparently be heard howling some forty miles away across the county border. What I am saying here is: take noise complaints seriously because they can get out of hand very quickly. If the complaints are justified, be aware that dog noise is a real problem to some people, and they may have waited quite some time before approaching you with a complaint. They might be at the end of their particular tether, and ready to involve the authorities. It is better to compromise on how you keep your dog than to lose her.

VACCINATION

Your puppy may have had her early vaccinations while with the breeder, or she may have come to you unvaccinated. Views on vaccination have changed radically over the last few years, and are likely to have changed further by the time you read this, so please take the following only as a guide, and be prepared to do your own research. Vaccination is a very thorny issue at time of writing, and people who want only to do the best for their dogs are at the mercy of much conflicting information and polarised views. I cannot – and would not – tell you what to do about having your dog vaccinated. All I can say is that you should do as much research as possible, and base your decision on the information that you have.

It used to be the practice for young puppies to have two injections of multiple live vaccine, given two to four weeks apart. Start times varied with different vets, but eight weeks and twelve weeks would be about average. After that, an annual booster was advised.

This has puzzled thinking dog owners, who reason that annual boosters are not required for human vaccinations, so why for pets? At the same time, immune-system illnesses are seemingly on the increase in dogs and other animals that receive annual booster vaccinations. Conscientious vets query this as well, but are between the proverbial rock and hard place, as both regulatory restrictions and the vaccine manufacturers insist that annual boosters are vitally important, and adverse reactions just coincidence. Some pet owners are not so easy to fob off, and an organisation called the Canine Health Concern (See Useful Addresses) sent out questionnaires to large numbers of dog owners, analysed the results, and put some force behind the argument that annual boosters were not only unnecessary, they were actually harmful in susceptible animals. Some enlightened vets started offering annual blood titre tests, which proved that immunity lasted a lot longer than previously thought, and while they were not allowed by regulation to recommend less frequent boosters, the results of the titre tests began to enable the dog owners to make an informed decision. Parallel to this, a lot of parents are querying the possible ill effects of multiple vaccinations of live virus in very young children, receiving a similar degree of fob-off from the authorities, and consequently public confidence in multiple live-virus vaccination programmes has plummeted.

Dealing now exclusively with dogs, several alternatives are available, but none is actively recommended to clients by vets because they are only allowed to put forward the old system of annual boosters. Radical reformers refuse to vaccinate at all, relying on keeping the dog's immune system as strong as possible as defence against disease – and we must remember that diseases such as distemper, hepatitis and parvovirus killed huge numbers of dogs before vaccines were found to combat them. Cynics amongst the old school opine that unvaccinated dogs only get away with it because they are riding on the coat-tails of owners who have their dogs vaccinated. Cynics among the radicals counter this by saying that vaccination spreads as much disease and illness as it protects against. And while these two groups face each other across a line in the sand, caring vets and worried owners cast about for other options.

One is to vaccinate puppies and titre test thereafter, only boosting if and when titres are low. Another is to use homoeopathic nosodes. The drawback with nosodes is that they are quite complicated to give, and not usually accepted by insurance companies, boarding kennels, training classes and competition groups, who mostly still insist on annual boosters. However, the good news is that recent research published in America by the American Animal Hospital Association and also the American Veterinary Medical Association has shown that vaccine-induced immunity lasts a lot longer than initially thought, and that vaccinating after the first booster at approximately fourteen months is pointless as it probably does not stimulate further immunity. It seems at the moment that a later puppy vaccination followed by a booster at fourteen months of age, and further vaccination only if indicated by immunity levels in blood titres, may well be the best way to go for now, but I recommend discussing the matter with an enlightened vet as new evidence emerges. Meanwhile, the authorities continue to beat the drum for the old system of two early puppy vaccinations and annual booster, and the radicals say that you shouldn't vaccinate at all. The only point on which they seem to agree is that if you don't do as they suggest, you are a neglectful dog owner and serve you right if your animal suffers from it. It will be interesting to see where we go from here.

NEUTERING

This is the other big decision that faces the new puppy owner. Pressure, both social and veterinary, to have your puppy neutered, is almost overwhelming. It is commonplace for the owner of a tiny puppy, bringing him or her in for her first health check, to be told rather than asked that they are bringing their new friend in for neutering at six months of age. Some practices even neuter earlier than that, which can result in incomplete development, both mental and physical, in the animal concerned. There are uncomfortable undertones of wanting to keep the dog a permanent puppy, as a sort of toy rather than a canine companion.

While the basis for a lot of neutering is the laudable desire to prevent the birth of unwanted puppies – which of course it does – and while there is no denying that dog rescues are stuffed with unwanted dogs, it does not follow that keeping a dog of either sex as nature designed it is in any way irresponsible. While neutering can be beneficial in a minority of cases, there is no doubt that the dog comes as a complete package, and that the loss of his or her 'bits' can have consequences that reach further than the immediate inability to cause offspring. Let's have a look at the details.

THE BITCH

Most bitches come into season around six months of age, and thereafter cycle twice yearly, each oestrus period lasting three weeks. While some are so accurate that you could set your watch by them, others cycle irregularly and some rarely or not at all. The greyhound family often does not come into season for several years, and tends to cycle only once a year after that, though often for four weeks rather than three. Some bitches have heavy seasons, some light; some have a high sex drive and some little or none. Quite a lot of bitches differ in the details from season to season. Spaying removes the uterus and ovaries, so that the bitch does not come into season and is incapable of being mated. It is irreversible. However, sex hormones are made in other parts of the body too, and some spayed bitches still exhibit season behaviour at the appropriate times, and are still attractive to male dogs, some of which may try to mate her and do her damage.

Most people have a bitch spayed three months after the first season, trusting that she would have had a six-monthly cycle. As mentioned above, some veterinary practices and especially some dog rescue organisations spay the bitch before her first season, though many vets question this practice due to problems of immaturity and hormonal development, which can result in many health issues later in life.

Chemical Spaying

It is possible to use drugs to stop the seasons in the bitch, but this does involve regular injections, which do have some quite nasty side effects. It is not often recommended nowadays.

The Season

The first sign you will have of your bitch approaching season is that she will stop to urinate more frequently when on walks. This is to tell passing male dogs that she is about to become interesting to them. At the same time, her coat will become very soft and shiny from increased female hormones in her system, and she may become skittish or downright disobedient. Some bitches experience a distinct PMT and are total ratbags until the season starts. If you are observant, you will see all these signs of approaching season.

The season proper is said to start from when the bitch starts to spot red fluid from her vulva. This is called 'showing colour'. Some bitches are so fastidious about clearing up after themselves that the less aware owner can miss this part of the season; other bitches are messier, but really there is very little problem around the house even so. If your bitch is allowed on the furniture, you'd best put covers over it, and remember to shut your bedroom door. But even if there are splashes here and there, it is easily cleaned up with a cloth and cold (not warm) water.

Male dogs will approach the bitch at this time but she will snap at them and repel their advances. Almost all males will back off, but if one presses his suit, she could well bite him. After a week or so of this – but varying very much between different bitches – her vulva will be very swollen and the discharge less profuse. All the books I've read say that it becomes straw-coloured at this time, but my own bitches have always spotted red all the way through the season. The bitch is now ready to mate, and will accept male dogs. The fertile period can be short in some bitches – just a couple of days – and long in others. Normally, the tenth to the fourteenth day is the most fertile time, but I've known bitches to be mated at any time through the twenty-one days of the season, or even a week later, and become pregnant. Always make due allowance for Murphy's Law, and don't take any risks. Remember that an animal that is only fertile for a short time in the year will usually have a correspondingly high need, and some bitches will go to incredible lengths to escape. I have a friend who was quietly eating his tea one afternoon when he saw something white flash vertically past the window. It was his whippet, who had jumped out of the bedroom fanlight. Not all bitches will strive to leave home and find a mate, but be aware that it can happen, and take suitable precautions. I have used Dorwest Scullcap and Valerian on my in-season bitches, and find it does make quite a difference in calming them down without sedating them.

Assuming that your bitch does not mate, her season will finish and her vulva shrink back to its customary dimensions after three weeks, though my own experience is that for some reason she will continue to smell desirable to male dogs for another week or so, and some will try to mate her. If one succeeds, you will at best have a pregnancy you didn't want, and at worst, a bitch with internal injuries. If you live in an area where people let their dogs stray, this can be a real nuisance. Though accidents can happen in the best-ordered households, unwanted puppies are usually a result of irresponsible ownership, rather than unneutered dogs.

False Pregnancy
Many bitches follow a season with a false pregnancy and phantom pups. This can be barely noticeable, or so convincing that you start to wonder if there has been a mating. Bitches can put on weight and at the appropriate time, demonstrate identical frantic nesting behaviour to that of the truly pregnant bitch. I have even known one to regurgitate food for her 'pups'. Bitches may become possessive over the nesting area, or carry soft toys about and nurse them; physically, they often come into milk to a greater or lesser degree. Some, of course, do nothing at all.

A few dog behaviourists make a really big deal about the phantom pregnancy, saying that the bitch should not be allowed to nurse her toys or guard her nest. Utter nonsense! Just let her get on with it: it will all be over in a very short time. The less people bully her, the better she will be. She may not want to come for walks while

False pregnancy

her 'pups' are new, but if she does, take her out and tire her out. Reducing her food at this time, coupled with lots of exercise can mimic the natural state of a bitch that has lost her litter. Nature in these cases puts the bitch first – after all, she can always have a litter next time – and the milk dries up. If she is really uncomfortable with milk – and even a maiden bitch will produce milk – there are homoeopathic remedies that will help her, such as Prolactin 30c given three times daily for five days. Other than this, leave her in peace if she is grouchy, and see that everyone else does as well. Be particularly careful with visitors and children.

Blackmail
Apart from the seasons, which are not really that daunting to deal with in the majority of cases, some vets will try to blackmail bitch owners into having their bitches spayed for medical reasons. First, they will tell you that as the bitch is hormonally 'quiet' at the midpoint between seasons, all that spaying does is extend that time. If only it were that simple. Hormones ebb and flow in your bitch all the time, and surgical interruption causes all manner of effects on coat, metabolism and temperament. A few spayed bitches can become decidedly stroppy. Coats can become more profuse, and change colour. Spayed bitches tend to show increased appetite, but unfortunately put on weight more easily, so the conscientious owner has to work hard to keep the bitch's weight correct, and the less caring one lets the dog become obese.

Cancer

There, I've said it. Big C. Have your bitch spayed, and she will not develop ovarian or uterine cancer, which is true – you can't get cancer in an organ you no longer have. Worryingly, there are still information sources that tell you spaying before the first season will lessen the chances of mammary cancer. If you have your bitch spayed and she doesn't develop mammary cancer, you cannot be sure that she would have if you had not had her spayed. The truth is that some bitches, spayed and unspayed, develop mammary cancer, and some do not. Prevention of mammary cancer is not a good reason to have your bitch spayed. The only evidence of a procedure that prevents mammary cancer is an indication that bitches who have borne and suckled a litter are much less likely to get it. Oh dear. And the reason behind the pressure to have dogs neutered was to prevent puppies being born, wasn't it? Best not to research that aspect too scientifically, then, as the results could be counter-productive.

Pyometra

This is an infection of the uterus that will kill if left untreated. Again, if there is no uterus, it cannot get infected. During the season, extra help can be given to the bitch in the form of raspberry leaf tablets such as those from Dorwest Herbs, and homoeopathic Echinacea given throughout the season and for a week beyond. 'Pyo' is by no means as common as pro-spayers would have you believe, and the subject is covered in Chapter Eight.

The Big Secret

The dark secret that is almost never mentioned when people are being persuaded to have their bitches spayed is that a proportion of bitches suffer from urinary incontinence as a direct result of the operation, either immediately or later in life. The manufacturers of the main drug used to treat it put the figure at twenty per cent, but opinions vary. The problem ranges from a few drops of urine leaked while the bitch is asleep to lakes of it every time she lies down, and a few poor creatures dribble urine constantly. Apart from the ramifications of keeping a house dog with such a problem, the bitch will suffer burns to her skin and discolouration of her fur from lying in her acid urine.

Research of spayed bitch incontinence done at Bristol University by Dr Peter Holt gave interesting results. Hormone treatment of affected bitches in one experiment had to be discontinued because a disproportionately large number of them became aggressive; hormone treatment is seldom offered nowadays possibly because of these results. Dr Holt concluded that the condition often had surgical causes in that it was customary to reattach the bladder with a single stitch, and that using a second stitch would make all the difference.

Other treatment options are further surgery, a choice of drugs, homoeopathy and acupuncture. If drugs are used, homoeopathy can be given to support the dog's system. If your own bitch is affected, it can be very trying; seasons once or twice a year are nothing compared to urinary incontinence twenty-four hours a day every day of the year. However, it is to be hoped that surgical techniques for spaying will improve, because there is no doubt that a spayed bitch cannot get pyometra, and she cannot get pregnant. If you doubt your ability to keep your bitch away from male dogs during seasons, spaying is still worth considering – but do talk it over with your vet. If your worries about the possibility of incontinence are treated dismissively, be concerned: it might be a relatively small percentage of bitches that is affected, but you do not want one of them to be yours.

THE MALE DOG

Neutering the male dog involves the surgical removal of both testicles. It is irreversible. In male puppies, the testes appear (drop) at any time after three months old, though some may take longer. They may appear and disappear for a while, or one may come down and the other take its time. Sometimes, one testicle does not drop at all, and rarely, there can be only one testicle there in the first place. Castration is recommended in these cases because a retained testicle runs the risk of becoming cancerous quite quickly, and the condition is inherited: these dogs should not be bred from. Castration is recommended for normal dogs because it supposedly reduces aggression, straying, and of course, the dog cannot breed, which prevents unwanted puppies. It certainly does that. It also alters the coat, and as with spaying, the dog needs less food but has more appetite, so the owner has to put in more effort to keep the dog at the correct weight.

Straying from the home is usually preventable by having sensible secure fencing at an appropriate height, or by keeping the dog in a pen or run when he cannot be supervised. Some dogs are very good at escaping, and may need the security of a closed door between them and the front door at all times, and no windows left open. Preventing straying while being walked is a straightforward matter of training.

I must stress that most male dogs are not in the habit of straying, from home or when being exercised, unless they get the smell of an on-heat bitch. Even then, the majority will not follow, if they have been trained properly. If you have one of the very few that does take off after bitches, then castration may or may not cure him, but should be done to stop him from mating with the bitches he follows. Some breeds have much higher sex instincts than others, and some individuals do as well, and these sorts need a little more application from their owners if you are to live together amicably. A few dogs will howl incessantly if there is an on-heat bitch in the vicinity. Castration for these sorts of dogs is justifiable, but they will still need to be trained, and confined responsibly. To have a dog castrated in order to let him stray does little to reduce his nuisance value to others, and he may simply disappear one day.

Aggression is a different matter entirely. Broadly speaking, aggression relates to fear, status or territoriality. An owner can be 'territory' as well as a place, and some dogs get aggressive when other dogs approach their owner, or if the owner fusses those dogs. Territory can be places where the dogs are frequently exercised, or the house and garden, the car, or most of the street. Fear aggression is displayed by the dog which has no safe place to go, and is often seen when dogs on leads meet. If they were off the leads, they would be able to get out of each other's way, but on the leads they are fearful. Of course, there are times when dogs have to be on leads, and owners should ensure that they cannot get at each other: likewise, a dog on a lead meeting a dog off a lead almost guarantees conflict.

Dogs that are establishing status (dominance aggression) will posture, skirmish, and occasionally fight. It looks and sounds bad to the human owners, but such spats are normally just noise and spit, unless one or both dogs are unsocialised and so giving off or responding to the wrong signals, or if the owners start shouting, which will gee the dogs up. Some breeds and individuals are much more likely to start a fight than others, and owners should be vigilant and avoid flashpoints such as confined spaces.

Castration is unlikely to help with territorial aggression. With dominance and fear issues, it can sometimes make matters worse, because a castrated male dog is the lowest in canine social hierarchy, and liable to be picked on by both entire dogs and bitches spayed and unspayed. So a fearful dog will be more fearful because he is being attacked, and a status-seeking dog will fight to retain his place in the eyes of other dogs, which no longer accord him any respect. It is worth knowing that truly dominant animals do not fight – they have no need to do so. Their very bearing commands deference. It is the insecure dog that starts a fight, though a truly dominant dog will end it with a minimum of fuss.

Mounting

Some male dogs will exhibit mounting behaviour, which is generally found very embarrassing by their humans, and often precipitates a decision to castrate. This really isn't necessary. Adolescent dogs, and bitches too, will go through a highly-sexed time, just like every other adolescent you have ever met, and this quietens down with maturity in the vast majority of cases. It is a valuable behaviour, because during this time, the youthful male learns when it is appropriate, and that it is mostly not! Other dogs will tell him off in no uncertain terms. Dogs of either sex may demonstrate mounting; many bitches do this and it is not a sign that anything is wrong with them. Any attempt to mount humans, however, shows a discipline problem rather than a sexual one, because the human should be so far above the dog in status that the option should not even be considered. If this does occur, it should be vigorously discouraged, and the dog's training programme amended. Some male dogs will form attachments to inanimate objects like cushions; there is no harm in this so just give him his own cushion and let him get on with it.

Medical Aspects

As with spaying, castration's hard-sell is prevention of fatal diseases, notably testicular cancer and prostate problems, prostate cancer itself being extremely rare in dogs. These cancers are common in humans, but you don't see hordes of men queuing up to be castrated. Removing the testicles will certainly prevent them becoming cancerous; as with mammary cancer, you cannot tell with any certainty whether a castrated dog would otherwise have developed it. If a dog does develop testicular cancer, he can be castrated then; the condition is not all that common and usually straightforward to treat as long as it is caught early. There is some risk of castrated dogs becoming incontinent, but this is not nearly as prevalent as spayed-bitch incontinence. However, there are definite links with thyroid conditions and castration, and several other health issues too.

On balance, the medical arguments for castration do not add up to much, though, as with the spaying of bitches, it is easy money for the veterinary practice. Castration may sometimes be indicated for certain behavioural problems, though most of these can be overcome with good training, which is a far sounder investment in terms of the well-being of your dog. Particularly with young dogs, it is better to 'wait and see', keeping castration as a final option.

Some castrated dogs will react to a bitch in season; some can mate and even tie, but they cannot father pups.

Falsies

I almost regret having to mention this, but it is actually possible to have false testicles ('neuticles') implanted after castration. The main reason given for this ludicrous procedure is that some owners (usually male) feel that castration has made their dogs depressed. I doubt whether dogs hold such store by their fertility, though I imagine having plummeted down the status ladder would indeed be depressing. Sadly, falsies would make no difference in how one dog perceives another, as they determine sexual matters using their sense of smell. I can tell from the body language of my own dogs whether one that is approaching them is male, female, entire or neutered, and that is well before they actually meet. Canine scenting abilities are awesome.

Chemical Castration

If you are considering having your dog castrated for behavioural reasons, there is a hormone injection that can be given that is said to mimic the effects of castration. The effects vary: most of the people I have spoken with say that the surgical castration had considerably different effects from the injection. However, it is reasonable to say that if the injection causes the improvement that you are after, then surgery will as well.

Other Options

If the reason for considering castration is because the dog becomes obsessed with finding bitches, or if he lives with or near to bitches which come on heat, sometimes alternative treatment can help. However, none of these will prevent an entire dog from mating if he gets a chance: they simply take the edge off his sexual appetite.

WHEN TO NEUTER

If you have decided that neutering is what you want for your dog or bitch, then the next consideration is when to have it done. Despite the modern fashion for neutering as soon as possible, it is better for your dog's health if he or she is allowed to grow up first. Also, a lot of behavioural 'problems' that may have led others to recommend neutering, will disappear once adolescence is over. I recently heard of a three-month-old pup being considered for neutering because he was mounting other puppies at his puppy training class – but this sort of mounting is nothing to do with sex and everything to do with establishing pecking order in the puppy group. Just as there is more than one cause of aggression, so there is more than one cause of mounting – bitches will mount, too, in certain circumstances. At three months old, your pup is very much a baby, and while his or her behaviour should receive guidance, surgery is somewhat over the top, particularly as there is every chance of considerable health issues arising directly from such early castration. Regrettably, no-one seems interested in researching these negative outcomes to date.

TRAINING

If you put work into training your puppy from the first days you have her, she will be a pleasure to own all her life. Training does not turn a dog into a robot: it makes her easy to live with. I am constantly amazed at the appalling behaviour that people tolerate in their dogs. But you need to show the dog what behaviour you want from her – it is not enough to shout at her in your own language. Training classes can be very useful – if only to prove to you that there are dogs a lot worse behaved than yours – but they have their limitations. The best will show you the way, but you still have to put in the work every day, not just for the hour in the village hall once a week. Ten minutes a day is all that it takes to train a dog, but in that ten minutes – which you can take in two blocks of five if you want – you must be utterly consistent.

Research your training classes carefully before you commit to them. Dog training has come a long way in the last half century, and is still evolving, but not every trainer has evolved along with it, and many are using training methods that may not suit you or your dog. Letters after the name do not necessarily indicate a good trainer. Go along and watch some classes, and see how the trainer works. If that method seems to be acceptable, then go along with your dog. If you find that you have made a mistake after a few classes, don't compromise your dog's welfare by continuing just because you have paid for the full course – find another trainer.

Training

PUPPY CLASSES

Puppy socialisation classes are everywhere now, because the importance of your puppy learning to behave in social situations is at last being recognised. Find out about classes from your vet or from the community centre. These classes can be very good for the puppy in the one-dog or one-pet household, and good for the owners too, for they can apply themselves to learning dog body language in canine interaction. Avoid classes where puppies of all ages and sizes are allowed to play in one huge brawl, as smaller puppies may get hurt by larger puppies. Controlled play is what you should be seeing, with the owners able to call their puppies to them and then send them back to their game. Personally, I don't like to see puppies passed around from person to person, as it is only too easy to drop a wriggling puppy and damage it. If you have a nervous pup that prefers to sit under your chair or on your lap, I hope that you have an instructor that can cope with this, and let the pup come out of her shell in her own time. Some teachers are marvellous with the more extrovert breeds, but have quite the wrong attitude with more diffident types. At the end of puppy socialisation training, your pup should be able to interact comfortably with other dogs, showing no signs of fear or protectiveness, and to come back to you when you call. She should have learned to walk properly on the lead, sit and lie down on command; to my mind, that is quite enough for a little puppy.

LATER CLASSES

What you want to do next will vary. If you have ambitions for one of the canine leisure activities, such as agility or flyball, then you will need to find classes that will cater for you. If you have plans for a working dog, now is the time for working training, which needs a specialist approach. If what you want is a nicely-behaved pet, then continuation classes should teach your dog to walk to heel off the lead, to 'wait' and recall, 'stay' until you return, and the remote 'drop' where you can command her to lie down at a distance. This last could save her life one day. You might also want her to retrieve, be able to send her to a spot in front of you to lie down, and to find hidden objects, which she would enjoy. Most pets can get by just with walking nicely on the lead and coming back when they are called: if your dog won't do either of these, your relationship will be difficult.

The teenager

METHODS

Training is an important part of your relationship with your dog. There are plenty of training books and videos about, good and bad, and I would suggest that you read and see as many as you can, critically, and applying your own common sense. If the methods used don't sit well with you, try another way. If something sounds like arrant nonsense, it probably is. Beware the trainers who can only demonstrate their methods with one of the more receptive breeds! What trains a border collie won't have the same impact on (say) a beagle or a saluki. So far as the well-known trainers go, I would recommend anything by Dr Ian Dunbar, who is head and shoulders above most of the rest.

If you don't like the idea of classes, or can't get to them, another option is to have a trainer come to you and give one-to-one instruction. This is expensive, but often better value than a lesson in a large class of which you will maybe get five minutes of personal attention. Some of the value of classes is seeing the training issues of different dogs and how to tackle them: with your own trainer, you will be addressing your own dog's specific needs. Again, standards vary enormously, and the best trainer in the world is of no use if there is not the empathy between you.

There is, of course, no reason why you should not train your own dog entirely by yourself, and end up with a good dog at the end of it. I do this myself, though I do like a pup to attend some socialisation classes. However, I have been training dogs for a very long time. It is easy to have terrific misunderstandings with your dog, and to really stress your relationship, purely through incorrect communication. If you are a first-time dog owner, or your previous dogs have not been as well-behaved as you would have wished, there is a lot to be gained from attending classes or otherwise putting yourselves in the hands of a professional. I still do so if I need to – sometimes a different perspective on a particular issue can make all the difference, and the trainer doesn't exist who knows it all.

TEENAGERS

Puppyhood goes by so quickly. Before long, your soft, velvety pup, so eager to be with you, has grown into a gangly adolescent whose vocabulary is, like Kipling's camels: 'Can't – won't, shan't – don't!'. Many of the behaviours that you thought you had trained in – and out – will be gone – or back. Many teenage dogs are hooligans, and will test you to the skies. This is the main reason why so many dogs taken into 'rescue' are between six and eighteen months old. Please be patient and ride out the storm: it all comes to an end, and with dogs is a matter of months rather than years. I have one whose adolescent rebellion lasted about two weeks, whereas his mother's went on for over a year – but we got to the end of it at last. The adolescent dog may defy your authority, but at least she won't be taking drugs or getting into debt – and you can choose the company she keeps.

By the time she is two years old, all the tantrums and trials will be past, and you will have a happy, healthy dog to brighten your days. Will others with less vital dogs congratulate you on the results of all your hard work? Will they heck. They'll tell you how 'lucky' you are. Best get used to it now.

3 The Inner Dog

Feeding for health and good behaviour

Good health demands good food. You cannot get other than inferior health if you feed inferior food, though dogs are mostly tough of digestion and will survive and even look tolerably good while being fed all sorts of rubbish. As they age, however, it is payback time, and if they have been badly fed, they are likely to develop all sorts of illnesses that could otherwise have been avoided. Luckily for us, feeding a dog properly is neither difficult nor expensive. It does, however, demand a little more effort than feeding one badly, in the same way as feeding ourselves healthily requires slightly more application than opening a packet and guzzling the contents. If you have only ever fed commercial dog food, or never fed a dog at all, some of the suggestions in this chapter may seem at first sight to be out of the question, or a leap into the unknown for you. They were for me as well, and then, as is often the case, what I thought would be problems just melted away. Feeding your dog for health is not at all complicated, but it is necessary for me to go into the reasons in some depth so that you can see the sense of it clearly. Please read all the way to the end of the chapter before you draw your conclusions and decide whether you are willing to give natural feeding a chance. To start with, let's have a look at what your dog needs, and the easiest and best ways to supply it.

TEETH

Look at your dog's teeth, and you will see that they are all pointed, even the ones at the very back. The canine teeth, the long pointed ones at the front, are very large and have deeply-set roots. When the mouth is closed, all the teeth in the upper jaw should fit tightly into the gaps between the teeth of the lower jaw, the bottom canines coming in front of the top ones. These teeth are designed to work hard.

In some breeds of dog, the shape of the face has been altered so that the teeth do not fit so well. It is possible by selective breeding to alter the shape of the dog's skull quite easily. Thus some dogs are bred to be 'undershot', that is, the bottom jaw is longer than the top. This alters the dentition and may have an effect on the way the dog manages her food. It is said that bulldog type breeds had the undershot jaw bred into them so that they could hold a bull by the nose and still breathe; this means that the bull breeds should still have a powerful grip which is unaffected by the shape of the jaw. Toy dogs which have the same altered face shape, for instance the pug and the Pekingese, have it altered to make the face more like that of a human baby, and the 'squashed face' look in toy dogs tends to go with enormous eyes as well, for the same unfortunate purpose. So on the one hand, you have the jaw shape altered for a working purpose, and on the other, for fashion. Bulldogs no longer have to drive and hold bulls, and in consequence no longer have the physique to do so, and their dentition is now as questionable as that of a dog bred down to a strange shape or 'miniature' size purely for fashion. Such dogs will have a little more trouble in using and therefore keeping their teeth than a dog of working type. Indeed, certain miniature breeds have such appalling dentition that a full mouth is not required by the breed standard. The 'overshot' jaw can occur freely in some breeds as well, where the top jaw is longer than the bottom to the degree that the teeth do not fit normally into the mouth. Feeding either type of dog correctly so that they maintain whatever teeth they have in good condition is especially important

Back to those pointed teeth. They tell you that the dog is a carnivore. There are other parts of canine anatomy that will tell you the same, for instance a digestive system powerful enough to break down bones and strong enough not to become ill as a result of eating carrion, a relatively short gut which sends the food through quickly, and eyes set on the front of the head to give binocular vision, which only predators have. Therefore your dog is designed to eat prey that she catches. That does not mean that your dog is meant to eat only meat. Hide, hair, bones and flesh is what nature intended to keep your dog healthy.

Now, this might be squeamish stuff for the first-time dog owner, and difficult to achieve at first sight. Equally, there are people who choose a severely restricted diet for themselves, which is up to them as this book is about dog health not people health, but then claim that the dog is an 'omnivore' and can live on a meat-free diet. Dogs certainly can live on meat-free diets, but they will never be as healthy as dogs that eat what dogs were designed to eat. The owners can choose what they eat: the dog cannot. My opinion is that if people wish to subject their pets to an inferior diet for the sake of their own food fads, then that is bordering on cruelty. I would suggest that such people content themselves with pets that are meant to exist on meat-free diets, though even herbivores will eagerly eat meat and bones under certain circumstances, usually when there is some sort of dietary lack. But you want to feed your dog whatever is best for her, and also acceptable to you, which does not include throwing her an ox every couple of weeks and letting her chew her way through it. So, what options do you have?

COMMERCIAL FOOD

A huge pet food industry has grown up since Mr Spratt first started manufacturing dog biscuits, having watched starving street curs hanging around the docks in the hope of being thrown some ship's biscuit. From these humble beginnings, dog food has become available in all sorts of guises, and generations of pet owners have grown up with the idea that dogs are fed 'dog food' and that anything else, such as table scraps, is bad for them. The people who make dog food are assiduous in encouraging this belief.

DRIED FOOD

Commercial dry 'complete' food is extremely popular, easy to store, easy to feed, and strutting its stuff by telling you that it contains every conceivable vitamin and mineral that your dog could possibly need. It comes in kibble, chunks, or a sort of muesli of flakes, lumps and grains, in varieties for puppy, junior, adult, senior, hardworking, resting, dieting, or even specially designed to be fed to dogs with this

Dried food

illness or that, for instance sensitive skins, or kidney ailments. Should you add one scrap of any other food, you are told, you will destroy this delicate balance, your dog will become ill, and it will be all your fault. You might wonder, if you are of an enquiring mind, why this perfect food needs to have added flavourings, sometimes even molasses, to make it more palatable. You might feel edgy about the necessary additives and preservatives, or even wonder why a dog would need her food to be coloured. You might even pause to consider that people are urged to eat as wide a variety of fresh food as possible, and yet apparently the best food for your dog is exactly the same processed stuff at every meal.

Given that the high spots of a dog's day are her walks and her food, you might feel that you are short-changing her somewhat, rather as if you were taking her on exactly the same walk every day and not even letting her off the lead. And then you remember the white-coated, smiling scientist in the dog-food advertisements assuring you that this dog food is scientifically prepared and honed to perfection in its dietary constituents, and feel reassured, as indeed you are meant to. Dried food, is, after all, very convenient. It is convenient to sell as well, and a lot of people who should know what they are talking about, such as vets, kennels owners and dog trainers, have a good sideline in selling dried food. They will assure you that dogs don't need variety in their meals, and will be perfectly happy and healthy on the same rations, day in and day out, for all of their lives. I must stress that they are not trying to delude you. They believe implicitly in this food or that, and feed it to all of their own dogs as well as patients/boarders/pupils. It has to be true. The feed manufacturers said so.

WET FOOD

This is probably what your family dog was fed when you were a child. Open a tin, add some biscuits and there you are. The picture on the tin shows a happy dog, the words assure you that the meat is prime cuts of something or other, and there are many flavours to choose from, though all except the fish ones smell very similar. The food looks good in the bowl, and dogs that aren't keen on dry food will seldom refuse tinned, though you will have to mix in the biscuit – which is now called 'mixer' – or else they will just pick out the wet food and leave the rest. Despite all the vitamins and minerals listed on the tin, the mixer is essential, as it contains added minerals, and does a fairly good job of balancing out the wet stuff. If you read the tin, you will find that you are paying for a lot of water, and sometimes the content is described as 'beef (chicken, lamb, rabbit etc.) flavoured' rather than 'beef'. Which means that the 'meat' could be anything, and may well contain a proportion of textured cellulose.

As well as tinned food, you can get 'moist' foods in sealed pouches and trays. Dogs find these very appetising as well. You will be recommended to add biscuit to some varieties, whereas others will be 'complete'. Some will have added herbs, cooked vegetables and cereals, and make interesting reading. Some will describe themselves as 'organic' 'natural' or 'free from artificial ingredients'. All these meats have to be cooked, because they would not keep otherwise, and the vitamins lost in the cooking will mostly be replaced, sometimes with synthetic vitamins. Tins, trays and pouches of dog food are readily available in shops, and almost as easy to store as the dried varieties of food. You have quite a bit more packaging to dispose of, which could be important if you have several large dogs, or live in an area where refuse collection is restricted.

THE OTHER END

Poo watching is part of the Dark Arts learned by every dog owner and not understood by those who are outside the magic circle. You can tell a great deal about the health of your dog just by observing the final stage of her digestive process. While no dog mess is exactly attar of roses, it has to be said that the end result of feeding tinned food can be pretty dire to clear up. Some of it, rather disconcertingly, smells exactly the same as it did in the tin and some varieties are so highly coloured that they result in bright orange faeces. With dried food, the results are not quite so vile, though muesli varieties can go through largely undigested. It takes a longer gut than a dog's to digest cereal presented in a form that is still recognisable when in the food bowl.

WHAT IS IN IT?

The pet food industry dovetails nicely with the waste from human food outlets. Some, particularly the smaller concerns do indeed source their food from better origins, but for the most part, dog food owes a lot to supplies which are deemed unfit for human consumption, sometimes very unfit indeed. Reading the list of contents can be a shock. Most of the food may be cereal and pulses. If the 'meat' part of the label refers to beef, chicken, lamb or similar, then some of that will be found in the food, though legally it may be as little as four per cent and will include obscure parts of the carcase such as udders, feet and lips. If 'meat and meat derivatives' then the net can be cast wider, including such delicacies as, for instance, chicken feathers.

Periodically, you will see reports of scams whereby condemned food intended for the pet industry is illegally recycled as human food. This food is typically in an advanced stage of decomposition when it is diverted into the catering industry, confirming many pet owners' concerns about processed pet food. Now, it doesn't actually harm a dog to eat most carrion, but you were probably under the impression that the meat used in dog food was fresh. Equally, dogs are quite happy to eat bits and pieces that don't come near the human catering side, such as udders, chicken feet, sheep ears or whatever, but you might not wish to be paying premium prices in order to feed your dog this way. Look at the larger dog food manufacturers and note their links with the human processed food industry. Think about it.

NATURAL FEEDING

This represents a quantum leap for the dog owner who has happily fed commercial food until now. Please be brave, and I will lead you through the options. The health of a dog which has been fed natural food is so much better than that of a commercially fed dog that few people making that leap return to their old ways, particularly once they know a little more about commercial food. Those who do, do so mostly because commercial food is quicker and leaves more television time, though some do so because they are on the receiving end of outright hostility from people with a vested interest in promoting unnatural feeding. Before we condemn these professionals, I would like to make clear that most of them are sincere in their beliefs. Vets especially get little training in dog nutrition, and what they do get usually takes the form of a series of lectures by, and a visit to, a manufacturer of commercial food. In the UK the only veterinary-recognised qualification in canine nutrition comes from a course taught by a well-known dog food manufacturer. Vets who have studied on their own, and crossed the divide whereby they promote natural feeding for canine health, are caught in an unenviable situation. Not only are they vilified by less enlightened members of their own profession, but also if they pass on the glad tidings to their customers, they need a far larger client base than normal because the dogs rarely become ill with the diseases that are rife in dogs fed on a lesser diet. My own local practice found that reducing vaccination and promoting natural feeding led to a much larger client base but not a corresponding increase in turnover as all the patients were healthier. Dogs that are injured or need surgery heal much more quickly with the vigorous immune system that natural feeding gives them. Dogs from breeds that are prone to skin conditions, digestive ailments and glandular malfunctions usually never develop them, or only when in extreme old age. Those teeth that we talked about earlier do not develop tartar, and so the annual 'scrape' under anaesthetic that is the regular ordeal of so many dogs just isn't necessary. Nor is toothpaste, tooth brushing or tooth extraction; in fact a whole corner of the pet care industry becomes obsolete. With healthy teeth, a dog does not have toxins leaching into her system that she would have had with a mouthful of rotten ones, nor does she face the risk of an anaesthetic every year. Natural feeding means that dogs are far less likely to get overweight, and their meals satisfy their hunger for longer. Well, that's enough preamble – you want to know what to do.

RAW MEAT WITH BONES

Let's start with the really daunting subject. Your dog needs to eat raw meat with raw meaty bones. Raw meat by itself is lacking in important minerals, which are provided exactly as nature intended by bones. Your dog will enjoy sawing off the cartilage and ligaments on the ends of the bones, and eating whole the softer bones, such as ribcages. She will split larger bones and extract the marrow, which is also very good for her. Once you have seen your sweet pet crunch through the thighbone of a calf with one bite, you will look at her in a completely different light. What sort of raw meat should you feed? Any sort at all, though remember pork tends to sour more quickly than other meats, and unless it is organically raised, will have far more drugs in it than lamb or beef, which are pretty nearly organic in the UK, however raised. Although your dog is well equipped to eat carrion, she lives with you, in your house, maybe shares your furniture or even your bed, and you are not as strong in the digestive system as she is. So give her fresh raw meat to eat, for your sake. If she chances upon something well rotted when she is out on a walk, she will probably devour it with glee, maggots and all: her digestive system can cope, but yours may not, so try not to let her lick your face.

Some folk will tell you that raw meat will turn your dog vicious, or make her smell bad. I can assure you that neither is the case. Cooked meat now and again will do her no harm at all, but it will be missing important nutrients which the cooking process removes, and also will be too soft to give her teeth and jaws a good workout. Raw meat acts as a natural dental floss because of its texture. Serve it in a lump: your dog needs to chew on it, and cutting it up into little cubes is a waste of your time. You may be shocked to see what big chunks of meat your dog can swallow. Some dogs overdo it on occasion, and have to vomit the meat back up in order to make a better job of it at the second attempt. This is normal dog behaviour: they are designed to do this. The pack feasting at a kill is vulnerable, and so the dogs swallow as much food as they can, to regurgitate it later in a safer place. Food is carried to puppies this way as well. If the spectacle makes you feel unwell, look away: your dog will come to no harm by it, and it will soon be over.

ORGAN MEAT
Heart, liver, kidney, 'lights' (lungs and trachea) and sundry other red bits are very rich feeding, especially full of vitamin A. This is one of the vitamins which can be harmful in excess, and so offal should not be fed more than once a week. Dogs adore organ meat, and a weekly treat will do no harm at all.

Tripe can be fed much more often – if you can get it, and if you can stand the smell. Tripe is the stomach casing of ruminants. While fresh meat simply smells of meat, there is no denying that tripe smells vile to people, and wonderful to dogs. I have an idea that tripe was invented to test how much you love your dog. Green tripe, which still has the vegetable matter from the animal's last meal clinging to it, is especially good for them, but it is difficult to get now due to tiresome regulations about the handling and sale of meat. Washed tripe is what you are most likely to find, and your dog will still enjoy it. Tripe is easy to digest but not particularly nourishing; feed it as often as you like, but be sure to feed red meat as well.

BONES ALONE
Now bones, and here be dragons! You and I have been subjected to a raft of received

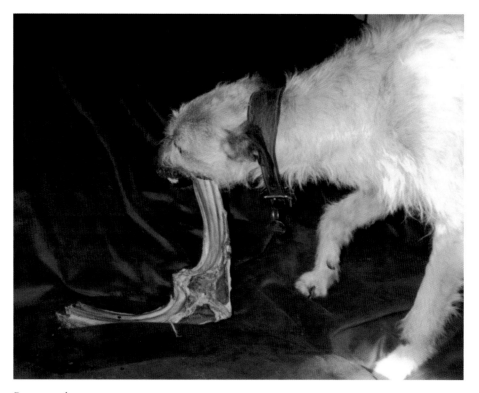

Raw meaty bones

wisdom about feeding dogs bones, and all of it designed to frighten us off doing so. The bones will puncture her intestines. They will block her gut completely. She will break her teeth, or choke, or turn nasty, or all of these. And yet…wild dogs, foxes and wolves seem to survive eating bones, don't they? Next door's cat seems to get away with eating whole small animals and birds? What really are the dangers?

First of all, I must stress that cooked bones are indeed dangerous, and must never be fed, not even if generations of your family have fed generations of dogs on cooked bones. They and you may have got away with it so far, but there is no need to go looking for trouble. Cooking alters the structure of the bone so that it splinters, and also can impact in the gut, causing a blockage. Cooked bones will indeed break teeth. So, no cooked bones, please. And not just any raw bones will do either. First of all, the best bones are from young animals. These bones have all the vital nutrients in them, but are softer than the bones of mature stock, and so can be crunched right up and eaten completely. Thus they provide maximum occupation, nutrition and roughage. How do you know if the bones that you can get are from young enough animals? If they are from animals that are sold for human consumption, then they will be the right age, for only young animals are sold in butchers' shops.

Equally important is that these bones have meat on them. This serves two purposes: the meat will be ripped off the bone by the dog using her incisor teeth, the little ones right at the front, and so provide exercise to jaw muscles, neck muscles, front feet which hold the bone, and the haunches which balance the activity of the forequarters. The whole dog is getting a workout, and in smaller dogs, a good meal of raw meaty bones provides as much exercise as a walk. Next, the other teeth are brought into use by the dog crunching up the bones, which cleans teeth and gums. But the other important feature of using meaty bones is that the meat and bones eaten at the same meal means that the meat pads the bony matter as it is eaten, which of course cannot happen if bones are eaten dry.

What Type

Rib bones of large farm animals are very good. If you have a source of wild rabbit or game, it is better either to cook the meat and take it off the bone, or else grind the meat and bone up in a mincer and feed it raw. This is because wild creatures get a lot more exercise than farmed stock, and the bones tend to be denser. Also, you cannot guarantee that the meat and bones are from young animals. If you are worried about worms from wild rabbits, cooking will kill these where they occur, or else freezing for four or more weeks at a temperature of minus 20ºC or lower will render the meat safe. Having working dogs, we get enormous amounts of wild rabbit, and have an industrial mincer to deal with them. Minus heads and intestines, the rabbits are ground up fur and all – good roughage – and then frozen. If you really are worried about feeding bones, then mince the lot as we do with the rabbits, which retains all

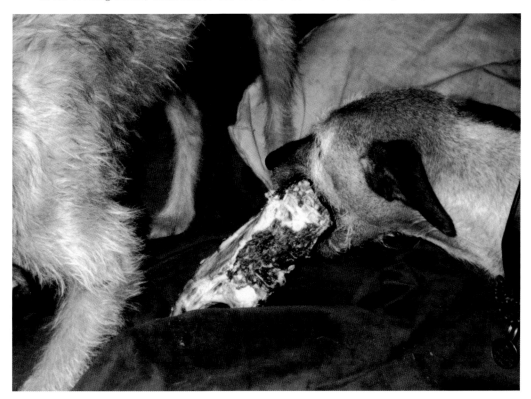

Raw meat as dental floss

the nourishment of the bones but of course lacks the tooth-cleaning and exercise provided by feeding the whole bones. If you mince the whole carcase, do not then cook the mince, but feed it raw, because of the bone content. I'm going to say this once more: do not feed cooked bones in any form – and this includes the 'roasted bones' that you can get in some pet shops.

Breast of lamb fed raw is marvellous for putting the weight on a skinny dog, and if chopped into small pieces, ideal for weaning puppies or starting a dog out on the voyage of natural feeding. Probably the most popular way to start is by offering a raw chicken wing. The smallest dog can cope easily with these, and puppies love them too. But, I hear you say, you always thought that chicken bones were deadly and should never be fed. I was brought up with that idea as well, and it is completely wrong. Raw chicken wings, or boned-out carcases from the butcher, are ideal feeding for dogs. The myth of chicken bones being fatal to dogs is a pervasive one, and I admit to lying awake listening for the sound of dying dogs the first time I fed raw chicken carcases, but now, many years later, I can tell you that raw chicken carcases and wings are an excellent food for dogs. The myth persists: one lady of my acquaintance had her butcher deliver a strong lecture on the dangers of feeding boned-out chicken carcases to dogs, and he refused to sell her any. However, she now gets chicken carcases from this shop, the butcher being under the impression that she makes a lot of soup. Her dog is fit, healthy and bursting with life on her 'dangerous' diet.

Marrow Bones
A lot of people think that a big beef marrow bone is a dog's dream, but in fact, these bones are best avoided, except with a teething pup. Marrow bones can cause wear on a dog's teeth, and a greedy dog could break off too much of the ends and swallow a large lump. Particularly avoid the marrow bone sawn in half by a helpful butcher, as a dog with a narrow bottom jaw can get it stuck in the hole as it tries to extract the marrow. Marrow is sensationally delicious to a dog. I referred earlier to my dogs cracking open bones to extract the marrow, which is what they will do quite safely with smaller bones such as legs of sheep or calves, but the huge marrow bones of a grown beef steer should be avoided.

The End Product
Meat fed with bones produces healthy, slightly dry faeces, which at first might make you think that the dog is constipated. In fact, this is the correct consistency for the output, as it exercises the bowel muscles and automatically empties the anal glands. It is very rare for a dog fed on natural raw food to have anal gland problems. Meat fed on its own, especially organ meat, will result in a dark, moist motion. Horsemeat, offal and red-fleshed game can cause loose, tarry faeces unless it has been 'hung' before feeding. Such meat is best fed with vegetables, of which more shortly.

Precautions
Yes, there are risks in feeding raw meat and bones, but equally, it is perfectly possible for a dog to choke on kibble. Feeding raw meat and bones does need a little common sense in certain matters.

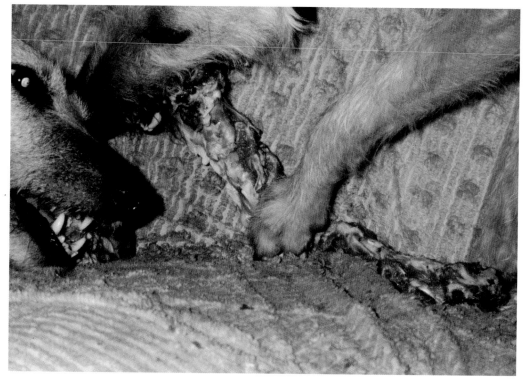

Eating bones together – only allow this if you are sure of your dogs' temperament

Don't feed dogs unsupervised. This is a good rule whatever you feed: you want to be sure that each dog gets her correct rations, and that shy or slow feeders are not bullied out of their meal by others. By observing your dogs eating, you will notice at once if there is something wrong with one of them, which you might otherwise not see if you just put the bowl down and walk away. Remember that bones are valuable to dogs, much more valuable than most other possessions, and certain types of dog will try to steal the bones off the other dogs, precipitating a fight. We have a terrier whose dream it is to own every bone in the world. Feed the dogs a sensible distance apart from each other, call them by name and give the bones out in order, top dog first, to lowest dog last, and if you have a troublemaker, feed her on her own, in a different room, kennel, or a closed dog crate. My own dogs (except the terrier) will cheerfully eat bones jaw to jaw with each other, but few dogs have this good a temperament, so do not allow this unless you are cast-iron sure that you will not get a fight. Dogs bear grudges just as much as people, and if a dog is continually bullied out of her bones, she will wait her time and one day deliver a furious attack on the thief. Dog fights are the owner's fault, not the dogs', for dogs will always behave like dogs. Avoid the situation ever developing by supervising meals properly. You might consider that processed dog food only causes disputes amongst the greediest of dogs, and come to the conclusion that you would rather feed processed food because the natural food seems to make the dogs aggressive, but this is not quite right: the truth is that the natural food is very much more desirable than the manufactured version, and it is worth a dog's while to eat as much of it as she can.

Very occasionally, a piece of bone can get stuck across the roof of a dog's mouth, or down the side of her jaw. This is easily rectified, and on the few occasions that one of my dogs has needed help, she has run to me straight away, pawing at the offending object. I have had to sort out a ferret with the same problem at times, and I can tell you I would much rather put my finger in a dog's mouth than a ferret's, though the latter have always been just as well-behaved about it as the dogs. This is another reason for being present during feeding times.

Dire warnings are given by vets who are opposed to the feeding of raw meat and bones, that we are exposing ourselves and our dogs to terrible infections, notably salmonella, E. coli and campylobacter. Now, these are all very nasty germs indeed, so should we be worried? Let's get it into proportion by remembering that a dog with a strong immune system is extremely resistant to all of these, designed as she is to eat carrion, if necessary in an advanced stage of decomposition. What about us frail humans? Again, these infections are all around us, and people in normal health are very resistant to them. You don't, after all, hear about farmers, pest controllers, butchers or abattoir staff going down with these infections on a regular basis, and you are exposed to all of these germs far more often than you will ever realise. However, it is right to be careful with hygiene in respect of all food, and normal sensible hygiene practices of washing hands, kitchen utensils, chopping blocks and dog bowls separately will be quite sufficient. Disinfect if it makes you feel more secure, but it really isn't necessary. If, however, there is someone in your home with a weak immune system, then be careful to keep them away from the dog food purely as a precaution. Frankly, though, there is more potential for infection in the average restaurant.

After a bone session, be sure to clear up any bits that might be left lying around. These might serve as the catalyst for a dog-fight, or attract blowflies and small vermin such as mice, and dried-out fragments of bone become sharp and might cause injury, especially the shards of a larger bone that has been cracked open by your dog in order to slurp out the delicious inside. If you don't like touching the bits, either put on rubber gloves, or slip your hand inside a plastic bag, in the same way as you clear up after your dog when out walking. Yes indeed, it is a little more trouble than filling a bowl from a sack, but for the little extra of your time, you are getting a much healthier dog, and incidentally, a happier and more fulfilled one as well.

VEGETABLES AND FRUIT

You are not off the hook yet! Your dog also needs vegetables and fruit in her diet. Dogs which have access to a variety of plant life will graze extensively, and should be allowed to do so. Some people do not like their dogs to graze because sometimes the dogs vomit afterwards, but this is an example of dogs self-medicating. Vomiting for a dog is not the unpleasant process that it is to us humans, and occurs in all healthy dogs. If the stomach is uneasy for any reason, the dog will seek out emetic herbs to eat, and rapidly get rid of whatever was bothering her. Usually she vomits up bright yellow bile and froth, which is normal; occasionally she will eject a knot of worms, which tells you that you have a job to do. Each dog has a pattern with this sort of

Grass is important

Hogweed

Cleavers

vomiting, normally two pukes in rapid succession and then everything is over and forgotten about. She can, if she wishes, eat again straight away and keep the food down – that's how efficient a cleanser herb-induced vomiting is. Food vomited and immediately eaten again has received a double dose of digestive enzymes, so you see the vomiting is in fact a very efficient way of processing food. Common herbs for stomach cleansing are couch grass (sometimes known as dog grass), lungwort, and common hogweed (not the giant variety). Dogs will also eat a wide variety of plants which do not cause vomiting, but are nutritionally important to them. Favourites with mine are green wheat, goosegrass (cleavers), chickweed, and sundry grasses that they choose and are very fussy about. If it is not the right grass, it simply will not do. In addition, my dogs have free access to the herb garden, though they have to be fenced out of the vegetable garden or they would lay it waste in a matter of days.

All this is in dogs that are fed a natural diet of meat, bones and whole-carcase in the shape of minced rabbits, so they really do need the extra nutrients in the vegetable matter. I have noticed that dogs fed on commercial food graze quite frantically, in contrast to the gourmet-style picking and choosing that my own animals display. Many dogs also hoover up the manure of vegetarian animals, which is revolting to us but, let's face it, only part-digested vegetable matter which is of use to the dog. Again, I find that my dogs don't do a lot of this, but dogs which are not fed vegetables will often frantically gobble down any manure that they can find. Mine

Picking blackberries

Eating a pear

rarely vomit bile as long as they have had their vegetables, and the morning after a meat meal often shows that the bile has been carried through the digestive system and ejected with the faeces. Dogs will go out of their way to eat fruit such as windfall apples, or pick their own blackberries. All species of wild canid will eat freely of fruit and vegetable matter as long as it is the right sort of vegetation. It used to be thought that wild members of the dog family would eat the stomach contents of the herbivores that they killed, and fulfil their vegetable needs that way, the digestive process of the prey animal having broken down the cellulose of the vegetation to a state where the carnivore can benefit from it. Then studies were made of wolves in captivity, and the stomach contents of wild dingos and wolves which had been killed, and it seemed as if they did not do this. The captive wolves in particular would eat neither the stomach contents nor the large intestine. Beware the conclusions of the scientific experiment that does not go far enough! Different studies on different species of wild dogs in captivity showed that they were much more likely to eat what wolves rejected – but studies on captive animals are never the whole story, and it is not always easy to monitor the dietary – or other – habits of wild groups. Wild and domesticated canids are selective about the vegetation they eat, much more selective than they are about the flesh they consume. If they haven't access to what they need, they will not eat vegetation for the sake of it. With regard to stomach contents: some will eat it, some not. The large intestine is never popular, but the small is one of the first things to be eaten at a kill. Wild canids will feast on fallen fruit, and some will pick their own as well: the scats of British foxes are full of sloe stones and the remains of elderberries and crab apples in season. If you have ever tried to eat a raw sloe, this will give you a new respect for foxes.

Unless rotted or half-digested by something else, vegetable matter cannot easily be digested by your dog, and will be excreted mostly in the same lumps that it was swallowed as. For your dog to access the nutrients in full, it is necessary to break down the cellulose that locks them in. We cannot digest cellulose easily either, which is why we cook most of our vegetables, and herbivores have long and unwieldy digestive processes which have evolved to do a similar job. The easy way for us to give dogs vegetable matter in a form that they can extract maximum goodness from is to break down the cellulose by mincing, lightly cooking, or processing the vegetables through a liquidiser. Even light cooking will destroy some of the more delicate nutrients, and so dedicated natural feeders tend to mince or liquidise the vegetables. This might, at first, make panic rise in your chest at the thought of yet another job to do – but it is honestly not that awkward. You can either liquidise a week's worth of raw vegetables and fruit in one go, and freeze in portion sizes, or whip up some each day. The total of extra work is around an hour a week for our five dogs (four large, one small) which time is more than offset by their hardly ever having to go to a vet. An hour a week isn't much in return for all that they give us, is it?

What sort of fruit and vegetables? Almost anything, but avoid the onion family, which contain a substance that is bad for dogs, and the jury is out on potato – some sources say not at all, some say cooked but not raw. Recent research in America indicates that grapes and raisins are toxic to dogs, which came as rather a surprise to

Vegetables and fruit ready for liquidising

Sharing a banana

me as I have fed mine both for years. Until more research is done, it is better to err on the side of the angels and avoid feeding these; I still give mine a few grapes, but it is up to you whether you want to take the perceived risk. Most dogs dislike citrus fruit, though I know a Labrador (it would be a Labrador) that eats whole oranges. Too much of brassicas – the cabbage family – can depress thyroid function: it takes a lot to affect a normal dog, but if yours is on thyroid medication, be careful. Do not feed Brussels sprouts whole, as they can obstruct the intestine if swallowed.

Don't feed rotten fruit or vegetables, though you can certainly source your dog food cheaply from greengrocers' stock that has come to its last day of sale. It is a kind gesture to make room in your garden for dog grazing as well, with a few favourite grasses and herbs. Dogs will happily help themselves to fruit, or hoover up windfalls; you may need to put the fruit bowl out of reach in the house if you do not want that raided as well.

With my own dogs, it is interesting to note that, if fed a meat and bones-only meal, they graze extensively the following day, whereas if I feed fruit and vegetables with the meal, the grazing is only cursory.

Although the most nourishment is taken from crushed vegetables, dogs enjoy the exercise and occupation afforded by eating whole vegetables and fruit. Ours love cauliflower, cabbage stalks, broccoli, carrots and any fruit – in fact it is impossible for us to unzip a banana, no matter how quietly, without attracting an audience of dogs that looked to be in a deep sleep when we sneaked up to the fruit bowl.

OTHER FOODS

Other foods may be fed in moderation, if they are the sort that a wild dog would encounter from time to time. A few eggs will do no harm, though raw eggs will cause appalling wind in susceptible dogs! One of mine is a terrible egg thief, and has been known to appear beside me on walks carrying an egg that he has liberated from a mallard nest. Scrambled egg is one of the best ways I know of settling a runny tummy, and is easily digested by a convalescing dog. Nuts and seeds will be eaten with glee, but should only form a very small part of the overall diet. Don't let your dog shell her own nuts as she may damage her teeth or swallow an indigestible shard of shell. Dairy products are not really good for dogs, but they do love them. When training, small pieces of cheese can be offered as occasional titbits, and the odd dollop of natural live yoghurt can be included in a meal from time to time, but milk should be avoided unless circumstances are exceptional. Cow milk is very good for calves, but not other animals, not even puppies, and causes scour (severe diarrhoea) in most cases, as dogs lack the stomach enzymes for digesting it.

TITBITS AND TABLE SCRAPS

There is no harm in your dog having the odd bit of 'junk' food in the form of titbits – as long as these are kept to a minimum – and nor is there any harm in giving your dogs table scraps, as long as these are alcohol-free and preferably sugar-free as well. After all, if the food is good enough for you, it is good enough for your dog, provided you eat a healthy diet as well. If you are a committed junk-fooder then avoid inflicting your worst excesses on your dog. I have often noticed that people see the vast improvement in their dog's health that results from natural feeding and feel motivated to clean up their own diet as well. That can't be a bad decision, can it? Avoid giving chocolate: the theobromine in it can kill dogs. If your dog adores chocolate – one of mine would sell her soul for it – give the chocolates that are made for dogs and which have had the theobromine extracted, and only a few of them as a special treat.

CEREALS AND PULSES

Dogs don't need cereals. Wild dogs would only be able to eat cereals either from consuming ripe grain on the stem, or the stomach contents of a prey animal that had been eating ripening crops. In neither case is the food readily or frequently available. Processed cereal is never available, and yet what is in almost every commercial dog food, and in large amounts? Pulses would not be available either, except in green form. Dried pulses, especially soya, can cause bloat in susceptible dogs because one of the ingredients they break down into are saponins, which foam and expand in the gut. Cereals and pulses are added to dog food because they are cheap, and have good keeping qualities. Recent dietary research suggests that mature-onset (type 2) diabetes in humans can be precipitated by a diet high in cereal-based carbohydrates and reversed if caught early enough by eschewing these completely; given the accelerating incidence of diabetes in dogs, we might one day find that the same applies to these as well. It is a big leap of the mind to realise that dogs really do not need to eat cereals, the words 'dog' and biscuit' seemingly being made for each other, but they do not. Apart from the occasional titbit, none of mine ever eat cereals, and nor do any dogs that are fed the natural way.

We all enjoy junk food at times . . .

. . . epecially if it has been stolen

THE REAL WORLD

Most of us lead busy lives, and from time to time find that we have run out of raw food for our dogs, or forgotten to get that day's rations out of the freezer. Occasional forays into the world of commercial food will not be harmful for your dog, so just do whatever is expedient, whether it is opening a can or cooking up a panful of leftovers, adding gravy (not processed – it is full of salt) or olive oil and some cooked vegetables. Natural feeding is a lifetime mission, so there is no need to worry that all the good that comes from feeding your dog properly will be undone by providing the occasional emergency meal of lesser ingredients.

INTRODUCING NATURAL FEEDING

Plonking a raw bone down in front of a dog that has been used to kibble can result in quite different reactions. Some set to immediately, deeply grateful that you have at last got the message. Others look at you in horror – what on earth do you expect them to do with THAT? Like people, some dogs can be very conservative in their tastes, especially if they have not been introduced to a variety of food as puppies. Weanling pups, by contrast, know exactly what is good for them, and will fall upon raw bones like tiny wolves, often growling and shaking them to 'kill' them. Similarly, some dog owners make the transfer to natural feeding with hardly a ripple, and others find the whole concept alien, especially if the thought of raw meat and bones makes them feel squeamish. Some people have been edging towards natural feeding for years, by adding extras to their dog's food because a dish of dry lumps looks so unappetising, and so the final step is not so frightening for them. Others rather enjoy the fact that their dog is a faddy eater, and only likes this while it turns its nose up at that. Yet, properly introduced, natural feeding turns the most finicky pooch into a dedicated trencher. Take it step by step with me.

First, mix a tablespoonful of raw mince with a tablespoonful of pulverised raw fruit and vegetables. Give your dog half of her normal ration of whatever she is used to with the raw food mixed in as thoroughly as you can. If she wolfs the lot, then the job is done – just cut right down on the old food day by day, adding more of the new. If she picks out her old food with an expression of deep suffering, then take the bowl away once she has decided that she has finished, offer no more food of any kind until the next meal, when you give the same amount of raw food and a quarter of her normal ration. Hunger is a wonderful condiment, and most dogs make the changeover within a couple of days. Once she is cheerfully eating the mince and vegetable mix, give her a chicken wing with it, and follow the same procedure if she rejects it. Soon she will be eating the chicken wings first. Then you can proceed to offering a meaty bone on its own at one mealtime, having fed half rations the day before so that the dog is hungry.

Mince is easier for the nervous human owner to handle as well. Mince is comfortingly familiar and also mixes well with the vegetables. If you can eventually progress from minced meat to giving chunks of raw meat, so much the better, but if the mince is all you can cope with, it will be a good diet for your dog as long as vegetable matter and plenty of raw meaty bones feature in the diet as well. Mince is also easy to get, and there are several sources of raw mince for dogs, from the pet mince sold by some butchers to the different types of mince (rabbit, tripe, lamb, beef) that you can buy from the better sort of pet shops. Don't confuse this mince with the processed tubes of cooked meat that pet shops supply, as the latter is not suitable for inclusion into a natural diet – reading the label will tell you why. It is even possible to buy pulverised vegetable mix, which is a handy stand-by although a bit more expensive than liquidising your own, and Dorwest Herbs makes a powdered supplement called Easy-Green which is palatable and full of good green herbs.

BALANCED DIET

One of the big concerns that people have about changing to raw food feeding is whether they have the skill to feed a properly balanced diet. All the commercial dog food manufacturers trumpet the proud fact that their products are scientifically balanced and contain all necessary nutrients to keep your dog healthy. No wonder people feel daunted at the prospect of taking on the responsibility for themselves. Here is the secret: you don't need to. Wild animals do not eat food that is scientifically balanced at each meal, and neither do you. So long as your dog, in the space of a week, is getting raw meat, raw meaty bones, and pulverised fruit and vegetables, her nutritional needs will be admirably met. She does not have to have all of these in one meal – indeed, it is far more convenient to mix raw meat and vegetables at one meal, and feed the meaty bones meal separately at another. What proportions? You can be as flexible as you need to be, but I like to feed them bones one day and meat with vegetables the next. If I am short of one or the other, no harm is done by two or more days of the same food.

It is important to remember that, no matter how 'balanced' and 'scientific' a processed 'complete' meal is, there is no such thing as a complete metabolism. Animals use their food according to their individual bodies. Some will wax fat on the same amount of food that will starve others. We all know people who struggle with their weight although they eat modestly, and people who can eat large amounts while staying lean. It is exactly the same with dogs. Some breeds are very much more energy-efficient than others, and individuals within those breeds can need vastly different food intakes to stay the same size as each other. How much of the new food, then, do you feed in comparison to the commercial diet that had recommended amounts for each breed on the label? To start with, feed a little more than the volume of commercial food that you have been using i.e. fill the bowl slightly above the level you usually do. If the dog leaves some each time, she is having too much. If she finishes the food, and seems to be getting too lean, give her more. If she finishes the food but seems to be putting on weight, give her less. It sounds suspiciously simple, but that's all there is to it. Dogs maintain a healthier weight very easily on the raw food diet. Dogs, especially neutered dogs, that have had severe weight issues and seem to get fat on fresh air, can now eat their fill and rediscover their waistlines. Types that have never held their weight well gradually fill out and get a real shine to their coats. Feed your dog properly, and you will find that good health follows effortlessly.

So does good behaviour. Commercial dried food is very high in protein and energy. Dogs do not need protein levels up in the high twenties and even thirty-plus per cent, not even growing puppies. Ordinary raw meat is surprisingly low in protein: the high-protein dog foods were evolved for such hard-working animals as huskies, pulling sleds for hours in freezing temperatures. Feed pet dogs this high and you get behavioural problems in many of them. The artificial additives in processed food can also have a similar effect on your dog to that which they have in children. Whenever I have people coming to me with severe behavioural problems in their dogs, my first question is 'What are you feeding her?' and you would be amazed how often the problems go away completely once the dog is on a better diet.

OBESITY

Obesity in the pet dog is probably the number-one health problem nowadays, and all sorts of serious illnesses can follow. Your dog's life will be shortened considerably simply through letting her get overweight, and if growing dogs are allowed to get too heavy, they will reap a terrible harvest in the form of distorted joints. Conversely, if dogs are kept to a correct weight, or even slightly underweight, they are much more likely to stay sound in body. Controversial Australian vet Ian Billinghurst (see Recommended Reading) reckons that, even in breeds where such infirmities as hip dysplasia are normal, the condition can often be avoided simply by never letting the dogs put on too much weight, as well as being careful with the exercising. He also states that puppies should only grow to seventy-five per cent of their potential. This almost heretical view challenges the Show world, where some breeds of dog are bred larger and larger with each generation, and breed profiles are amended ever upwards in terms of size. But many normal-sized dogs are allowed to become far too fat, and certainly my most difficult task in the production of this book has been to find dogs to photograph which are not overweight – not just a few pounds overweight, but dangerously, unhealthily fat. Show ring dogs are much fatter than they should be, and pet dogs are even fatter than that. Owners who are dedicated to maintaining their own figures seem unaware that their dogs need to keep their weight down as well. It is difficult when those big brown eyes are looking at you every time you seem to be near food, and it is so easy to post titbits down a dog's throat, but please resist. Dogs love exercise just as much as food, and it is far better for them to have a run than extra food. If you must give titbits, for instance when training, break each piece as small as you can, so that the dog's overall food intake is not significantly increased. It is possible for dogs to become overweight on a natural raw food diet, but it is much harder for them to do so. The food is much more demanding to eat, much more satisfying to the 'chew' needs, and takes longer to pass through the body. Often, all the weight-reduction a dog needs is to change to a healthy diet, and the pounds will drop off without any further effort.

You do not need to weigh a dog to find out if she is the right weight. You should be able to see the last rib and if you can see the last two, that is also good. The ribs should lie under the skin without a layer of fat atop them, and be easily felt by your hand as you slide your dog's nice loose-fitting hide over the ribcage. A clearly-defined 'waist' should tuck-up where the belly goes between the hindlegs, and at the front, the slope of the shoulder should be clearly visible. No excuses. No dog is 'meant' to be fat, cuddly, rounded or any other euphemism. Your dog, however bred, is an athlete, and should look vibrant, fit and ready to go. If your dog's spine is sunk in between two layers of fat either side of it, if she looks as if you could lay a table on her back, if the legs come out of an apparently boneless sausage shape, if she waddles when she walks and puffs when she runs – she is too fat.

Working fit – few dogs reach this kind of fitness

Too thin is not so unhealthy, and is easily remedied by offering more food. If she can't eat more at one meal, feed her more often. If every rib can be seen clearly, if the spine stands clear in a row of knobbly bones, if her hide hangs off her hip-bones, she may be too thin, or, if a particular breed in a state of complete fitness, she might be exactly as she should be. Sighthound types, especially salukis and similar breeds, look extremely lean when working-fit, and these dogs will indeed show every rib and protruding hip-bones, with spine clearly defined. This should not be confused with emaciated, which has no condition on at all. Look again at that bony sighthound, and you will see big, rippling muscles along either side of her spine and down her hindquarters, with shoulders in proportion but not overloaded. Sometimes, it is a medical necessity to keep a dog slightly underweight: I have at time of writing an elderly lurcher who, at the end of a long working life, has sustained damage to the joints in her legs, as athletes often do. To prolong her quality of life, I keep her very slightly underweight. If you want to drop some weight off a dog on the natural diet, feed more meaty bones, vegetables and less flesh; if you want to put some weight on a very underweight dog, feed more fatty meat e.g. breast of lamb (just give her the whole side to chew) and chicken.

FEEDING ROUTINES

How often should you feed your dog? Ideas have changed very much in recent years. It used to be thought that dogs should be starved one day a week, the reasoning behind this being that it was considered that wild dogs would not kill every day. This flimsy logic does not take into account the small animals, e.g. mice, that such dogs could catch, or the carrion, berries, invertebrates, leaves and roots that they might eat. It is, however, a great money-saver in that the dog is not fed for fifty-two days a year! Again, some people make a religion out of feeding the dog at exactly the same time each day. So now you have a dog that is starved one day a week because of a theory on wild dogs, but which must be fed at exactly the same time each other day and never mind the wild dogs. Then we have the old-fashioned type of dog behaviourist who insists that the family eats before the dog to stop the dog getting ideas above its station. Given the hectic lives that most of us lead, this all seems complicated bordering on impossible. Relax. The truth is far easier.

Feed the dog at times that are convenient to you. There. That is all there is to it. What you feed your dog is far more important than when you feed her. Once she is out of puppyhood (puppy feeding is covered at length in Chapter Seven) feed once or twice a day, whatever suits you, and fit in her meals with your own life. Unless you are home all day, or keep staff, you will find it very difficult to feed your dog at exactly the same time each day, and it may well be more convenient to feed her before you have the family meal – if indeed your family does eat together. People who work their dogs need to feed them to fit in with their work, for a dog should not work or even be exercised on a full stomach. I have had a lifetime of feeding dogs, people and other animals at random times, and believe me, as long as they get enough of the right type of food at some stage during the day or night, they will be fine. My own method is to feed once, in the evening, after the last walk of the day, unless the dog is working that night, in which case she will have a light meal twelve hours or so beforehand. Dogs have good clocks in their heads, and if fed to a strict routine, will become edgy just before the witching hour, sometimes to the extent that they become a real nuisance, but dogs fed to a free and easy system will be much more relaxed about waiting for their meals. Very young, very old, and convalescing dogs will need to be fed little and often, according to their specific needs, which are covered in detail in the relevant chapters.

THE SHY FEEDER

Certain breeds of dog are noted for being difficult to feed, just as certain other breeds are canine dustbins. Some individuals can be awkward feeders, too. Sometimes this is due to the dog finding that if she fusses over eating her food, she gets lots of attention, and is subsequently offered food that is more to her liking. Sometimes it is a sign of illness. Often it is a sign that the wrong food is being offered, and I have every sympathy with dogs that won't eat dried food, but hang out in hopes of being offered a few pieces of fresh meat. People who have never had to deal with a shy feeder might tell the hapless owner that no dog ever starved itself to death, but the truth is that some will definitely starve themselves to a point where their physical development may be affected. And some dogs have the measure of their soft owners, and will manipulate them shamelessly into all sorts of unsuitable behaviours – only the best fillet steak, cut up into little cubes and fed by hand – which are equally detrimental not only to the dog's health (a diet of straight meat is deficient in essential nutrients) but to her relationship with her owner. The old-fashioned dog behaviourist will say that the food bowl should be left down for no longer than ten minutes, then taken up and nothing else offered until the next meal. This is often a sensible course of action, and the manipulative dog will pretty soon learn to stop trying her owner out and eat the food. It remains true, though, that some will simply ignore the food altogether, and others are dainty eaters that like to nibble and sift at their food, have a bit of a rest and then eat some more.

I make two observations here; one is that it is cheaper to feed something that your dog will eat rather than engage in a perpetual battle of wills that ends each meal with food thrown away, and the other is that neither you nor I eat what we do not like. Giving the dog food that she will eat is not 'giving in' but being sensible – providing that food is nutritionally sound. Assuming that you only offer the dog her meal, and that she shows little or no interest in it despite not having eaten anything else that day, and does this for several days, look at the rest of the dog. If she is bright-eyed, wet-nosed, shiny-coated and active, she is unlikely to be ill. If by contrast, her hide is dull, tight on her skin, she is lethargic, maybe her third eyelid is partly across her eyes, you have a sick dog. Is she drinking a lot? Panting excessively? Drooling, coughing or sneezing? Not wanting her walk? Hunched up in a dark corner? Time to go to the vet. When she has been checked over, maybe blood-tested, and the problem found and sorted, try not to be steered into feeding whatever commercial food the surgery sells as a sideline, but take a good look at what you are offering. If I can't persuade you into changing over completely to a raw food diet, at least give her some raw meat, bones and vegetables with whatever you normally put out for her. If she eats that, and most do, she is telling you what she needs. If she still won't eat more than a few mouthfuls of anything, and you are sure that she is well, it is time to look at the rest of the picture.

First of all, what are you putting the food into? Plastic bowls may give off fumes, hardly detectable to us, but vile to the dog. Metal bowls are cheap to buy and easy to keep clean, but the brightness or the noise can really spook some dogs, especially those which have been in rescue kennels, where the rattle and clang of metal bowls can become inextricably linked in their minds with the din of barking and shouting and general noise stress. Earthenware bowls are solid, fume-free and quiet, and most dogs seem to be happy with them. Where are you feeding the dog? Do you have other dogs? Some dogs will eat better with other dogs around them as 'competition', but others, especially very submissive dogs, will lose all appetite when having to share dining space with more dominant types. Is the place where you feed your dog peaceful, or is it a hub of family comings and goings, shouting and laughter, radio and/or television on loudly? Try feeding the dog in a different room, or in the garden, or in a kennel on her own, and if she does not eat when alone, stay with her and read quietly while she plucks up the courage to eat. Some dogs – mine included – really appreciate human company when they eat. Offer just a spoonful of food in the dish, and add another once that has been eaten. Yes it can be a bit of an effort, but once you have started a shy feeder eating, you will be able to dispense with the details and offer a robust bowlful of food which she will eat – though you might always have to feed her separately.

I sometimes have a very nice dog to stay who is normally very spoilt with her eating in that she shares her owner's meals. She is always quite horrified to be presented with raw food, and almost shudders visibly at the hearty appetites of her country cousins. After the first day, during which she is obviously missing her owner as well as her gourmet food, the extra fresh air and exercise gives her an excellent appetite, and she becomes every bit as good a trencher as the others. I have, however, been informed that she will not eat the raw food diet at home, even when I have given her a 'doggy bag' to take with her! Other visiting dogs have launched into their healthy diet with eagerness, and refused to eat their processed food upon returning home.

UNFINISHED MEALS

If your dog consistently leaves some of her food, it may simply be that you are giving her too much. Dogs' stomachs are in proportion to the rest of them, and a heaped tablespoonful of food will be quite enough for a small terrier or toy dog. It doesn't look much, does it? Try using a smaller dog bowl, then the portion won't seem so meagre. If your dog gets too thin, give her more. It is the easiest thing in the world to overfeed a dog, and if yours only eats as much as she wants, that is likely to be as much as she needs, too.

WATER

We are often told that our dogs must have constant access to clean fresh water – wise words indeed, which make the average dog owner smile wryly when recollecting that the dog herself would rather drink out of puddles, stagnant ponds, scummy troughs, in fact anything but that pristine bowl of water. This is the dog telling you something again. While we are assured by the water companies that the water from our taps is the purest we'll encounter, our senses tell us differently. Tap water varies markedly from district to district, and whereas in some areas it is delightful to drink, in others it stinks of chemicals even to a human nose. You have to be truly desperate to drink the tap water where I live. If it is this bad-tasting to humans, think how much worse it must be to the subtle senses of your dog.

So do you fill her bowl out of the rain-butt instead? You certainly can do, but take the water from the top, where it is cleaner; the run-off from your roof might not be as free from chemicals as you think. Try to avoid allowing your dog to drink out of puddles, which can be contaminated with oil residues, agrochemicals, even anti-freeze, which latter can kill your dog. Stagnant ponds and the like might be safe drinking but can be full of similar filth, or a nasty type of blue algae which will make your dog ill, or a myriad of lesser organisms which will have you and your dog up half the night with D and V (diarrhoea and vomiting). While you cannot wrap your dog in cotton wool, it is a sensible precaution to prevent her from drinking standing water of any type. You are fairly safe with water from troughs where livestock drink regularly and so keep the water moving through, and with running water from brooks. There are other peculiarities to take into account with these sources of water. Cattle in particular can be very possessive of their water trough, and cattle and dogs don't mix; with streams, you need to watch out for litter, some of which can be contaminant and some of which can cut your dog if she goes in for a drink. There is a particular type of

Drinking

Enjoying running water

human that seemingly must dump rubbish in water, and some of this rubbish is very dangerous to dogs.

While it is sensible to be aware of water availability when you walk or work your dog, it is much safer to carry water for her. Keep some in the car for when you return, but also it is useful to teach your dog to drink from a child's feeder bottle. This is easy to carry in a pocket, non-spill and not too heavy; while it doesn't carry a lot of water, it can keep your dog's thirst under control in an emergency, until you get back to your car.

What about at home? I am not going to suggest that you give your dog bottled water (although they do enjoy it!) but if your tap water is like mine, filtering the water will make it much pleasanter to drink – try for yourself with a glass of filtered and unfiltered water – and the more your dog drinks clean water, the less thirst she will have for water from dubious sources. Filtering out the chemicals sometimes means that you filter out useful minerals – can you ever win? So another way of making water pleasanter to drink is to put one or two quartz crystals in the bottom of the bowl. Cheap and easy to obtain from New Age type shops, these can be put in the bottom of the water bowl, or else in a jug of water that you leave to stand for an hour or two and then use to refill the water bowl. Crystals last for ever, and all you have to do is clean them under a running tap from time to time. I use clear quartz, rose quartz and amethyst, but you can use pretty much whatever takes your eye, as there is plenty of choice. Would your dog eat the crystals? Nothing is impossible; all I can say is that I have never known one to try, but maybe if you have an exceptionally

Crystals to purify drinking water

greedy dog, it is better not to use these. The only time I have ever known a dog to do anything with a crystal was one day when I was out and my beloved had not noticed that the water bowl was empty. My old dog picked one of the crystals up and spat it into his lap!

The same applies with water bowls as with food bowls: plastic types give off fumes and metal ones are noisy. Earthenware or toughened glass are pleasantest for the dogs to drink from. Place the water bowl in a sheltered spot that is easy for the dog to reach and you to see, but not in one of the main traffic routes of the house. If your dog is kennelled and tends to play with the water bowl, make a frame for the bowl to hold it secure, and give your dog a bone, some cardboard boxes to chew, or some toys. The exception to all this is if your dog is one of those breeds that is addicted to water, such as the Newfoundland, in which case you just have to grin and bear it, as playing with water is what they do.

Changing your dog's diet to raw food is likely to be the biggest, bravest leap into the dark that you will have made in all your time as a dog owner. Therefore, may I suggest a couple of books and websites to help your research? (See Recommended Reading) This is radical stuff, and some exponents, myself included, can be evangelical about it, but I can assure you that your dog will be so fit and healthy once she is eating properly, that you will wonder why you ever hesitated. Yes, it is a little more time and trouble, but you will save that time in not going to the vet. except for routine checks, because your dog is so well.

4 The Outer Dog

Workshop manual for body care

here is something about a really well-cared-for dog that takes the eye at once, and yet it would be hard to pinpoint exactly what makes the dog look and act so well. In truth, very little work is involved, but what needs to be done is to attend to the little tasks at once, and then they never become big or difficult. A comfortable dog is a happy dog, but one that itches, has paintstripper breath or painful feet is never going to look well. And if she doesn't feel well, she won't behave well, either.

COAT

The coat is the first thing that people notice about a dog – indeed, if you are choosing a puppy out of a litter where there are several different colours, it can be difficult not to let the coat colour influence you above all other considerations. Most puppy coats change in texture and colour; if you have a pedigree pup, you can judge pretty well how she is going to look as an adult, but crossbreds can be full of surprises, mostly pleasant ones. Coats that need professional stripping and clipping are outside the remit of this book: I'd suggest that you put yourself into the charge of a good dog groomer, and either learn to prepare the coat yourself, or budget to have it professionally attended to at whatever intervals are recommended. Some coats are so profuse that the dog spends much of its life miserably hot, which needs to be considered if you live in a warm climate but have always had a yearning for that particular breed of dog. Sometimes a compromise is possible with the shearing of the dog's coat, though if you wish to show the dog, then the coat must be endured, and sculpted as the breed specifications state. If you are very houseproud, remember that a thick coat can bring a lot of the garden indoors with it, and a spell of wet weather will decorate your floor and walls with mud. White coats stain with food and body secretions, and black coats fade to red at the tips of the hairs if the dog spends time in the sun. Sparse coats can mean that vulnerable areas of dog, such as ears, can suffer from too much exposure to the sun as well, and of course thin-coated dogs will feel the cold.

Exaggerated coats (unless on show dogs, where they cannot be altered) need trimming around the genital area for hygienic reasons. Anywhere that could be stained with faecal matter, semen or urine, even down the insides of the hindlegs and under tummies, would be better off for keeping short, and male dogs should have the hair trimmed carefully from the urethral opening of the penis. Bitches on heat can keep themselves cleaner without dreadlocks around the vulva, and if the bitch is to be mated, it helps to have the target area clear. Some breeds would be more comfortable for a reduction in the hair around the mouth, which has a tendency to become stained and matted with food. Sometimes a little trimming around the eyes and inside the ears is helpful, for runny eyes can make the dog sore, and pendulous over-furred ears may create the kind of warm, moist environment that bacteria and parasites love. Plucking can be preferable to cutting, as the dog does not need sharp ends of cast hairs working their way into ears and eyes. Ask a professional groomer to show you how to do this.

Check that eyebrows do not curl round into the eyes. Feet with too much hair can be a misery in muddy conditions or snow, and with some dogs, the whole coat will tangle and pill with mud or ice until the poor creature looks like a wattle and daub house. Unkempt coats can hide parasites and make them more difficult to deal with, and in extreme cases can result in 'fly-strike' where a particular type of fly lays its eggs, usually around the soiled tail end, and maggots hatch out and start eating.

As well as keeping the dog more comfortable, these attentions will reduce 'doggy' smells and stop you racing the dog into the house to try and clean her up before she wipes herself on the furniture. Seen to every week, it is very little work, just a matter of attention to detail, but once a coat gets out of hand, it can be painful for the dog and difficult for the owner to return it to a suitable state. In extreme cases, dogs have even had to be sedated before the knots and tangles could be cut out of their coats. Seek the advice of a dog groomer: they have all the latest equipment, and a vast experience of handling different coats. The right brush or comb can make all the difference to keeping the coat within bounds, and why work any harder than necessary? Your dog will thank you for that as well.

Ordinary coats can still need a tidy-up here and there, and a regular grooming session will be enjoyed by your dog provided you are gentle and take care not to tug at tangles. Carefully tease these out, pulling against hair caught in your fingers rather than the hair roots in the coat. An ordinary flea comb is excellent for most normal coats, especially if there is an undercoat, and will gently strip out dead hair with no effort. You can also buy a loose-toothed comb that does not pull hair but is an efficient de-matter. More profuse coats have all sorts of special brushes made for them. Comb or brush against the lie of the hair from the root of the tail, along the hackle line of the spine right up to the back of the head, and then comb the other way so that the hair lies correctly. Then do the same to the fleshy areas of the shoulders and haunches. Bony areas are more comfortably brushed than combed. When you tackle the hind end, support the dog under the belly with your other hand. There is a ticklish spot midway down the back that makes dogs waggle a hindleg as a reflex, so be careful of this area and neither dwell on it nor laugh at your dog's reaction. They can't help it, and it isn't pleasant for them. Swish swiftly across the place – firm strokes are less ticklish than light ones – and move on. Dogs like to be brushed under their chins and around their faces, as long as you use light strokes here. Remember when mother used to brush your hair? Don't press down as hard as she did. More vigorous massaging strokes of the brush will be enjoyed along the flanks and the fleshy places. Your dog will show you where she enjoys being brushed most: don't be surprised at some strange noises. Mine croon and moan with pleasure, others grunt or mumble, but these are essentially happy sounds. If you have taken on a second-hand dog that objects to being groomed, take note of the warnings she gives you because your face will be in the line of fire if she decides to strike. Make haste slowly and groom a little at a time, doing non-confrontational areas first. Grooming should be a pleasure for you, not a battle. If a dog objects seriously, a muzzle is a wise precaution, and you might consider using a calming remedy before you start, such as Bach Rescue Remedy, or Dorwest Herbs Valerian Compound. Groom a little of the difficult areas each time, rewarding non-reaction by moving immediately to a less touchy area. Patience is the way here, as it usually is with animals. Often an animal that dislikes the brush or comb will respond positively to massage, and this can be used to get the animal accustomed to being touched all over. The brush or comb can be introduced for short strokes after the massage, or you can progress to massaging with one hand and brushing with the other.

Even a dog with a coat like a whippet's will benefit from regular grooming, which will stimulate the hide and remove dead skin particles. A semi-soft brush like a horse's body brush will be adequate for a smooth, thin coat. The majority of dogs have harsh guard hairs over a softer undercoat, and some dogs, such as Labradors, have a waterproof outer coat that is quite greasy. Frequent grooming has several important points in its favour: first of all, the dog learns to be handled all over in a pleasurable manner. I cannot begin to stress how important this is. There may come a time when your dog has to be similarly handled by a stranger, such as a vet, and everyone's experience of this will be a lot better if the dog is used to being touched all over. Next, while grooming, you will notice any lumps or bumps. Some of these might need attention. Long-term lumps may suddenly start to grow larger, or new ones might form. Some lumps are abscesses, or caused by thorns which need pulling out. As a rule of thumb, a lump that feels hot and that has appeared suddenly indicates a foreign body, a sting, an allergic reaction or an abscess, whereas a cool lump that grows slowly is a tumour. Most tumours are harmless and better left alone, but your vet is the best person to advise you about these. Grooming will reveal the presence of any beastly biters, of which more shortly. You will see if hair has changed in texture, colour or thickness. Losing hair can be a temporary hormonal matter, or might be indicative of a more serious problem, such as mange, or a glandular condition.

Grooming within the pack environment is a cosy exchange of intimacy, occurring right across the hierarchical strata. Dogs are very comfortable with grooming each other. Often the privilege is extended to the human family, too, and should be accepted as the gift that it is, though the rapid nibbling of the incisor teeth that is so valued between dog and dog can be rather uncomfortable if performed directly on soft human skin. Some dogs will hold you down like a puppy and lick with considerable pressure. Grooming is a very bonding experience between dog and owner, and dogs that are correctly groomed in a non-confrontational manner will delight in the experience. Mine all come running when they hear the word 'brush'!

BATHS

If you groom correctly, your dog may live its whole life without ever having a bath. One justification in my opinion for immersing a complete dog and shampooing it is if it has rolled in something obnoxious – and even then, you can get away with spot-cleaning, by rubbing tomato juice or ketchup into the offending areas (I'd wear rubber gloves if I were you) and then shampooing and rinsing them clean. Show dogs have to be bathed a lot, but the show ring is a different planet. Bathing a dog, even with the gentlest of shampoos, strips oils from the coat and can alter the coat texture if done often. Sometimes bums and ends have to be washed, but that shouldn't mean a bath. However, if a dog has wilfully and with great pleasure immersed itself in smelly, adhesive mud, a severe hosing-down may be the only solution.

HORMONAL CHANGES

I touched briefly on hormones affecting coats. With some breeds, spayed and castrated dogs will grow a different coat from the one they had in their complete days, the coat usually being softer and more profuse. This change is irreversible. Temporary changes can happen as the result of a bitch coming on heat, where the coat becomes silky and very shiny, or from changes associated with pregnancy and suckling, where in some bitches the coat will thin and partly fall out. Illnesses associated with the thyroid, pituitary or adrenals can often show in the coat before they manifest any other symptoms.

MOULTING

It can come as a shock to first-time dog owners when they find just how much a dog can moult. There are times when the house and car seem entirely covered in dog hair, despite your best efforts, and you will marvel at how a single dog hair can get under, in or through the most hygienic of food wrapping. Dogs moult most when casting their winter coats in the spring, though they will moult in autumn to a lesser extent. Between times, just like we do, they will shed a certain amount of hair every day. When you think of it, the domestic dog has so many changes of temperature to which she has to adapt. Is your house centrally heated? Does the heating go off at night? Does the dog come in during the day but sleep out of doors? Do you have the heater on in the car when driving with your dog? It is no wonder that some dogs' systems give up completely and the result is a continuous, noticeable moult. Very regular grooming will help get out the dead hair, and if you can keep your dog from extremes of temperature so much the better. Of course, the family will complain if you keep the heating down for the sake of the dog! There is no doubt that dogs kept permanently out of doors have much better coats than those which go daily from heated to unheated environments, but most of us like to have our dogs with us in the house. The choices are simple: more dog hair or less heat. But if moulting really bothers you, there are breeds that don't shed hair, such as the poodle or the bichon, and breeds that only have a little in the first place, such as the Chinese crested and the Mexican hairless. Both types need extra care: the former need professional stripping and grooming, and the latter feel the cold and need protection from the sun.

TEETH

A dog's teeth are awesome in design, with roots set deeply into the jaw, and each serration in the upper jaw matched to fit into the lower. Every tooth is pointed: there are no flat molars for chewing, and dogs do not need to chew their food. Tear and swallow is the way, to get as much meat down in as short a time as possible, for the pack around its kill is vulnerable to larger predators. Healthy, clean dog teeth are easy to maintain, yet what vets and show judges see most of is filthy mouths full of stained teeth, tartar build-up and gum disease. Makes you feel sick just reading about it? Makes the dog very sick, too.

I am about to alienate a whole industry here. It is not necessary to clean a dog's teeth with a toothbrush and special dog toothpaste, and for goodness' sake don't use human toothpaste, which is full of alarming chemicals that no-one would put in their mouths if they realised. Special dog 'chews' and toys with suitably dental names are as much use in curing or preventing dental problems as the proverbial chocolate teapot. It should not be necessary for a dog to go under anaesthetic every year and have her teeth scraped clean. A dog will go her whole life without any but the most minimal tooth care, so long as she has raw bones and raw meat to chew on. These clean the teeth naturally and so easily that I have seen really bad mouths come right with no other help at all. There is other help, though, if you have inherited a dog with a dreadful mouth full of tartar. Homoeopathic Fragaria works in most cases by softening the scale, though you may have to use it for a few weeks before you see results. If this does not help, then aloe vera gel rubbed into the tartar with a finger should produce a softening effect when used over several weeks too. The tartar can then be gently scraped off with a fingernail, or a dentist's scraper padded with a twist of kitchen paper (you do not want to scrape the surface of the tooth and create a 'key' for future tartar to cling to) or you can leave it for the bones to scrape clean as your dog chews them. Ever seen the teeth of working foxhounds? Even the oldest hounds have spotless teeth, because their diet is raw flesh and bones. Take those same hounds and feed them on commercial dog food, however, and you will get mouths as dirty as any pet fed on cakes and other unsuitable items. It is no kindness to feed your dog sugar-laden 'goodies' – they are not good for us either, but at least we can choose how much to eat of them, and take steps to rescue our teeth afterwards. The staining that affects so many dog mouths seems to come directly from the dyestuffs added to commercial food so that it appeals to the human buyer!

Occasionally, accidents befall teeth, which chip or break or die in the jaw. Dogs which chew obsessively, the sort that dismantle house walls and doorsteps, damage their teeth, as do dogs that try to pull their kennels apart. Terriers are notorious for damaging their teeth by such actions as tearing at roots while digging, and if allowed to scrap, will often leave teeth behind in the hides of their opponents. Incisor teeth are particularly vulnerable. Some dogs teach themselves to use stones as toys, which is really bad for teeth, and should be discouraged if at all possible by the provision of safer toys to carry about. Kicks from large livestock don't do teeth any good, which is yet another reason for never taking risks with the big fellows. Luckily, for the most part, no treatment is needed for damaged teeth: they may offend the owner's eye but they seldom affect the dog. If a tooth has died in the jaw, showing discolouration from healthy ivory to bluish or brown, keep a watch over it just in case at some stage it needs veterinary treatment, (See Chapter Eight) but they seldom do. Dogs are better off than we are in that respect.

Be careful with the toys that you provide for your dog. Before you ever let your dog near a toy, stop and think what effect it will have on her teeth. Will it splinter? Is it hard enough to break them? Could a tooth get caught? Could she bite bits off and swallow them, or make the toy small enough to get stuck in her throat? Never let a dog play unsupervised with these toys. No toy is completely safe – no life is completely safe – but your dog is less likely to do herself damage chewing on cardboard boxes (remove staples first, please) or raw vegetables than she is on brightly-coloured plastic or rubber.

NAILS

Your dog's nails are her football studs, there to help her keep her purchase on the ground when running and cornering. Too long, and she risks damaging her toes because they will be pushed out at wrong angles: too short, and she will not have enough grip when she runs. Inside each nail is a long fleshy centre with its own little blood supply, known as the 'quick', and a nail cut too short will bleed impressively, not to mention landing you with a yowl and a woebegone look from the dog. Very neglected nails just keep growing and curling around, and extreme cases have been known to penetrate the dog's foot. These can be tricky to bring back to normal, but by trimming a little more off each time, you can improve the foot considerably. Received wisdom states that the quicks will shrink back every time a little more nail is taken, but my own experience with neglected feet is that they only do so up to a point, and the foot never returns to how it ought to be.

What is the correct length? The nail should just touch the ground when the dog is standing normally. Too short is better than too long, but there should ideally be a little nail between the quick and the ground. White nails are easy as the quick is clearly seen, but black nails are a misery to keep right. Some dogs have such symmetry of foot that the nails are kept short without human interference, and some dogs attend to their own pedicures by nibbling away at excess nail. Some feet have to be trimmed right from the start, though, and other feet change their shape as the dog ages or is injured, so that we have to trim the nails then for the sake of the dog's well-being. An old kennelman's tale states that once you cut the nails, you will always have to, and I have heard people say this as an excuse for their dogs' awful feet. It is nonsense. Trim the nails if you need to, leave them if you don't, but don't let your dog suffer one moment through neglecting her feet.

Note what your dog's feet look like. The nails are not in line, and nor are the toes. From the outside of the foot, you see the corner toe, which is short, then the longest toe, the next longest, and then the inmost toe, which is the shortest. Therefore, trim each nail according to its toe position and do not try to make the nails align, because they don't. Different breeds have different feet, from the long toes of the saluki to the compact bunch on the Australian cattle dog, or the splayed toes of the GSD. Front feet are larger than hind feet; some breeds are remarkably dextrous with their forepaws and use them as 'hands'.

If your dog's nails are soft and flaky, look first for a health or dietary cause. If she has the all-clear, it may just be the way you are cutting the nails. Guillotine cutters

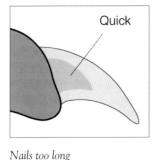

Nails too long

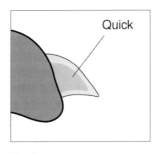

Too short

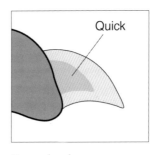

Correct length

leave the nail stronger as they slice from bottom to top. In other cases, scissor-action clippers can be preferable, especially if you are trimming a nail to shape. If you file, draw the file from base to front of nail: sawing from side to side weakens the nail. However, some black nails are so strong that you have to file them any way you can!

Sometimes nails break off, or split, or even get pulled out completely, and treatment is covered in detail in Chapter Eight.

DEWCLAWS

All dogs are born with these on the front – they correspond to the human thumb – and some have them on the back. Rear dewclaws are residual, loosely attached pieces of gristle, and if they ever served a purpose, do not do so now, except in the case of a very rare Swedish multi-toed dog (Lundehund) which uses its plethora of toes for scrambling across wet rocks on the shores. For the rest of the canine population, the rear dews are better removed at birth by a vet, as they will otherwise only catch in things and tear. There is great controversy about front dewclaws, however. Many dogs have these removed at birth, the idea being to avoid injury later in life. The dewclaw in a newborn puppy is soft and gristly, and its removal is quickly accomplished without causing trauma to the infant. Dewclaw removal in a grown dog, however, is a different matter. A general anaesthetic is necessary, and a surprisingly large incision has to be made, for the front dewclaw is a toe in its own right, and the whole digit has

Use of dewclaw in turning

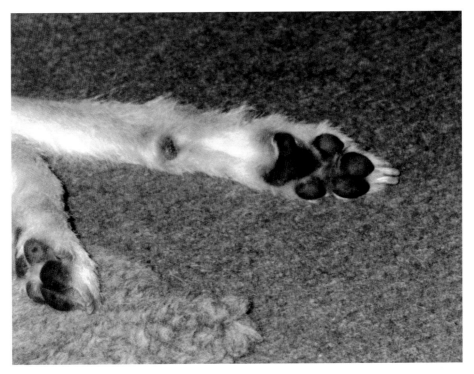

Stopper pad

to be removed. There follows an appreciable convalescence, for the place is awkward, tight-skinned and not well fleshed, and correspondingly difficult for healing. So why do my dogs, and very probably yours, have the dewclaws left on?

The decision is the breeder's. With some breeds, dewclaw removal is the fashion, especially with certain working breeds, with others it is never done, or else just the rear dews are removed. If you have a dog with the front dews on, you will see just how much these toes are used, and having seen that, you will be reluctant ever after to have a dog with its dewclaws off. The dews are used in grooming, in holding items that the dog is eating, when the stud dog holds on to the bitch in mating and when the bitch holds a pup down to groom it. Running dogs, especially sighthounds, use the dews when cornering at speed, the whole of the pastern bent to the ground and the dewclaw standing out at right angles, reminding one of a motorcyclist who corners touching the ground on one knee. I would not wilfully remove such a useful part of my dog. But do the dews get injured? Yes, as much as any part of any dog can get injured, but certainly they are no more susceptible to damage than any other toe, and in my own experience, a great deal less than some bits, so long as the nails are kept to a sensible length. If you breed a litter of puppies, you must take a decision about dewclaw removal, but if you buy a dog from someone else, than the decision has already been taken for you. I'd say don't fret about it either way. If your dog still has her dews left on, trim the nails when you trim the rest of them, and that will probably be all the worry that the dewclaws will cause you.

STOPPER PADS

Take a look at your dog's front feet at the back of the wrist joint, and you will see a spongy circle of tissue that is known as the 'stopper pad'. When your dog brakes, the pastern (wrist) bends and the pad touches the ground, giving added stopping power. With fast dogs, the stopper pad can sustain a fair bit of damage, especially on rough ground, and as it has a rich supply of blood vessels, it can bleed every bit as dramatically as any of the other pads. Luckily, the bleeding cleans the wound, and the dog can easily reach the place to lick it, so the majority of stopper pad injuries heal easily, though they can be rather an alarming sight the first time they are hurt.

FOOT CARE

Dog feet are tough and largely trouble-free, but there are a few things to watch for. Puncture wounds can easily go unnoticed until infection has built up inside the foot and the dog becomes lame, and foreign bodies can enter the skin between the toes or where the nail meets the toe at the cuticle. Get to know how your dog's feet look, and then you will notice at once if a toe is swollen, or else the body of the foot is larger than its opposite number. Massage your dog's feet gently, so that you recognise how they should feel. If the dog squeaks or snatches her foot away where normally she would enjoy her massage – you have found a problem. First aid for feet is covered in Chapter Eight.

If you have been running your dog on farmland and discover too late that it has been sprayed, or the council has salted the roads, rinse your dog's feet off thoroughly before she goes into her bed. Tar from the beach can be removed using copious amounts of petroleum jelly, 'like to like' being a useful rule of thumb when you are up against a problem like this. If your dog has walked in anything that you think might be toxic, put some Bach Crab Apple in her drinking water for a few days, to help her eliminate anything that she may have taken in through her skin. If your dog goes lame for no readily apparent reason, check the foot out very thoroughly indeed before you search higher for a problem.

TAILS

Your dog talks with her tail. Watch that tail in all its moods, and you will be streets ahead of other people in understanding your dog. Observe when dogs meet, how the carriage and action of the tail precedes more doughty body language. A wagging tail by itself does not always mean a happy dog: if a dog is snarling at you and the tail is wagging, believe the mouth not the tail. A high wag challenges, a low wag is placatory, which can easily slip over into 'I warned you!' a circling wag is anticipatory, a tail straight out behind means that your space is more welcome than your company. Tails don't 'talk' in isolation, of course: their meaning is fine-tuned by other body language: posture, ears, eye contact, raised hackles. A properly docked dog, that is, one where only the last third of the tail has been removed, is still perfectly capable of signalling with its tail. Dogs of guarding breeds such as the Boxer, Dobermann and Rottweiller, which are traditionally docked very short indeed, were so presented because they then had less body language for the human to interpret, and thus seemed fiercer, and also so that there was nothing for a human to get hold of if attacked. These are all round-bodied smooth dogs, and having had dogs attacked by both Boxers and Dobermanns, I can vouch for the fact that there is very little indeed to get hold of except ears, which latter were also traditionally cropped in these dogs' country of origin. (Ear cropping is illegal in UK.)

For the most part, however, you will be encountering dogs with enough tail to 'read' and also enough tail to get damaged. A simple precaution is to always be aware of the tail when you greet your dog upon your return home, or otherwise make her happy, and see that she has enough space to wag without hurting her tail. Long whippy tails sustain damage very easily, and because the tail is well furnished with blood vessels but not well padded with flesh, an injured tail will bleed like blazes. Nor is it the easiest place to bandage. Bathing with salt water will help most tail injuries, and bandaging a plastic syringe-cover over the affected part helps to protect it while it heals, but tail damage can be the devil to get right as it gets opened up again so easily, especially if you have a happy dog. Always think 'tail' when shutting the car door or boot with the dog inside, or after the dog has jumped out, or when shutting doors at home. Some dogs are very tidy with their tails and tuck them out of the way, and others leave them all over the place, so be careful when you are walking near the dog, and train your children to be as well. Apart from it creating a great deal of upset, broken and cut tails take a lot of mending, and sometimes have to be partially amputated before they will heal.

SKIN

Sometimes referred to as 'the largest organ in the body' skin is an excellent barometer of your dog's health. Some breeds are very much more prone to skin conditions than others, and as a general rule of thumb, white animals have more delicate skins than dark, but any dog can have skin problems because the skin has so much to do in the way of cleansing and protection. Dog skin can be black, pink, or a mottled combination of the two, lighter skins usually but not always matching lighter coat colour. Healthy skin is smooth, sweet-smelling and shiny. If a dog is inordinately itchy, to the extent of scratching or chewing holes in her skin, or the skin forms little lumps, or weeps, or smells foul, something is not right and needs assistance.

Skin changes can mean that one or more of the main eliminatory organs needs some help, so once you have tackled the obvious issues, if your dog's skin problems persist, or if there has been a sudden change in skin smell, texture or colour, have her blood and urine tested to see if there is some kind of an internal problem. Even a simple infection, easily cleared, can show first as a change in the skin. The great thing with skin is that there are only ever two problems with it: something on the inside trying to get out, and something on the outside trying to get in.

EXTERNAL

Your dog can pick up all manner of skin irritants, especially in the domestic environment. Household cleaners are very strong, so be sure that you rinse floors thoroughly before your dog lies on them, give dog bedding an extra rinse in clear water before you dry it (without fabric softener, please) and rinse dog bowls out an extra time before they are used again. Farm chemicals can affect a dog's skin, so keep off sprayed fields and don't let your dog lie in or drink from puddles on arable farmland. Likewise if you do your own motor maintenance: keep your dog away from chemical spillages and fumes. There are also many lurking parasites hoping to make a living on your dog, and dog owners wage a constant battle against these. Parasites and dogs – or any other animal – have evolved to live in symbiosis with each other, which makes it very difficult to keep them separate. This is one area where natural remedies on their own are not enough, because it is 'natural' for the parasites and the animal to co-exist. Natural it may be: desirable it isn't, and too many parasites of any kind make your dog's life a misery and probably yours as well. Here are some ways you can improve on nature:

Fleas

Everybody's favourite – you only have to mention fleas and everyone starts itching! Fleas are a problem all year round, but they peak in Summer. As well as causing intense itching, they are the vector for some kinds of tapeworm. There are lots of different species of fleas, but most of the ones that you see on your dog are cat fleas, dog fleas being comparatively rare. Cat fleas will bite people as well.

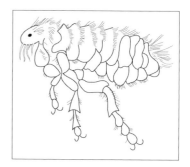

Flea

If you suspect fleas, take a flea comb and a sheet of white tissue paper, and comb some of the hair from around the top of your dog's tail root. Spread the combings out on the paper. You might see a flea wiggling about, and if you are quick, you can crunch it with the back of your thumbnail. You might see lots of black dots, which are flea dirt. If you make these wet, they will show blood colour on the paper. If you don't see anything, comb the rest of your dog and check the combings in the same way. Favourite areas for fleas are behind ears, around the tail root, along the hackle line, armpits and groin, and tummies. If you have one of those dogs that likes to show off her tummy, do a flea check when she does. There is no shame in your dog getting fleas: it is not a reflection on your management. The best-kept dogs get fleas. There is a lot of received wisdom about fleas, such as the reason that they are more prevalent nowadays is because of carpets and central heating. Well, I've yet to see a rabbit bury with either, but they are always full of fleas. Then you are told to clear your house of fleas because they don't live on your dog but in your house. This is true up to a point, and it is a help to vacuum your house viciously, but that by itself will not resolve a flea problem. Fleas do live on your dog as well, and particularly on your cat: cats are flea reservoirs and should be treated for them with every bit as much vigour as the house and dog. The snag here is that every time your dog (or cat) goes out, she will pick up a whole new crop of fleas – so flea treatment should include something that deters the fleas from getting on your dog, and something that kills them when they do. Old-fashioned flea sprays and spot-on drops contain organophosphate chemicals, which are based on nerve gas, and can have some very unpleasant side-effects on both dogs and humans. More modern flea treatments are safer, but that is not to say that they do not carry some risk, especially if you are treating a puppy. There is a huge choice available, of sprays, drops, and even substances that you put in your dog's food. I would say, however, that it is best to avoid using anything where the flea has to bite the dog before it (the flea) dies, firstly because it is the flea bite that makes the dog itch, on occasion so badly that she ends up with an allergy to flea saliva, and secondly – well, do you want to give your dog something so toxic that it gets into her bloodstream and kills insects that bite her? I also avoid any substance that requires me to keep the dog in a different room after treatment, or away from naked flame, not to touch her or sleep in the same room as her, and to wear full protective clothing when I apply the chemical. Yes, there really are flea treatments that include these comments on their instructions. There are still a few products available that are safe to use on young puppies, and that don't require you to keep your dog in a nuclear fallout shelter afterwards. Frankly, you will have to use one of them – my own experience with repellents and natural treatments is that they only work up to a point, and that sooner or later, you are going to have to use chemicals. My vet comments that all homoeopathy does for fleas is make them very healthy!

When I use a chemical flea treatment, I prefer a spray, and I only use it in the most flea-friendly areas rather than spraying the whole dog, Thus I cover from back of ears down the hackle line up to and including the tail root, armpits and groin, and it seems to do the job well enough. Most of my dogs only need the chemical spray once a year – I have found 'Frontline' perfectly satisfactory, and there are several others that will do the job just as well – but one of them must be very sweet-tasting, and I have to back up his annual Frontline treatment with a herbal spray called 'Xenex', used monthly if it is a bad flea year. I also use the flea-comb with great application.

AROMATHERAPY

If ever a little learnin' is a dangerous thing, it is with Aromatherapy. As a qualified Aromatherapist myself, I cringe at some of the advice I read in the dog magazines. Yes, there is quite an arsenal of insect-repellent, even insect-killing Aromatherapy oils, but these oils are strong medicines and not automatically safe. For example, almost all of them must be greatly diluted before use. Furthermore, most of the really effective insecticidal oils are not safe to use on pregnant and lactating bitches. Others are not suitable for animals that are on certain types of medication. Then there is the issue of smell – surely with an animal as sensitive as a dog, it is bordering on cruelty to make her wear such powerful, volatile scents? Much as I love Aromatherapy, I do not consider it suitable to use on animals in this context, with the exception of lavender oil used as stated below. As a treatment given for a specific condition by a qualified therapist, Aromatherapy can hold its own with any other discipline, but for repelling parasites, there are ways that are much pleasanter and safer for your dog. First Aid use of Aromatherapy is covered in Chapter Eight.

FEEDING

Adding garlic and brewer's yeast or Marmite to your dog's food will help repel fleas and other biting insects, but used alone, these are not sufficient to counter fleas at peak times. Natural garlic can upset some dogs' digestions, as can odourless formulas, but I have had good results using Dorwest Herbs' garlic tablets.

FLEA COMB

The flea comb, used diligently, is very good at getting rid of those fleas that are on the dog, and is of course quite harmless. Keep a container of lukewarm water, to which a few drops of lavender oil have been added, by the side of you, and also a sheet of white paper. Dip the comb in the water, then comb the dog thoroughly, especially along the hackle line, behind the ears, and all around the tail, under as well as over. As the comb fills with hair, remove the hair onto the paper and check for livestock, which can be executed with the back of a thumbnail. Dip the comb again before you start combing. If you are too squeamish to crack the fleas, remove the hair from the comb under the surface of the lavender water, but take care to sink any fleas you find, as they are small enough to jump off the surface of the water. Such is the hunter/gatherer instinct in most people that the daily pursuit of the flea can become quite addictive. However, the flea comb is only effective until your dog goes out again and collects a new lot of little lodgers.

FLEA COLLARS
Some of these are impregnated with strong insecticides, which kill fleas, and some with natural repellent oils. The insecticidal ones certainly do kill fleas, but you may not wish to have such strong chemicals on your dog, especially if they are organophosphate based. A good use for this sort of flea collar is to put it in the vacuum cleaner bag, so that fleas vacuumed up will be killed. They are also handy in the wardrobe for dealing with moths.

The repellent collars and bandannas rely on strong-smelling oils, which smell very pleasant to us but probably are not so nice for your dog, and certainly interfere with her own sense of smell. With these and the chemical collars, some sensitive dogs become sore around the area where the collar is in contact with the skin.

Flea collars, whether insecticidal or repellent, are in any case only effective for small dogs, as the active ingredients only travel for approximately a foot away from the collar.

Ticks

Ticks can be picked up all summer long, especially in areas frequented by deer or sheep. Ticks are members of the spider family, and when unfed, look like tiny spiders. Once they have sunk their heads under their host's skin and had a good feed, only the swollen abdomen shows, like a wart. If left alone, they will then drop off and crawl away. Ticks are happy to feast off us as well as our dogs; unlike fleas, they cause no irritation when they bite, and so can go unnoticed. They can spread a number of unpleasant diseases in animals and humans alike, the most common of which is Lyme disease, which in man shows as a localised rash where the tick has been, accompanied by flu-like symptoms which can leave the sufferer feeling very ill for weeks. Ticks are therefore best removed as soon as possible.

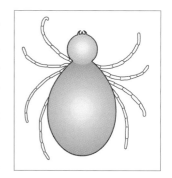

Tick

There is a great deal of received wisdom about ticks and their removal, most of which is nonsense. An engorged tick is easy to remove simply by gripping with the fingernails as close to the skin as possible, and then, being careful not to squeeze the tick's abdomen, giving a half-twist counter-clockwise and pulling sharply. You will almost always extract the whole beast, which you can then crush. Other ways are to spray the tick with flea spray, or, remembering that ticks breathe through their abdomens, plaster the bit you can see with something that will seal off the air – butter, olive oil, petroleum jelly, nail varnish, hair or deodorant spray – and the tick will suffocate, loosen itself and drop off shortly afterwards. Dabbing on neat spirit, tea tree oil, perfume, meths, anything like that will also make the tick loosen. You can also buy a metal device that tweaks out ticks just as well as using your nails. Sooner or later, someone will tell you that a lighted cigarette end held against the tick will make it let go. So it will, but it will also hurt the animal in which the tick is embedded, and make it wriggle, so that an accidental burn might result.

What if you don't get the tick's head out? You will be regaled with all sorts of horror stories of terrible infections that will result, culminating in your animal developing huge abscesses that need surgery. Relax. Nature isn't so stupid. If the head is left in, dab the site with neat tea tree or lavender oil, and leave the rest to the immune system. A small pimple will form that has the tick head neatly contained, and will eject it in a matter of days. You can, if you wish, give homoeopathic Silica orally and/or Bach Crab Apple in the drinking water, to help eject the foreign body, but it will happen in any case. I have taken in rescue ferrets that looked like armadillos with the number of ticks they had on them: their immune systems were weak from starvation, dehydration and parasite overload, and yet never did I have one develop abscesses from having ticks removed and the occasional head being left in. Simple ways work well, as long as basic cleanliness is observed – no picking of scabs or similar grisly human/monkey behaviours, please. Cleanse the area and leave it alone.

Mites

At certain times of year, mites can make your dog's life a misery, especially harvest mites, which can be seen as little moving dots around the paws. If your dog is intensely itchy about her feet, bathe them in salt water and add just a couple of drops of tea tree oil. Other mites can come from poultry or small birds, and if you bed your dog in hay or straw, small bloodsucking things can live in there as well.

Ear mites are commonly found in dogs, the first signs being an unpleasant smell from the ear, maybe accompanied by a brownish discharge, or the dog scratching her ears or shaking her head a lot, carrying her head lopsided, presenting you with an ear that she wants cleaning, or grumbling if you try to touch her ears because they are sore. There are several ways of treating this unpleasant nuisance: Thornit powder (See Useful Addresses) is excellent, or aloe vera gel, or a little olive oil with a few drops of lavender oil in, and there are several ear washes that you can get from your vet. If you have a cat, they are often symptomless carriers, and many a case of recurrent infection can be traced to the family cat. Therefore all ears (except human) in the house should be treated at the same time, whether perceivably affected or not.

Itchy Weeds

There are several weeds that can cause intense irritation to your dog, the most common being nettles. Tiny nettles that you may not even have noticed have great stinging power, and a dog with 'nettled' feet can spend several hours scraping the carpet and trying to find somewhere cold to lie down. Giant Hogweed is another common irritant. If you suspect your dog has come into contact with stinging weeds, bathe the affected areas in cool water to which a few drops of lavender oil have been added, soothe with aloe vera gel or bathe with nettle tea.

Foreign Bodies

Ears are also beautifully designed to take in grass seeds and similar herbage, and some grass seeds are equally well designed with sticky barbs that work their way deep into the ear. This is intensely painful for the dog. Veterinary help is required, for the dog will have to be sedated while the foreign matter is extracted. If your dog tells you that an ear hurts, get help at once, because delay may cause swelling which makes the object more difficult to extract. As a preventative, don't let your dog run about in long grass at seed time, and particularly not in fields of crops (See Chapter Eight).

Mange

There are two types of mange commonly seen in dogs. The most common is Sarcoptic mange, also known as 'fox mange', though the mites will bite other animals as well. It is extremely infectious, and is easily caught by dogs that are active where mangy foxes live. We can get infected by the mange mite too, and irritant rashes on exposed areas like arms will result. It itches like blazes, but neat lavender oil gets rid of it at once, if it is caught in the early stages. Obviously, if infected animals are in the household, they need to be treated or the human infection can recur. Left alone, the mites die on people anyway, but I wasn't motivated to put up with the itch long enough to find out.

Mange in rescue dog

Demodectic mange mites are cigar-shaped (sarcoptic mites are oval) and thought to be present in all dogs, but it is comparatively rare for them to cause a problem. Passed from bitch to pups after whelping, demodectic mange will sometimes show in the suckling bitch and often clears up spontaneously. This type of mange can also occur when a dog is very stressed, physically or mentally, including by illness. The condition is not contagious, but a result always of another problem.

Mange is identified by means of a skin scrape taken by your vet. who will advise treatment accordingly.

INTERNAL MATTERS

What is not commonly understood is that most skin problems are the result of something on the inside trying to get out. The skin is a great cleansing organ, and where other cleansing organs are stressed by disease or circumstance, the skin may be called upon to do more work than usual. We notice that the dog's body scent has changed and become stronger, or that her skin has changed colour. Skin eruptions may well follow, possibly leading to hair loss and weeping sores. The dog responds by chewing at the irritation 'making it worse' but what else can she do? There are many causes of skin problems, some of which are simple to deal with. Cleansing herbs may be given, such as Dorwest's Garlic and Fenugreek, and Bach Crab Apple in the water will assist cleansing too. Chopped and cooked nettles in the food are good cleansers, and dogs will often seek their own herbs in order to detoxify themselves, couch grass, cleavers, common (not giant) hogweed and parsley being favourites. I let my dogs help themselves from the herb garden, and they will graze certain plants to the roots on occasion. However, cleansing by itself will not help unless the cause of the problem is found and addressed, and if there is a lot of internal muck, the act of cleansing will make the skin condition seem temporarily worse as it is expelled. This is known as a 'healing crisis' and can seem alarming if you are not prepared for it. What I often hear is on the lines of: 'The stuff you said to try made it worse and then it sort of got better on its own'. What really happened was that the cleansing forced all the foreign matter out of the skin, so that it looked worse, and then the body was able to heal itself. By contrast, some conventional treatments, typically steroids, suppress the cleansing process so that the condition appears to clear up, but in fact the stuff that needs to come out of the body is trapped within; as soon as the suppressing medication is discontinued, the condition appears to recur as the body tries to deal with it again. This creates a vicious circle of continuous drug treatment. Consultation with a holistic vet can often be very successful by working with the animal's system instead of suppressing its natural immune reaction, and should be the first port of call when problems recur.

Worms

If your dog has worms, it does not mean that you are an inadequate dog keeper or that you have done something wrong: all dogs – in fact, all animals – are exposed to worm infestation at birth, and often in the womb, constantly re-infected all their lives and mostly suffer very little from it. Like fleas and other external bloodsuckers, worms have evolved to live in symbiosis with their hosts. We don't care for this, however,

ABOVE: *Skin problem caused by food allergy*
BELOW: *And after changing to rawfood diet*

and so we treat our animals regularly with substances that expel and preferably kill the worms. There are also some concerns that, if children do not grow up with dogs, their immune systems cannot cope with dog worm eggs, which develop into migrating larvae, and there have been sporadic cases of children whose eyesight has been affected. Although such cases are extremely rare, we still worm our dogs with this in mind.

The situation regarding treatment is similar to the flea problem in that natural remedies, while they will help to reduce the worm burden, are not enough on their own to do the job. In fact, old-fashioned wormers like areca nut expelled worms so violently they could harm the dog. Mucus and toxins put out by an excess of worms can be implicated in skin problems such as eczema as the dog's system seeks to expel them, and again, a consultation with a holistic vet can be very helpful in such cases.

There are two main types of worm: tapeworms and roundworms, and you should treat your dog for these with something such as Drontal-Plus between two and four times a year. Sometimes you will see tapeworms in the dog's faeces, and then you know you need to worm, regardless of when you last treated your dog for them. As the name implies, tapeworms are flat like tape, and what you usually see are small wriggling segments about the size of a rice grain either in the faeces or around the anus. Roundworms are, as you would expect, round, the shape that we expect to see when worms are mentioned, and they are most often seen in puppy faeces, though a dog with a severe infestation will sometimes vomit them up as well. If you have to dispose of wormy muck, burn it, for worm eggs are tough and will live in soil for quite some time. Worming your dog is therefore not just a matter of doing what is best for your dog, but also very much an environmental concern.

Wormy dogs can look 'poor' with staring coats and pot bellies, but it is also possible for a dog to show no external signs of worms at all. Between worming, feed a few raw pumpkin seeds every day, which helps to create a hostile internal environment for worms, and plenty of raw vegetables, especially spinach. It is also thought that, while good health equals fewer worms, sometimes those worms that proliferate in an unhealthy intestinal environment may even have a beneficial effect by cleaning the gut. Once again, we need to keep our minds open and an eye on new research.

Other Worms

Now that we don't have such stringent quarantine restrictions, dogs are bringing in worms and other parasites with which we are not so familiar, such as heartworm. If your dog has been abroad, or in contact with dogs that have recently returned, and you suspect that she is unwell, see your vet and explain the circumstances. Some of these worms require specific treatment, and the sooner the better. Meanwhile, you can carry on feeding the worm-repelling herbs and seeds, as everything will help.

VISITING THE VET

A well-kept dog should not need to visit the vet often, and for the first few years of your dog's life, your vet will probably only see her for an annual check-up. It is sensible to find a vet in whom you have confidence before you actually need him or her, and there are some things you can do to make the veterinary visit as trouble-free as possible for both sides of the table.

Obviously you will arrive in time for your appointment, and made sure that your dog has emptied herself before you go into the waiting room. Please come equipped to clear up after your dog, and if, despite your efforts, she soils the car park or waiting room, tell the staff at once so that it can be cleared up – otherwise you will have started a problem which means other dogs will smell where your dog has been and try to add to the mess. Once in the waiting-room, do not let your dog roam on a long lead, terrorising small pets in carrying boxes, irritating other dogs or blocking access routes – most waiting rooms are rather small as surgery space is more important. Don't let her sniff other dogs – the waiting room is no place to be sociable. Other dogs may be in pain, or carrying unknown infections. If you suspect that your dog has something contagious, don't bring her into the waiting room at all, but arrange with the reception staff to take her directly into the surgery when her turn comes. Likewise with a bitch on heat – you don't want to start male dogs trying to scrap or mark. If you have to bring your children to the surgery, please see that they sit quietly (bring along some toys or a book for them) rather than running around making a noise – sick animals are very stressed by this sort of thing. Also consider that some of the owners might be very distressed as well. It is quite upsetting enough sitting in the waiting room with an animal that you suspect has reached the end of the line, without having your and her feet under constant attack by galloping, squealing children.

Long before you ever need veterinary help, you should accustom your animal to being touched all over. Play with her toes, her tail, peer into her mouth and ears, lift each leg gently and put it down again. Brush her coat the wrong way and then brush it flat again. There is rarely an excuse for bringing an animal that is difficult to handle into the vet. If, however, you do have one of these, warn the staff and either bring a muzzle or be prepared to see your dog restrained. Some vets never need to use anything other than their personality to disarm a dog, but if others wish to save themselves injury, I have every sympathy with that.

Surgery-induced amnesia is common to all of us, so write down what you want to ask about if you think your mind is likely to go into standby as you walk through the door. Your vet won't mind at all if you pause to refer to notes. Likewise, if you are not sure about what has been said, do ask, and if you get home and can't remember something, the reception staff won't mind looking up your notes and telling you what you need to know – but please be considerate and don't telephone at busy surgery times.

LOOKING THEIR BEST

You reap an enormous reward for very little effort when you keep your dog in good condition. Healthy dogs are so vital, so alive, with their shiny coats, bright eyes and sparkling teeth. Take a look at the dogs that you meet when out walking, and see which ones are getting the best care. As the dog ages, it becomes even more important to look after the small details of her appearance, not for the sake of vanity, but for good health and comfort. It works for us, too.

5 Exercise

How much, how far, how often

Going for a walk with your dog is one of the best times you can share together. Never mind dinner, the truth is that walks are the high spot of your dog's day. Mine, too. Seeing the world through your dog's eyes, watching her enjoy the smells, meeting other dogs, running for sheer joy, is a great intimacy. She will turn to you, eyes glowing, mouth half open in a grin, saying as clearly as she can 'Isn't this fun?' So how much exercise should you give your dog, where should you go, and when? It is not as straightforward as you thought before you got your dog.

HOW MUCH

People tend to think that big dogs need more exercise than small dogs, but in most cases that is not so. To get an idea of how much exercise your dog will need, look at what job she was bred for. Terriers had to follow the hunt, often keeping up with the hounds, and then go to work underground. Terriers will go all day. Border collies were designed to run up and down mountains, rounding up sheep. It is hard to tire out a collie. Spaniels and Labradors put in a full day's work finding and retrieving game: they need a lot of walking. Pointers, setters, and the Continental gundog breeds have bottomless stamina for their job. This type of dog will need at least two long walks each day, and hard weather is of no matter to them. They are bred for endurance.

Others are bred for short bursts of incredible speed: greyhounds, whippets, salukis, lurchers, galgos, and so on. You can see this in the shape of them – lean and sensationally aerodynamic. They will need to run. They do not need to run for long, but when they go, they need to be able to really stretch out, to twist and turn, and burn up their energy. Afterwards, they will happily sleep until you pick up the lead again. They are not fond of wet weather, and it is unwise to take them out in the heat of the day, but they must have that exercise – so you will be getting up early in summer.

Little lapdog types are full of 'go' but will be happier with shorter walks as long as there are at least two in a day. Dogs which have breathing issues such as bulldogs will not need long or fast walks, but still need to be exercised to keep them healthy – you will be proceeding at a much more leisurely pace, but the dog still needs the stimulus of new smells to sniff and dog friends to interact with. Some folk think that a dog can manage without walks if they have a large garden, but if you want the dog to get exercise from being in the garden, you will have to join in by throwing balls, or hiding toys for hide-and-seek. There is the side-effect of a trashed garden from this sort of fun. Not all dogs will humour you by playing with you – while GSDs and collies will join in happily, don't try it with a saluki unless you can take rejection. The main problem about expecting the garden to be your dog's universe is twofold:

Providing entertainment in the garden

she won't be able to socialise with other dogs, and she won't have the mental stimulus of new smells and experiences. Both of these are vital to her mental health. If you have ever been ill for a long time, and unable to get out, you will understand at once.

So – how much exercise? Ideally, the minimum is two walks per day, in which your dog can have some freedom to run and explore safely and without causing upset to anyone else. The dog should never be out unaccompanied, and should not be out of your sight, nor should she be at a distance where you cannot control her. A dog should never be allowed to 'take herself off for a walk'. If you can manage more walks, be sure that your dog will be delighted. If you truly cannot manage two walks per day, think very hard before getting a dog.

PUPPIES AND GIANT BREEDS

Although these still need their daily walks, it is bad for their growing frames to have too much exercise. Puppies of non-giant breeds will toddle happily along with you for a leisurely fifteen-minute walk two or three times a day, and that will be quite enough for them until they are six months old. Between six and twelve months, the walk can be increased until the pup is having about an hour at a time, but this should be walking, not jogging or following a bicycle. Two dogs of similar age will exercise themselves very nicely by running about while the owners have a leisurely stroll and chat, but pups of significantly different ages and/or size should not be allowed to romp together because of the risk of injury. Puppy exercise should be educational as well as fun: use these outings to teach your puppy about the outside world. Sit on a bench and watch the traffic go by. Stand outside the school and let her see and hear the children. Wait by the level crossing and let her see the trains, and by the bus stop to see the buses. Go to a local show or fete and let her see large numbers of people. Give her plenty of space and do not overwhelm her with these new experiences: start a reasonable distance away and move closer over the weeks until you are at the stage where she will board a bus or train to go one stop and then come home again (not if she is going through a travel-sick stage, though!). She won't automatically like everyone she meets any more than you do, so don't force her to submit to being petted if she is not the type of dog that enjoys it. Were you ever made to kiss people you didn't like when you were a child? Dogs need respect for their feelings, too. Young puppies should not be taken on long walks, or made to dash about after a ball or toy, but they do need to hone their social skills with other dogs, meet a variety of people, and get as many new experiences under their belts as possible. These experiences should be designed to build their confidence, not undermine it, and if the pup shows signs of disquiet, the owner should not force her, but take her back to a stage where she is confident and move more slowly forward from there.

Giant breeds have special needs in terms of how much they are allowed to exercise, because they have been artificially bred to be much larger than the optimum

Giant breeds – limited exercise for these deerhound pups

Puppy socialisation

size for a healthy dog. These must not be allowed to run with other dogs as there is a very real danger of damaged limbs, and nor should their joints be stressed by being walked for long distances. Twenty minutes at a time for the first year of their lives is quite sufficient for such animals, and then exercise should be gradually increased until they are two years old. Again, this should be walking exercise interspersed with the dog choosing her own pace off the lead, but not being made to run at a speed dictated by the owner. Most giant breeds are not fully mature until three years old, after which they can have as much exercise as any other dog until they start to slow down through old age.

Both young puppies and giant breeds should not be encouraged to run up and down stairs, and nor should they be allowed to leap out of the car onto a hard surface. Jumping into the car is all right, and so is running up and down slopes, but baby joints are vulnerable and a lot of damage can be done by these otherwise harmless practices. Activities such as 'Agility' should not be attempted until the dog is fully mature physically, especially if of a breed that suffers from hip and elbow problems, and for giant breeds, it is not suitable at all. In the home, be careful if your puppy shows a propensity for climbing onto furniture and then jumping off it, and keep doors shut that lead to rooms with such temptations. Some pups are easier than others: one of mine would jump onto work surfaces and window sills like a cat, and I once found him on the mantelpiece. If you have a dog like this, pad the landing areas with rolled-up duvets or similar. Precautions taken now will go a long way towards saving your dog from a painful old age through arthritis.

FURTHER AND FASTER

Once your dog is fully grown, she will relish more exercise and a faster pace, maybe more than you can comfortably manage. Some people take the dog out beside a bicycle, but this is in fact illegal, as is having her running alongside a car, unless you are off the public highway. Curiously, it is legal to exercise the dog on the highway if she is running beside a horse. All of these ways will be enjoyed by your dog if you can find places to take her where it is legal, but there are safety issues, so she should be well enough trained to keep beside or behind you rather than running ahead, with the potential of being hit by car or bicycle, or trampled by the horse, if she stops or swerves suddenly. If you are using public rights of way, remember so are others, and a pack of mountain bikers or a posse of horse riders can come at speed out of nowhere. I used to have great fun exercising my lurchers behind a horse or the old farm van when I had access to plenty of private land on which to do it, but time moves on and land gets sold, and I have to walk now!

WHEN

Dogs don't really mind when they are walked, as long as they get out at some time. It is not necessary to stick to a particular schedule; much as you love your dog, she has to fit in with a host of human responsibilities. However, a well-exercised dog is a

Further and faster

darned sight easier to have around the house while you get on with other things, and if you have to leave the dog for a few hours, it is sensible to have given her a good walk immediately beforehand. Mine go out at first light, and then I have all morning to myself until lunchtime, when yawning, stretching and wagging tails indicate that I need the recreation of another trip out. If it is winter and daylight is short, we have the second long walk then: if summer and hot, then a quick round-the-block suffices until the cool of the evening and our proper walk. If you are tied to office schedules, then walking in winter will become difficult as daylight decreases. We live in the real world, and you can only do so much, but try your best to get your dog out twice even if only for a short run, and then be sure to make up for it at weekends. You can still have your well-earned lie-in and leisurely breakfast if that is what suits you, but after that, your dog's wellbeing should come before any household chores – which after all can be done in poor light if necessary. Invest in a good coat and hat, some stout boots and a few towels, and you will find that walking in the wind and rain is exhilarating rather than a penance. You can certainly walk your dog in the dark – I do – but the safety of this depends very much on where you live. If traffic is your concern, reflective strips on your coat are a good idea, and you can get these to go on your dog's collar and lead as well; it is also helpful to carry a torch. You can even get dog collars that light up. If you feel vulnerable walking in the park or countryside, perhaps you can team up with other dog walkers and go together. Don't let your dog off the lead in the dark unless you are very sure of her obedience, for darkness awakens the natural dog hunting instincts, and there will be wildlife moving about at these times.

Always feed after the walk, not before. There are two main reasons for this, one physical, one mental. It is harmful for a dog, or any other animal including us, to exercise with a full stomach. At best it will cause discomfort and digestive difficulties, and at worst (especially with large and giant breeds) it can cause bloat, which has the potential to kill your dog. The second reason is that a hungry dog is more obedient! If you are going through a tricky patch in your training, a dog that is hungry will be more inclined to pay attention, and will want to stick close to you and come home with you. Then feed the dog and let her rest. That is how the natural dog operates – out on the hunt (walk) with lots of exercise on an empty stomach, then the kill (dinner) then sleep.

PROFESSIONALS

Nowadays a lot of people walk dogs as a business, which can be helpful if you work long hours. They will collect your dog, walk her, and drop her off at home again. There is no regulatory body for dog walkers: anyone can set up as one, so before you entrust your dog to the walker, it is wise to do some homework. Check, for example, that there is adequate insurance cover, in case of mishap. Is the walker taking your dog out on her own, or taking several dogs together? If the latter, how are the dogs confined in the car? Are they kept separate, or all in a bunch? Where will they be taken, will they be let off the lead and if so, all together or individually? Are you happy for this person to have access to your house while you are out? If possible, go for a walk with this person and your dog, to see how the other dogs interact with the walker. A good dog walker can make all the difference to your peace of mind, but a bad one can cause all sorts of problems. It is sensible to give the dog walker a list of your training commands so that s/he can control your dog, and also to advise of any peculiarities such as if your dog is afraid of or aggressive towards certain types of dog. If you don't want your dog let off the lead, make this clear. Expect to pay extra for your dog being walked on her own, which is money well spent in my opinion. If you want your dog walker to undertake additional tasks, be prepared to pay for them; I know a dog walker who was forever being asked to do extra jobs, from washing and drying the dog on rainy days before she went back indoors, to feeding the goldfish and clearing the week's dog mess off the lawn! Most dog walkers will only walk the dogs.

WHERE

This is surprisingly tricky, and before you ever commit yourself to a dog, it is useful to do some research on places to go for walks. Beaches and recreation areas are sometimes restricted or even forbidden, fields are busy growing crops and livestock, and woods can be full of wildlife. There may be public footpaths through this area or that, but there will be times when the use of these footpaths is not sensible, such as if there is a Shoot in progress, or cows with calves (far more dangerous than cattle without) or even when the paths are so muddy as to make using them a penance. It is irresponsible to let your dog chase livestock or game, and especially important to either have your dog under close control or on a lead when walking through areas where these are. Cattle and horses can be particularly aggressive towards dogs, and unless you know that particular ones are not, I'd say keep out of fields that have them in. If you thought the field was empty, and now that you are halfway across it you are

Careful with cattle

Steady with sheep

Placid with poultry

being approached by cattle or horses, this is one occasion when you should let your dog off the lead, so long as you are sure she will not chase. If attacked, she can run faster than you, and get out of danger. Cattle will rarely attack a human without a dog, though it is worth remembering that the big one with the ring through its nose is generally a bull. Always have your dog on a lead in a field of sheep, or if the footpath takes you through a farmyard, which latter may have loose poultry and cats about. Don't assume that because your dog is friendly towards people that she will not have a prey-drive – all dogs are predators.

If you are walking through woods, keep a good lookout for deer – you do not want your dog to chase these. Get into the habit of checking for the presence of deer where woods and fields meet, and always go over stiles and through gateways first. If you cannot stop your dog chasing, have her on the lead. Better that than a dog killed by chasing a deer across the road. In the countryside during April and May, there is especial danger of your dog encountering fawns, which are left concealed by their mothers. Every year, nice-natured family dogs like yours kill large numbers of fawns – be aware that this happens and take suitable precautions. Equally, don't let her terrorise ground-nesting birds, some of which are legally protected and all of which should be left in peace to breed.

CAR SICKNESS

Few of us are lucky enough to live within walking distance of suitable exercise areas, and even if we do, there comes a time when the dog needs to be taken somewhere by car. Young puppies are almost guaranteed to be travel-sick, and like young children, they mostly grow out of it. A variety of natural remedies is available to help with this, which are covered in Chapter Eight. As well as these, try the dog in different cars, in case it is the suspension of that particular car which is causing the trouble, and with a different driver, in case it is your driving! Sometimes a dog can go further on a journey with straightish roads than on switchback changes of gradient and camber. Sometimes a dog will travel better secured in the front seat area (safest in the passenger seat footwell) or with the dog crate in the exact centre of the car rather than over the back wheels where the motion is most pronounced. Simply having the windows partly open to allow a constant stream of fresh air can make a difference, too. If you are travelling alone, put the dog in an indoor kennel or travelling box, ensuring that there is a blanket over the top to make it dark and cosy as well as eliminating outside vision. Line with newspaper and then towels, old sheets, or similar easily washed or discarded items. Make sure that the container is securely fixed and doesn't slide about in the vehicle, see that the dog can face the direction of travel, and if possible is able to see you. If you can travel with a companion, then that person is duty bound to talk encouragingly to the dog throughout the journey. Please don't put the dog in an enclosed boot: apart from being illegal, there is a possibility of her inhaling exhaust fumes, which won't do her any good at all. If the travel container is by the sound system speakers, do without the radio, for the dog will otherwise suffer with her sensitive hearing. Try to avoid taking the dog out by car on hot days.

If the dog is very travel sick or frightened in the car – it is unfortunate that, for most dogs, their first few car rides involve going to the vet – then a programme of desensitisation is necessary. Start with the dog in the car and the engine off. Sit there and read the paper, then unload the dog and go back indoors. Progress in stages to

Car safety

having the dog in a stationary car with the engine running, driving to the end of the road, then around the block, and finally to a place where the dog can be walked, as close to home as possible. Rescue Remedy used daily during this spell is usually very helpful for dog and driver! If the dog is really hysterical, then homoeopathic Ignatia 30c may be of assistance. Ensure that car journeys end in nice experiences and build on what you achieve day by day, and gradually the problem, in most cases, will go away.

HAZARDS

On the beach and in parks, look out for dangerous litter such as broken bottles and hypodermic syringes, and litter from picnics, especially cooked chicken bones. By lakes and rivers, be careful of discarded fishing tackle. Still water sometimes develops a toxic form of algae, which is blue; keep your dog out of the water if so. Walking through shallow streams is a delicious experience for your dog, but watch out for broken glass and rusty metal. Standing water and puddles may be contaminated with chemical run-off from fields. Keep to the paths on farmland, because there may be discarded bits of machinery waiting lethally in overgrown areas, and also people may quite legitimately be shooting. Oh dear, is there anywhere to walk your dog? Of course there is, and I am just advising you to be on the alert instead of pootling along with your mind full of human matters. With sensible precautions and your normal good manners, walks with your dog can be just as much fun for you as they are for her.

BASICS

Well, you need a dog of course, and a lead. Or perhaps a harness, or one of the headcollar-type leaders, or maybe an extending lead? And of the ordinary leads, do I mean one with a clip, or a slip-lead, or a choke-chain, or a half-choke, or...? Let's have a look at leads.

Dogs don't usually come ready lead-trained. Though some walk naturally to heel, most resent the lead when they first encounter it, and either pull, fight or flop. While you are dealing with this under the guidance of your dog-trainer, you may be using various helpful devices such as those listed above. The only one with which I would take issue is the extending lead. This is the badge of the person who cannot be bothered to train their dog. It is also risky. The nylon cord may have the strength to hold a runaway truck, but the nickel clips do not, and neither does the plastic handle. The arresting mechanism sometimes fails, with catastrophic consequences for the dog – some have run into traffic, or jumped obstacles and broken their necks. Please don't use this dreadful device, but work at your lead training. Your aim is the dog walking confidently to heel on a slack lead. I prefer the slip leads, as a collar can come off over a dog's head unless it is tight enough to make her eyes bulge; also my dogs' collars are loose anyway, partly to stop them getting hung up in undergrowth (I once rescued a dog that had been trapped for two days in a ditch, with a branch through her collar) and also to stop anyone stealing them by grabbing hold of their collars. If, however, you prefer a lead with a clip, then provided your fingers are still nimble, these are just as good. Harnesses and headcollars are many and varied: take a good look before you buy. Nylon harnesses sometimes rub: be on the lookout for worn or sore patches on

Cooling off

Hazard – farm machinery

your dog's coat or skin every time you take the harness or headpiece off. Follow the instructions of your trainer, and you will soon be able to discard these because your dog will be walking nicely. Be careful though, when you let your dog off the lead, because you do not want her to get caught up. Best to take the harness or headcollar off as well – which means of course that she still needs her ordinary collar on. I recommend always using leather collars: not only are they softer than synthetics, but they can stretch, which means that if your dog does get caught up out of sight, she is likely to be able to struggle free of a leather collar.

LEADS

The lead that you choose should be comfortable for you to hold, and you will need more than one – the lead that got wet on your morning walk may not be dry by the afternoon one. There may be occasions when that lead has to hold the full strength of your dog, and with that in mind, check how it is made, for a cheap lead that will break is no economy. Is it stitched, glued or riveted? If the former, are the stitches single or double? How well is the clip attached? It may cost a little more, but a leather lead made by a saddler will last fifty years, if properly cared for, and will be strong enough to hold the strongest dog. The rope slip leads that I favour come in varying qualities too – as ever, you get what you pay for – so check the stitching at either end frequently, even if it is covered by a little leather or plastic sleeve. If you use a clip-on lead, check the collar for wear at the fastening. It takes seconds, but is so important. There is little as numbing as holding the end of a broken lead while your dog careers into danger.

Holding The Lead

Yes, there are better ways of doing this. It is natural for a human to hold the lead the 'wrong' way, passing from the dog through the thumb and forefinger to the palm. Held like this, the lead can easily be pulled through the fingers. Similarly, if the loop of the lead is held in the fingers, it doesn't take much for the dog to pull the lead out of the owner's hand. Instead, take a leaf out of the horse riders' book, where reins of a similar size to your lead will be sufficient to contain the energy of half a ton or more of eager horse. From the dog, the lead should be taken between the third and fourth fingers, across the palm and then held lightly between finger and thumb. Should you need to hold on to a lunging dog, simply closing your fingers will give a very strong grip. For extra safety, take the loop of the lead in one hand, passing your wrist through it, then have the lead across your body and hold with the horseman's grip in the other hand. This will enable a normal person to hold a normal dog in any everyday situation. Do not wind the lead around your fingers or thumb, because a sudden leap from the dog could break one or more of these.

It is popular practice to hang the lead around your neck or diagonally across your body when the dog is enjoying free exercise. This is terribly dangerous. Anyone with evil in mind simply has to grab the lead as you pass, and you are in serious trouble. Have the lead in your pocket. You might lose the odd lead, but it is better than being mugged.

IDENTIFICATION

By law, your dog must wear a collar which carries your name and address, and she must wear it at all times when she is out, unless she is a working dog and actually working. This law is so old that it does not mention telephone numbers. Of course, a telephone number is much more useful if you find a stray dog, so it makes sense to have this on the collar as well. I prefer not to have my dogs' names on their collars, as it is easier for people to steal them if they know their names.

Most people have an engraved identity disc hanging from the dog's collar. This is cheap, easily obtained, and will last for years while remaining legible. The discs come in a variety of sizes and are made in metal or plastic. The metal ones can jingle, which is annoying for an animal with the acute hearing of a dog; I solve this by taping the top of the disc. A popular alternative is a hollow barrel-shaped container within which is a piece of paper on which you can put your details. It is an extremely small piece of paper, and I for one have difficulty in putting the information on it in a legible manner. However, the barrel is small and neat, much easier for little dogs to carry. These barrels come undone very easily, and there are two ways to deal with this: one is to put a dab of nail varnish on the thread before you join the two halves of the barrel together, and the other is to make sure that you have bought a barrel with an indentation in the bottom which will take a screwdriver, and so screw the two halves together very tightly. I always do both. Don't be tempted to use glue, as one day someone might need to get that barrel undone and read the contents. Barrel or disc, both come with a flimsy split-ring that soon falls apart, so what I do is change it for the much more robust split-rings that you get on key-rings. It is also useful to write your telephone number on the collar itself, in case, despite your precautions, the identity disc or barrel falls off. This could rub out and will need renewing from time to time.

Tattoos
Dogs can be tattooed in one or both ears, or on the inside of a thigh, as a type of permanent identification, and then the details are held on a national register. The tattoo is not done like a human tattoo, but instantly with a type of punch machine. It is painful for just a moment, and then done. Collars can come off or be removed, but a tattoo is there for life, and if your dog is lost and then found, you will have a reliable means of proving yourself her owner. Tattoos can be altered or defaced by unscrupulous people, and some dogs have even been abandoned with their ears cut off, but these cases are extreme. By contrast, relatively few people would bother to check the inside of a strange dog's hindleg for identification, but that does include kennel staff. If you would like to have your dog tattooed, you can check at your veterinary clinic or with your dog training club for a list of people qualified to do this.

Microchipping
Another popular method of permanent identification is the microchip. This is a small inert electronic chip slightly larger than a grain of rice, which is inserted under the dog's skin with a special hollow needle. When scanned with the appropriate receiver, it will show a number unique to that dog, and you as the owner can be traced. Microchipping is slightly more expensive than tattooing, and the chips have been known to migrate to different parts of the body in a significant minority of cases. Some of us are uneasy about inserting a foreign body into our dogs, especially one that might move. If a dog is chipped while she is still growing, the very act of growth can move the chip, just as scars move during growth. A big drawback is that many dog rescues do not bother to scan for a chip, or do not scan properly. Scanner manufacturers recommend an extensive scan procedure, but the sad reality is that in many cases, an overworked kennel hand swipes the scanner vaguely around the dog's neck area, to a background of blaring radio and barking dogs – hardly conducive to hearing an electronic bleep. Neither tattoos nor microchips are foolproof or tamper-proof, but in most cases they will help you to prove that a 'found' dog is yours, whereas if you have neither, the task is much more difficult. Have your dog's chip scanned when you take her to the vet for her annual check-up, to see that it still works and has not moved. It is also sensible to check with the registration body that they are still operating their twenty-four-hour service for reporting lost dogs, as there was a case not long ago when two companies working in partnership went their separate ways, and as a result, dogs that had been registered for years were taken off both registers without clients being notified. The new register was moved to a different country, and only open during that nation's office hours. Fortunately, a popular dog newspaper raised the issue, and the other company re-registered the dogs free of charge and confirmed the twenty-four-hour service availability.

Incidentally, even if your dog is tattooed and microchipped, she still, by law, has to have your name and address on her collar.

SECURITY

Dog theft is a perennial problem, and although certain breeds seem to be stolen more than others, any dog is vulnerable. Dogs are stolen for a variety of reasons, none of them pleasant, and often sold on within hours. As there is no central point of contact to report stolen dogs, and in the eyes of the police dog theft is of little importance compared to other crimes, the dog theft victim is very much on his or her own at a very distressing time. Organisations such as Lurchersearch and Petsearch will handle information on all types of dog theft, not just lurchers (See Useful Addresses), putting up posters can sometimes be very productive, and all dog rescues in the area will have to be contacted on a daily basis as often they are not good at passing information on. Prevention being better than cure, treat your dog just like any other precious possession: never leave her tied up outside a shop, or alone in the car, and if you leave her in the garden, make sure all access points are padlocked. Nothing will deter a determined thief, but security arrangements that delay and make theft difficult will help against the opportunist.

COATS

Dogs seldom need coats when out exercising, though some owners feel better for putting coats on dogs. Most dogs have a more than adequate jacket of their own, and are healthier for the air getting to their hide. Even a thin-skinned whippet can keep herself perfectly warm by running around, and the brisk walk to and from the exercise area should be enough to keep the circulation going. Elderly dogs, however, do like a coat on bitter days or if there is a keen wind, and there is some justification for a coat on whippet types if it is raining hard. Dogs are very good at converting body fat to warmth, and another good reason for not coating a dog while walking her is to keep her weight down. If your dog is coated and you let her off the lead, take her coat off as well to stop her getting caught up, or injuring herself if the coat swings round and she puts a leg through it. If your dog is old or infirm and you put a coat on her, make sure that it is long enough to cover her whole back. Some dog coat manufacturers such as Country Mun (See Useful Addresses) build a curve into their coats to follow the shape of the loins, which is much better than a straight coat for warmth and fit, and also lets the rain drain off. You note that I am referring to coats while exercising. If, however, your dog is a thin-coated type and would be standing around a lot, such as if you are spectating at a winter event, a coat is definitely a good thing. Wet muddy dogs benefit from a coat on the drive home after exercise, too, and you will have a dry cosy dog at the end of the journey. Coats are useful at night in the winter if your dog sleeps outside, or your house is not heated at night. In fact, dog coats have lots of sensible uses, but out on walks for a normal lively dog is not one of them.

OVERHEATING

At the other end of temperature extremes is the risk of your dog overheating, which is much more likely in temperate climes than suffering damage from cold. Treatment for this is covered in Chapter Eight. Dogs overheat distressingly quickly. They do not sweat over their whole bodies as we can, but lose most of their heat through their tongues and pads. Sighthound types, which produce bursts of incredible speed, have minimal or no coat underneath, to aid dissipation of the heat they produce when they run. To avoid heatstroke, which can kill your dog, never exercise her in the heat of the day or leave her in a car on even a warm day – parking in the shade, having the window open and a bowl of water available does not stop the car from turning into an oven. Even if you have the dogs in the car with the windows open as you drive (but not so far open that the dog can jump out, please) it will not take very long in a traffic jam for your dog to become severely distressed.

Dogs need shelter at home, too, and most prefer to be indoors when it is very hot. Given the opportunity, some will alternate a spot of sunbathing with cooling off in the shade, under a shrub or inside the house, but if your garden does not allow for this, it is better for the dog to be indoors in the cool than outside with no chance of getting away from the sun. Kennels and sheds can become insufferably hot very quickly, and so can open lawns.

Another area where heat can be a problem occurs when the dog is the beloved companion of an elderly person. Often old people feel cold all the time, and simply do not realise when the weather is sweltering. Consequently, the dog can be taken for her constitutional in the midday heat, or left to lie in a hot conservatory or patio. Equally, elderly people can have the heating on indoors all year round, which can cause all manner of health problems in their pets. Clearly, this is a difficult area in which to intrude, but for the welfare of the animals, some sort of compromise – the dog having access to an unheated utility room, perhaps, or the planting of some decorative shade in the garden – needs to be reached.

Beware of overheating

VARIETY

Do your best to keep walks interesting for your dog. Some breeds need constant entertainment, or else they start looking for it themselves, and become troublesome. Vary the walks as much as you can: even going the same route but starting from the other end can make a difference. If your dog likes to chase a ball or Frisbee, then take one and use it for part – not all – of the walk. The dog will be watching you all the time in case the toy is about to appear, rather than the toy being a feature of the entire walk and therefore less interesting. Dogs like to walk with other dogs, just as people do in company too, so team up with other dog walkers sometimes. Choose your walking friends carefully though: you do not want your dog to copy another's bad behaviour, or be the victim of aggression. Dogs that are especially fond of scenting will appreciate some rough ground to snuffle through, especially if there are rabbits about, and sighthound types will enjoy a good gallop.

Some breeds of dog are very excitable, however, and too much stimulation will have them coming back from their walks in a state of fizzing over-agitation. Thus when you bring them home, instead of being ready for relaxing or sleeping, they will be hyper and on the very edge of controllability, maybe taking several hours to calm down. This does not mean walk them less, but walk them differently. Throwing the ball or toy may be replaced by hiding it and then sending them back for a 'find', and walking freely may with advantage be interspersed with heelwork, wait-and-recall, or sit and stay. Let me just explain the differences in those two disciplines: 'wait' means 'remain where you are and await the next command' and 'stay' means 'do not move – I will come back to you'. Please don't mix these different commands, as it will be confusing for your dog. By giving such dogs plenty to concentrate upon, as well as spells where they can sniff around and generally behave like dogs, you are ensuring that the interest of the walk is maintained, and also the fact that the dogs are concentrating on you and not on getting into what a human would construe as mischief. As you near the end of the walk, keep matters very calm and relaxed, so that the dog is also calm and relaxed, which is quite different from being bored. Bored dogs are at best under-stimulated and at worst will invent ways of brightening up their walks, which will probably not brighten up yours. Remember that walking your dog is not just about keeping her physically fit, but also adding mental stimulation to her life.

ANTICIPATION

Most of the troubles that affect dog owners out on walks occur because they are not paying attention. Watching out for wildlife or sudden cats should be second nature to you. Some dogs adore children and will try to greet any child they meet, but some parents can't cope with this – indeed, some children and adults are terrified of dogs – so it is better to get your dog into the habit of coming back to heel when others approach. Equally, some children will approach dogs, often at a run and making a lot of noise, when the dog would rather they did not, so it is useful to be able to send your dog away while you field the child. Don't keep your dog on a lead on occasions like this, because leads alter the power of a dog. A frightened dog that cannot run may snap. Conversely, dogs that are bullies will feel empowered by being attached to their owners, and skirmishes between canines are a racing certainty if they are of similar status and one is on a lead. Learn to read dog body language, and be aware that issues that are small to you may be very significant in dog dynamics. A few days ago I witnessed a very avoidable dog-fight that I could see happening a hundred yards before it actually did. Approaching a kissing-gate from one side was a boxer – an entire male – on a lead, and at an equal distance in the other direction, a male crossbred bull terrier off the lead, with the owner carrying a Yorkshire terrier. Both dogs would reach the gate at the same time, and confined spaces are flashpoints between dogs; however, neither owner held back. I moved my dog – an entire male – to one side, and sat him, because I could feel the tension building up between the other two. Both dogs met in the confines of the kissing-gate, and a noisy scrap ensued. The seriousness of the fight is usually in inverse proportion to the noise, so little damage was done, but my dog squeaked at the Yorkie. He only does that for one reason, and it transpired that the little terrier was on heat. The owner should have realised that the bitch being on heat had increased the protective instincts of his male dog, and the presence of another male in a confined space was sufficient excuse for a fight. Dog walkers should be vigilant for this sort of thing.

HOLIDAYS – UK

For many of us, the dog is so much a part of the family that going on holiday without her is unthinkable. There are many holidays that can be taken in Britain that include dog-friendly accommodation and long walks in lovely scenery. The best of these are marvellous, but as ever, it pays to do some homework.

Not all hotels are as dog-friendly as they seem on their advertisements. Most do not allow dogs in dining areas, and some are not keen on the dog being in the bedroom when the owners are not present – which poses a problem about what to do with the dog when you eat. Some expect the dog to live in the car when she is not walking with her owners, and do not allow dogs in the rooms at all. Sometimes (I was caught out like this) there is no garden to the hotel, and so the dog must be taken out into the streets to empty herself each time. Many hotels that do accept dogs also have dogs of their own; hotel dogs tend to be friendly, but if yours is not, or is nervous of other dogs, this might not be ideal. Of course, you will not take a bitch on heat into a hotel.

Some hotel and motel chains leave dog acceptance to the discretion of the manager. Now this can really lead to problems, especially if the manager who accepted your dog when you booked no longer works there, or is not on duty when you arrive. Even with a written confirmation, dog owners have been known to be fobbed off with an unhelpful comment about it being 'wrong' and there you are, expected to leave the dog in the car again. Some places will take 'small' dogs but not large – and the definition of a 'small' dog can be rather arbitrary. All I can suggest is that you arrive early and so have plenty of time to either renegotiate or find suitable alternative accommodation. Please don't leave the dog in the car: she may get stolen.

Holiday cottages may seem a better option, but again, it is necessary to check what is on offer. Some will only accept one dog, or you get the 'large' and 'small' dog discrimination. Then there is the issue of security – some places are not fenced, so your dog must be shut indoors for much of the time. Often, there is nowhere to exercise the dog safely: you might be on farmland where sheep are grazed, or the cottage complex might be sharing with an industrial park. There may be resident dogs that resent strangers on their 'patch' – farm collies are notorious for this. When you are out and about, be watchful for potential dangers: every year dogs are injured, lost or killed through falling over cliffs while chasing rabbits or birds, falling down disused mineshafts, going down fox earths or badger setts, or just running off and being unable to find their way back. If you cannot trust your dog's recall, she will have to spend her holiday on the lead. If you cannot trust her with livestock then you may not be able to use footpaths through fields, and if she has a strong chase instinct that you have not addressed, she will be a hazard herself to horse riders and cyclists. All the more reason to train your dog! Time spent on the puppy reaps huge dividends for the rest of her life.

TRAVEL ABROAD

Since UK quarantine regulations have been relaxed, many people are choosing to take their dogs abroad with them. In health terms, this is definitely not in the dog's interests. Regulations demand that she receives a cocktail of vaccinations and parasite treatment at each embarkation point, and she will be exposed to parasites and infections to which she has had no chance to develop immunity. Some of these may be brought home by her and shared with the indigenous dog population, and deaths have already occurred from this. You may be taking her to a climate to which she is not suited, and the actual travel, however accomplished, will add stress to her. Ferries and some trains demand that the dog is left in the car for the duration of the crossing; apart from the security aspect, the decks of a car ferry are full of fumes. No matter what the weather conditions, delays or other unforeseen circumstances, you will be unable to reach your dog during the journey. Some ferries claim that they supply 'kennels' which can be reserved at the time of booking, but in practice, these are no more than crates, and are often filthy from the distress of previous occupants. Taking livestock by air is very strictly regulated, but not for the benefit of the animals. You will have to supply a container of suitable strength and dimensions, see that the dog has been sedated, and trust to luck that she is loaded in the pressurised part of the hold, the right way up, and with nothing else blocking her air supply or erroneously loaded on top of her container. Collection at the other end can be fraught as well, with vital documents going missing or proving incorrect, or your dog being sent to the wrong area. Aviation is prone to long delays in certain circumstances, and your dog's drug may have worn off during the journey, or she may have become acutely distressed at being confined for so many hours and having to soil her box. It may seem rather fun to have your dog with you when you go abroad, but take it from me: I spent over twenty years working in the travel industry, and I'd never put my dogs through the risks of a journey abroad just for the sake of a holiday, or indeed a competition.

BOARDING KENNELS

One of the alternatives is to board your dog for the duration of your holiday. As with any other service, standards at kennels vary enormously, so do your research a long time before you need the kennels, and don't let geographical convenience come before your dog's welfare. The right sort of kennels will not mind you visiting before you book a place, and it is a good idea to visit at different times of day, to get an idea of the kennel routine. With some places, the dogs are locked away mid-afternoon and don't get a chance to leave their kennels again until the staff arrive the next morning. This can distress house-trained dogs trying not to soil their quarters, or turn a previously clean dog into one that empties herself all over the house upon her return. Old-fashioned kennel blocks offer the dogs little in the way of visual stimulus: often the kennelling allows the dogs only a door's width of outside vision, and the indoor kennel blocks look out onto blank wall. As a consequence, inmates bark constantly, because they are effectively kept in 'solitary'. Newer systems, where the dogs can see other dogs and something of the staff at work, are much more dog-friendly. Prepare your dog for boarding by booking her in for an afternoon, then an overnight stay, before you go off and leave her for a fortnight. Bach Remedy Walnut given in the water for a week before kennelling, and during the stay if possible, prepares the dog for coping with change.

When leaving your dog at kennels, do advise the owner of any peculiarities of character, likes and dislikes. Some dog owners like to leave a favourite toy or bed, but usually the bedding is neatly stored until the owner's return, for boarded dogs can act out of character when first confined, and a trashed bean-bag is often the first casualty. Diet usually goes by the board, kennel owners doing what suits the kennel routine rather than preparing sixty-four different meals per day, but it isn't for long, and once home again, your dog can make up for her fortnight of junk food, as indeed probably you will be doing also. When you have found a good boarding kennels, do your level best to be a helpful customer, for the right kennels and staff need looking after, and goodness knows, they see plenty of the other sort.

THE DOG SITTER

As an alternative to kennelling, you can employ a person to house and dog-sit for you while you are away, or else have your dog(s) in their own home. Both these options can work very well with the right people, and costs compare favourably with boarding fees if you have more than one dog. No matter how competent your sitter or how well-behaved your dog, accidents and unforeseen incidents can happen, so please make sure that adequate insurance is in place, and a legal form of indemnity is also useful. Make sure that your sitter is fully instructed: for instance, I once looked after two dogs for six weeks, having been warned not to let either of them off the lead. By contrast, I once looked after a dog that, I discovered after the owners had left, had bitten several people (she never bit me, but continued with her criminal career upon her owners' return). Your sitter will appreciate being fully advised about the dog's character, and it is better to leave too much information than too little. Details of local walks will be helpful, if someone is staying in your home. Be sure to check out character and customer references if using sitters, as there is no regulatory body; equally, don't be offended if they want to know more about you.

DOG PRIORITIES

Your dog enjoys her walk in ways that are special to dogs but not always acceptable to human owners. For instance, it is very pleasant to many dogs if they can roll in something that, to humans, smells disgusting. Fox muck is a great favourite, and badger muck smells even worse – or better, depending on your point of view. Equally, the eating of something well-rotted brings joy, though not to you when it is brought back up on the living-room carpet, and of course, the droppings of herbivores large and small are a very desirable snack to the dog. Meeting other dogs means much sniffing of bottoms and sometimes licking of genitalia. Small – sometimes not so small – life forms need to be chased and/or barked at. There are issues where dogs and owners should come half-way to meet each other, and areas where behaviour, however natural, is deemed unacceptable. You have the final say, but here is a guide:

ROLLING IN MUCK

You need to teach a 'leave-it' command, and keep your wits about you for that tell-tale shoulder-lowering. Should the worst happen, slathering the offending areas in tomato juice or sauce and then shampooing them with a good dog shampoo should restore a more acceptable smell. Damage limitation means restricting the dog's car access by travelling her in a crate, or having a dog guard. You may have to drive with the windows open.

EATING CARRION

This is most undesirable for a variety of reasons, the most important being not your living room carpet, but what the carrion died of in the first place, especially if it could

That fox muck moment

have been poisoned. You need that 'leave-it' command again. Or else teach a retrieve so that your dog brings its treasure back to you: then you can swap it for a titbit. Of course, this can mean getting hold of some pretty objectionable items, so if you are squeamish, keep a plastic bag or two in your pocket to slip over your hand before you take whatever your dog has found. Wet-wipes in the car are invaluable, too.

EATING MUCK

This is actually a good source of nutrition if from a herbivore, because it is vegetable matter broken down into an easily digestible form, and won't do your dog any harm. However, it can strain your relationship with your dog, especially if it has a lot of facial hair, a flat face, or likes to lick you. Once again, you need that 'leave-it' command, and constant vigilance. Occasionally you get dogs that like to eat all droppings, including dog muck, even their own. This is a lot more unpleasant than the ingestion of herbivore dung. Personally, I find that dogs on the raw food diet are not attracted to eating muck, but there will no doubt be the odd hard case that has found it such a pleasant habit that she will not give up. It then becomes a training issue.

SNIFFING OTHER DOGS

Sorry, you are the one who has to compromise here. There is no harm in it, and it is a very important part of dog-to-dog communication. And yes, they do have to sniff bottoms, sometimes more: it is their way of shaking hands. With male dogs, legs must be cocked after meeting. Sometimes this applies with bitches, too. If a bitch meets an on-heat bitch, there will be much sniffing, and the on-heat bitch's vulva may be licked by the other bitch. A bitch that cocks her leg to scent-mark with urine, or that interacts strongly with another bitch when on heat, or with an on-heat bitch, does not have anything wrong with her hormones. It's a canine matter, and perfectly normal.

'READING THE PAPERS'

The leaving of information for other dogs by means of urine and faeces is perfectly normal, and the examining of these scenting-spots is the dog equivalent of reading the papers, and also normal. As dog muck smells so loathsome to us, it is difficult to comprehend its appeal to the dog, and I can only think that the dog's enhanced sense of smell detects subtle nuances that make it pleasant. After all, dogs must wonder why we like music. Dogs that have something extra special to communicate will scratch up the earth next to their contribution, as if to underline it. This is not, as I have heard some dog behaviourists say, a sign of aggression or dominance, rather a way of shouting 'Read all about it!'. Male dogs demonstrate status by urinating as high as they can up vertical surfaces: female dogs advertise their availability with a series of 'call-me' pools. A puddle from a bitch on or nearing heat will cause interest in both sexes: deep sniffing will ensue and often a chittering of the jaws and drooling. If the pool is very recent, some dogs will even taste it. All perfectly natural: let it happen. However, when the dog is on the lead, constant inspection of scenting sites is irritating, and slows the walk down. It is also a good way of training the owner rather than the dog: dog stops, owner stops, dog moves off, owner does as well. I have an arrangement with my dogs: on the lead, we walk briskly and don't stop, off the lead, they have the leisure to sniff and mark.

CHASING

Again perfectly normal, but has to be moderated. You do not want your dog chasing farm livestock, someone's cat, or animals such as deer. Work with your trainer to teach your dog that sheep, cattle, horses and so on are forbidden, and learn to distract her with toys or games on walks, so that her interest is with you and not scanning the horizon for wildlife. Not all dogs will respond to this, especially those breeds with a high prey drive, and so you will have to be alert on walks, and put the lead on in risk areas – or keep away from them entirely. However, the need to hunt is hard-wired into your dog, and you will have a woefully frustrated animal if she cannot express any part of it. She can still chase rabbits (which go down holes) and squirrels (which go up trees) as long as you have a strong recall with her and can get her to stop and come back. In dangerous areas, such as near cliffs or large areas of forestry, keep her on the lead. And please don't think, as I have heard so often, that 'she only wants to play'. She is a predator, and deadly serious.

MUD AND WATER

Some breeds of dog adore water and will go out of their way to experience as much of it as possible. Breeds like the Newfoundland will even tip out their water bowl and lie in the result. If you have a water-loving breed, you will have to compromise on this. Of course, where there is water, there is also mud, and depending on the soil type where you live and whether the water is standing or running, your dog can be more or less like the Swamp Monster after her aquatic sessions. Compromise again either by allowing your dog to disport in reasonably safe, clear water and putting her on the

Friendly with cats

131

The mud moment

lead when you near the radioactive slurry that clings and stinks for days. It is unreasonable to get a water-loving dog and then not allow her a certain amount of bathing. You might consider adapting your back yard so that you can hose her down and dry her with ease when you come home. I have never understood, though, why cold filthy water is so desirable, but putting right the damage using warm clean water sparks apparent intense suffering in the dog.

BENEFITS

Although the walking is for your dog's benefit, in truth, you stand to benefit just as much, not only from the fresh air and exercise, but from an improved relationship with your dog. Be observant and watch your dog while exercising: when you know how she looks when she is on top of the world, you will quickly be able to spot when she is below par, and so do something about it before she becomes ill. Regular suitable exercise will strengthen your dog's immune system because she will be fit, and the increased circulation will benefit her skin and coat, not to mention her general health. She will also be happy – and happiness is a powerful force in the maintenance of good health.

6 The Older Dog

Health for golden oldies

Dogs live a lot longer nowadays than they did when I was a child. Strangely enough, one thing has not changed in that a dog over eight years old is, in veterinary terms, geriatric. Dogs living longer are old dogs for longer, sometimes for a third of their total span, and need a little extra care as befits such special friends. How long a life you can expect your dog to have, barring accident or disease, depends chiefly on her breed and size. As a generalisation, small dogs live the longest – sometimes well into their teens – then medium dogs, then large breeds, with giant breeds having the shortest life expectation. There are, of course, exceptions: crossbreeds and mongrels usually live longer in health than pedigree dogs, and some larger breeds that still work, such as greyhounds and salukis, generally expect a longer lifespan than most others of similar size. However, your dog will still be an old dog at eight years of age, and although she will probably have plenty of years left, you will need to treat her a little differently, much as she needed a different sort of looking-after when she was very young.

Smaller dogs generally live longer

FIRST SIGNS

When you live with a dog and see her all the time, it is easy to miss those first signs of ageing. Then one day you will look at her with new eyes, or maybe someone who hasn't seen her for a while will comment that she is going grey around the muzzle, or that she has quietened down from the way she used to be. Like people, individual dogs will age at different rates, and while some will slip serenely through their years, others will endure marked, sometimes sudden, changes in their health. Greying hair is often the first sign, creeping up the legs and face, more obvious in some types of coat than others. Your dog will lose the proud topline along her back, and as age progresses, will develop a distinct 'sag' in her outline. Her gait will alter: she may begin to pace, that is, move both legs on the same side with each stride, instead of diagonal opposites, and she may seem to 'pump' herself along with quick nodding movements of her head and neck. The angle that her feet strike the ground may alter as her wrists sag and her toes spread, one consequence of which will be that you will have to keep a close eye on her nails, which will not be wearing down evenly, or maybe at all. Her hearing may dull, and she will sleep longer and more deeply. Her eyes may cloud, seeing less and less, and her close and distance vision will alter just as ours does when we age. An observant owner will see the first signs of ageing and then be able to look deeper into the dog's everyday life, to make it more comfortable for her.

ACHES AND PAINS

Dogs are mostly great stoics about pain, because in the world of the pack, the weak members are either driven out or killed. It is not therefore safe to show infirmity. Your older dog may be in quite considerable pain from joints wearing out before you notice that anything has changed. Therefore watch your dog as she walks and runs, and see if her gait has altered. Is she taking shorter steps? Does she seem stiff upon getting up, does she lie down when you meet someone and stop to exchange the time of day? Does she seem to stand awkwardly, or have difficulty getting onto the furniture (if she is allowed) or up the stairs? Does she still jump eagerly in and out of the car, or is she now hesitating as if the spring into or the leap out is going to hurt? Does she sit on one side rather than firmly balanced on both haunches? Is she getting grumpy from pain? Does she have tremors, especially in her hindlegs? Perhaps she is worse for humid weather, or cold and wet, or all of them. All of this is a natural process of ageing – we go through it as well – and there is a variety of treatment available to help your old dog become more comfortable, without resorting to drugs. There may come a time when drugs are the only option left, and then it is still possible to use holistic methods in addition, to protect the body against the inevitable side-effects.

EXERCISE

Your older dog will still enjoy her walks, and what is more, the interest and exercise that these bring her will go a long way to maintaining her health, both mental and physical. However, she will not want to step out as briskly as she did in her youth, but rather potter and sniff and dawdle. Though her sight and hearing will not be so sharp, sense of smell seems not to diminish in the same way, and smells will be even more important to her than before. It is up to you to be patient and let her enjoy her walks in her own way. If you have younger dogs to exercise as well, you might prefer to take the old dog out on her own, so that she is not holding everybody up, or else take everyone out on a short walk so that she can enjoy being part of a pack, and then take the youngsters out for a faster hike afterwards. Although accompanying you on long walks, jogging, or cycle rides was once her joy, please be aware that she cannot do this easily any more. I have seen some pitiful sights of old dogs doing their level best to keep up with their beloved owners, though age, pain and infirmity have only too obviously claimed them. People can be so blind to this as well – I once gently remonstrated with someone who would take his ageing Labrador jogging every day, though her hips were ruined and she was clearly – to me – in great distress when she followed him as best she could. 'Oh, she loves going for a run' was the reply. Well, yes, once she did love going for a run, but how much more she would enjoy going for a walk now.

I know another person who takes his blind, deaf, arthritic spaniel on long walks and nags at her constantly to keep up (why? She can't hear him). She would far rather have a shorter walk more often, and plenty of time to investigate interesting smells. It is hard for us to acknowledge that our canine friend is getting into old age, especially when it seems that only yesterday she was a puppy, but we must. As your dog ages, she will elect to stay home from time to time, such as during cold, wet or windy weather, and so meet her halfway on this – as long as she has been out and emptied herself properly, forgo her usual walk until the weather is kinder. Dogs do not often age in a steady decline: she will be quite skittish and lively some days, and on others, she will look depressingly old. But exercise is important throughout a dog's life, and it is up to us to ensure that not only does she get it, but that she gets the right exercise for her needs and not our convenience.

FEEDING

The older dog will not be able to get as much nutrition out of her food as a young one, and her digestion may slow down quite noticeably. Because she is taking less exercise, her appetite should correspondingly diminish: if it does not, you will have to watch her weight. This is seldom an issue on the raw food diet, but if you feed processed food, you will be thinking about changing to one of the 'senior' mixes. Some old dogs get scrawny, some tend to put on weight, but there is no excuse for having a fat dog, and indeed, too much weight will stress her system and shorten her life. Older dogs do very well on the raw food diet, with little adjustment, but you may have to reduce her rations quite considerably if she is on commercial food. If that is the case, I would recommend feeding her twice or even three times daily, to give appeal to her day and not too long to be hungry between meals. An important consideration is that older dogs' digestions are often less efficient at absorbing vitamins and minerals from their food, and they consequently do not get enough of either. A good multivitamin and a trace mineral supplement can help them enormously, especially considering the demineralisation of commercial soils nowadays, with a consequent reduction of trace minerals in crops estimated by some agencies to be in the region of thirty per cent.

Older dogs have generally trained their owners to give them lots of treats and titbits as extras – I met a lady only this morning who, after telling me that her (rather rotund) spaniel would not eat her meal every day, added that she always had five biscuits of a particular brand when she came home from her walks. Now, these are treated. Your vet is the person who should be consulted as soon as you notice any growth, and then you know exactly what you are dealing with. A few lumps need removing straight away, but most, even the dubious ones, don't need any hasty action, just to have an eye kept on them and a regular check-up by a professional. Dogs don't notice how they look, so if a lump is better left alone but you find it unsightly, console yourself that you will soon get used to it as just a little more of your dog to love.

Lumps can also form internally. The older a dog – or person – gets, the more likely they are to have some form of cancer. These cancers do not always cause death: some are slow-growing and do not show any symptoms, while a few are aggressive and come from nowhere to take hold and seriously affect quality of life. Your vet will be able to test for these, and advise you on your options. What is important is to note any changes in your dog's wellbeing, particularly constipation, diarrhoea, blood in urine or faeces, difficulty in passing either, any sort of persistent discharge or odd smell – in other words, anything that would alert you to something being wrong if it occurred in your own body. Some breeds are prone to particular cancers, so if yours is one of these, you will need to be extra observant.

STATUS CHANGES

Very often, the first indication that you will have in the deterioration of health in your dog is from observing other dogs' reactions to her. If you have several dogs, you might notice that one is losing status within your home pack – this dog is ill. Similarly, other dogs that you meet out walking might mount, dominate or even attack yours seemingly for no reason. Dogs' senses are exquisitely fine, and they can tell when another dog is weak. Pack law then says that dog must be driven out or killed. Individual dogs may care for other individuals and help them when they are ill, but for the most part, the canine instinct is to kill the weak. This applies to most social groups of animals. There are many tales of dogs that have lived together for years turning on one of their number and killing it. The owner comes home to a bloodbath and a dead dog, or worse, no dead dog because the others have eaten it. Because we regard dogs as our dear friends, and it is tempting to see them as slightly altered humans, this is horrifying. But they are not slightly altered humans: they are slightly altered wolves, and their instincts, needs and drives are virtually unchanged from the wild state. We must not condemn them for this, but instead respect them for their otherness. If those distraught owners had only seen what was going on in front of them for probably quite some time, the situation could have been prevented by a shut door and a change or two in sleeping and feeding arrangements. Observation is the key: watch your dog or dogs at all times, and question any changes in behaviour. They occur for good reason. I have several times been put in appalling situations by people who did or would not take heed of warning signals between dogs, in one case being left to house-sit with one dog that was dying of undiagnosed cancer (the owner having refused to take him to the vet when he seemed unwell) and another, visiting dog that was intent on killing the old boy. The warning bells were loud enough: the young dog took to marking the old dog's territory, and I dared not leave them alone together for a minute, the problem being exacerbated by the fact that not one door in the house closed properly, and there was no way that the dogs could be shut away from one another. It was a nightmare week. With my own old girl, I have to be

MA
Som
vigila
as he
some
in re
best l
it a t
which
and a
hidin

SEI
Old d
have
for a
case i
the da
huma
world
she is
days a
standl
wall. I
any re
long a
obsta
extrao
touchi
speak
vibrati
place a
talk so
perhap
waking
sunny
and pr
the law
dogs ca
room,
express
us, the
recolle

ANC
As you

careful that she is not attacked by strange dogs while out on walks – it has happened several times – as the others no longer defend her. They have not yet joined in an attack, but pack law is pack law, and it could happen. When she has to be left in the house, she is kept apart from our status-seeking terrier; the others, being lurchers, are not into dog politics, and have no axe to grind with the old lady, who, frail though she be, is still 'top dog'. However, leaders only lead by the agreement of those who are led, and I watch the pack dynamics closely at all times.

SLEEPING

The older dog will sleep more and more of her day away, and deserves comfort in which to do it. Though her bed should be raised off the floor to eliminate chills and draughts, it should still be easy for her to get in and out of it. She will have grown out of the chewing and destructiveness of her youth, and so can be indulged with a duvet, perhaps, or a fleece blanket. Her skin will be thinner, and less well padded over the bones, and so a good soft bed will prevent pressure sores, which otherwise occur readily at elbows and hocks. Old dog bedding should be easy to wash, and of a sort that your dog can snuggle into, for old bones do feel the cold more. You might consider putting a coat on her at night, if you have no heating or it is switched off overnight, but it is better for her to have plenty of bedding rather than a coat, as she can come up for air when she is too hot. Kennelled dogs, surrounded by fresh air, appreciate a coat on cold nights. If your dog sleeps on the bed with you, she can use you as a hot-water-bottle whenever she needs extra warmth.

INCONTINENCE

Which brings me to the unspoken condition. Old age often – but not always – brings incontinence. Some people choose to have their dog put down at this point, and others work with the condition for as long as they can. If your dog has been allowed on the bed and furniture all her life, incontinence can be a major, heartbreaking problem; if she lives in a kennel, you will hardly notice. However, in its early stages, incontinence can be helped holistically, notably with both homoeopathy and acupuncture. You may well not see results at once, but then incontinence is a sneaky condition which creeps up over a long time, and sometimes takes a correspondingly long time to respond to treatment. Sometimes these methods will work for quite a time, but eventually fail, in which case there are several drugs available which can help. Consult your vet for advice, and if the initial treatment does not suit your dog, ask to try another way. Often, drug treatment can be supported with homoeopathy to reduce unpleasant side effects. Meanwhile, you can help by giving the dog plenty of opportunity to empty herself, remembering that a walk of a few hundred yards can have a miraculous effect, whereas standing around in the garden often achieves nothing at all. Sudden, dramatic incontinence, however, tends to indicate an infection, and responds equally dramatically to antibiotics or an appropriate homoeopathic remedy, eg Cantharis, so don't write your dog off just because she has had a series of 'accidents'. Dogs that have been clean all their lives get really woebegone at losing control of their bladder and/or bowels; try to be patient with them, and remember that it might be your turn one day – let's hope in that case you have a good vet to call upon.

of
so
wl
so
w(
ol
w(
op
th
wi
th
dc
dc
ar
sn
or
so
th
be

ha
an
w(
wr
qu
fol
fe\
tal
an
yo
be
sc(

S]
Bi
ler
ol(
bir
su[
hi[
de
big
Th
an
Cl

Some older dogs enjoy a new puppy

another. Some people will tell you that the arrival of a new puppy will rejuvenate your oldie, and give her a new lease of life. Or perhaps you might be of the mind that a second dog will soften the pain of loss when the time comes. Are these suggestions right? The answer, as ever, is 'it depends'.

Some older dogs, especially of the more playful breeds, will indeed benefit from the arrival of a puppy, but many, it has to be said, will not. Puppies have needle-sharp teeth and use them on elderly ears, puppies want to play when oldies want to sleep, puppies claim attention that was hitherto the sole property of the old dog, they make a noise and mess, and get fed more often. Visitors will arrive and coo over the puppy, while ignoring the quiet, greying old girl in the corner. Did they but know it, the elderly dog would so much have liked a greeting, too. The vitality and appeal of the new puppy can quite eclipse the older dog, and make her last months miserable instead of happy. Should you then get a grown dog instead? This would be even worse, for at least the oldie can exercise some sort of seniority over an immature pup, but a young dog in the full flower of her youth and strength will simply follow pack law and either ostracise or attack the elderly one.

If you are determined to get a second dog while your old one is still alive, then you will need to give some thought to keeping them apart enough to give each one personal space, and you should have sufficient time to commit to giving each the exercise requirements suited to her age, not to forget training the puppy. If you have a friend who gets a puppy, take your old dog to meet it and see how they interact. She might be quite delighted with the little one, or she might rumble a warning and move away. Even if she seems pleased with it, a puppy at home permanently is a whole different ball game from a puppy met on neutral territory. The old dog should have her own space which the pup cannot invade, and when puppy is fed, oldie should have a mouthful of food in her own bowl too. Visitors who come to see the puppy should be briefed to make contact with the old dog first. Signs of jealousy or insecurity, such as the old dog cramming herself in the puppy's bed, or scent-marking inside the house if the puppy has an 'accident' should be dealt with sympathetically. Jealousy is a horrible emotion: humans cannot deal with it, so don't expect miracles from a geriatric dog. Bach Rescue Remedy given to the older dog can be helpful, but if the situation escalates, there are specific Remedies which can assist, such as Walnut for coping with change, Agrimony for restoring inner peace, Holly for jealousy or Willow for resentment.

Will the second dog help you through losing the first? Again, a definitive answer cannot be given. If the arrival of the second dog upset your first dog, bereavement may give you another stick of guilt with which to belay yourself. If the second dog adored the first, then her grieving will magnify your own. However, another dog will mean that you have to get on with your life, will have to walk her and feed her and generally bother about something when you don't feel like it, and that is therapy in itself.

Old dogs sleep very deeply

take the help on offer, and don't feel bad either about grieving for your dog or for getting another when the time is right. These are all things that must be done.

SENSITIVITY

Some people are very much more sensitive than others, and will feel the spiritual presence of their departed pet. If this happens to you, do not fear it, but take it as a very great compliment. Dogs will often seem to sense presences as well. This is normal, and happens much more often than most people realise. You may be a down-to-earth sort of person, in which case it can come as a bit of a shock; alternatively you may be sensitive normally but not perceive your pet's spiritual visit, which can also be disquieting. Don't be startled if it does happen, nor feel rejected if it does not; you have had your time together, and it was infinitely precious.

STUD FEE

This should be discussed and arranged at the time you book the stud and advise when the bitch is due on heat. Owners of busy stud dogs appreciate as much advance warning as possible, to avoid their dog being over-used, so let them know as soon as the bitch comes on heat. The usual stud fee is either second pick of the litter after the bitch owner has chosen, or the price of one puppy. Money is usually required in full before the mating takes place – you can return the fee but you can't unmate the bitch. Occasionally people agree half the fee on completion of service and half when the pups are born, a free return if the bitch does not conceive, or a reduced rate for a male dog's first mating, but these terms are unusual. Mostly it is money up front and no variations.

The stud dog owner has no responsibility for the puppies or homing thereof, although some will send suitable people your way.

THE MATING

It is usual for the bitch to be brought to the dog. Professional breeders prefer the bitch to be left, but it is up to you if you want to do this. Personally, I prefer to be present, and then you know that the right dog has covered the bitch, which may not be the case if the chosen stud is reluctant. However, you should be aware that many bitches scream when mated, sometimes for several minutes. Also, some may snap, usually at

Soft cloth muzzle

the moment of penetration, at the onset of the tie, or when the dog dismounts. To avoid injury to stud or handler, it is quite common to muzzle the bitch, either with a bandage tied around her mouth or a soft cloth muzzle. Though it may fill you with horror to see your beloved pet restrained in this way, it has to happen: these are dog matters, and humans are only on hand to prevent injury. Do not, for goodness' sake, just leave the dogs in a shed to get on with it. The result could, at best, be a dog which refuses to mate for ever after, but sometimes instead is a dog ruptured from the bitch struggling during the tie, or one or both parties bitten. Sod's Law decrees that the accidental mating that takes place on a street corner, or from a stray that jumps into your garden, will likely go without a hitch and result in a pregnancy, but a planned union between carefully chosen dog and bitch has endless scope for disaster, and responsible owners do their best to prevent problems.

Professional breeders know what they are about, and should be left to get on with it, unless they ask for your assistance. If, however, this is a union between two pet dogs where the owners are on a steep learning curve and possibly the dogs as well, it does help if at least one of you knows what to expect, and I strongly recommend talking to a breeder or a vet who knows the practical aspects and is good at explaining them.

Sometimes the stud is brought to the bitch, and this is what I normally do with mine. However, it is best to be prepared for at least one re-visit, as some dogs will not cover the first time in a strange place. If yours is the male dog, never leave him behind to collect after the event, or a few days later. You have no control over what can happen; while most people are respectable, some are not, and he could be used on other bitches or even sold in your absence.

MECHANICS

The dog and bitch, when introduced, will sniff each other, and engage in lengthy foreplay, running about, putting forelegs over each other's backs and licking each other's genitals. This should all be allowed, as it helps the right sort of hormones to flow. The bitch should be flagging her tail and thrusting her rear end at the dog, who will be nibbling at her hocks and testing her acceptance of weight on her back with his chin or his front legs. When she stands and he is ready to mount is when the bitch should be muzzled if you are going to, and if there is a height discrepancy, the bitch should be taken to the prepared area where either one stands in a dip or the other on a raised platform. Obviously, the latter should be absolutely secure, as it is easy to put off a dog if not. The bitch must be held, and her owner is the best person to do this. Male dogs can easily back off from mating if interfered with too much, so the bitch should be held steady and the dog left to mount. Inexperienced dogs will sometimes try to get on the front or the side; it is better to swing the bitch round than to manhandle the dog. Likewise, if the target area is small, it is better to move the bitch's vulva into position than the dog's penis.

The dog will not be fully erect when he mounts, but as soon as he penetrates, he is. The first part of the ejaculate, which contains the bulk of the sperm, is passed during the thrusting of this first phase of mating. Then you get the 'tie', which is when the bulb at the root of the dog's penis swells inside the bitch, and she clamps her muscles around it. Immediately, the dog will turn until he is rump to rump with the bitch. This looks excruciatingly painful, but usually during this phase both become calm. The tie can last from a few minutes to an hour or more, but is normally about half an hour. During this stage, the dog continues to pump ejaculate into the bitch, which washes the fertile part deep into her. The dogs' quarters should be held steady at this stage so that the bitch does not struggle and injure the dog. The bitch controls the length of the tie because the dog cannot disengage until she relaxes and lets him. Presently she will allow this, and they part. The fluid that runs from the bitch's vulva at this time is not a cause for concern, and she should be allowed to clean herself up. There are startling old kennelman's tales of bitches being held upside down to stop the fluid leaking out, or even, heaven help us, a handful of nettles being applied to the bitch's vulva; none of this is needed as the important part of the dog's contribution has long gone on its way.

If there is no 'tie' there is still a fair chance that the bitch will conceive, particularly if it is an accidental union and you did not want her to, but it is not considered a successful mating. Best to try again the following day until you get a good 'tie'. Most stud owners will allow two matings on consecutive days if the bitch is prepared to stand.

Sometimes dog and bitch like to engage in 'afterplay' particularly if they know each other well, but mostly, the bitch goes off to be mysterious and female, and the dog forgets all about her. Put the bitch somewhere secure and go and have a well-earned cup of tea!

EARLY PREGNANCY

The usual pregnancy lasts sixty-three days, and though some bitches will give birth either side of this, most are very exact. The fertilised ova do not implant at once. The bitch will still be attractive and receptive to other male dogs, and great care should be taken that she does not mate with one or more of these hopefuls. In wolf packs, the female will mate with every male wolf she can during her oestrus, and the behaviour has passed down to the domestic dog – though at least her season is only half the length of the she-wolf's. The idea of this is to create as wide a gene pool as possible. Your bitch can mate with several dogs during her season, and have a mixed litter of puppies with some sired by each, which is not what you had in mind. When the ova do implant, they do this in the long uterine horns to either side. The pups will be carried high along the bitch's sides until the final stages of her pregnancy, which means that she would be able to look after herself better in the wild. Yours does not have to catch her own food, and does not need any change in her routine just yet, unless she is a working dog, in which case she should be exercised normally rather than worked. Do not feed any more than usual, for she will not need any extra rations until much further on in her pregnancy, and if she gets too fat now, it is added stress on her joints, and she may even have birthing difficulties. Overfeeding the bitch sometimes results in large puppies, which can lead to problems too. Better to let the pups put weight on after they are born.

At the start of the pregnancy, the extra hormones will cause physical and emotional changes: her nipples will stand proud, her coat may develop an extra shine and softness, and some bitches vomit a lot during the first week or so. She may become very quiet and private, wanting to be alone more, or else perhaps she will be extra clingy. Her pregnancy is unlikely to show until she is into the fifth or sixth week Some people like to have the bitch scanned, but there is not a lot of point to this unless there is a history of previous problems. Scanning will not make her pregnant if she is not, nor will it make her any more pregnant than she is. While the majority of pregnancies go through without a hitch, some foeti may be aborted or reabsorbed, so a bitch scanned with a certain number of puppies early on may give birth to fewer. Sometimes a puppy dies in utero and is mummified within the body until the bitch starts labour. All this is quite normal. Species that have multiple births can afford to lose a few. All you have to do is be patient, and soon you will know whether or not your bitch is pregnant.

LATER PREGNANCY

You can start to increase her food around the sixth week, feeding twice daily instead of once initially, though you will be up to four smaller meals a day by the time she gives birth. Aim for two-and-a-half times her normal rations daily, if she will take it. As the puppies take up more space, so she will not be able to eat so much in one meal, and she will need to empty herself more often. See that she has ample opportunity to do this: remember she is also processing waste matter from the pups, and it is not good for her to have to wait to empty herself. Her bowels might be a little looser than normal during this time, which should not be a cause for concern. She will start to alter in shape, and will find lying down more uncomfortable as she spreads. Many bitches solve this by spending more time upside down. You can feel the

Eight weeks pregnant

Two days before giving birth

unborn puppies under the skin between her hindlegs when she does this, and they can be very lively on occasion. It is very moving to lay your hands gently on her tummy and feel the little ones squirming against them. As she becomes heavier, she will want less exercise. She should still be taken out, though, because the mental stimulus is good for her, but she would prefer shorter walks now.

WORMS
Standard veterinary recommendation is to worm the bitch through the latter part of her pregnancy. However, there may be a slight risk to the unborn litter, and many vets opt for worming the bitch prior to the onset of the season and then after the pups have been weaned. The roundworm cycle is such that encysted roundworms in the bitch are activated by the pregnancy, and travel down the umbilical cord to infest the puppies. Some of these will encyst in their turn, and in male pups and non-breeding females they stay dormant. If a bitch becomes pregnant, however, the whole cycle starts afresh. No matter how well you have wormed your bitch in the past, the pups will have worms because of this.

OTHER DOGS
If there are other dogs within the family, you will need to be vigilant for any changes in status, or disruptive behaviour. The alpha bitch is the one that should be breeding:

153

if this is the case in your own little group, all should be tranquil. But if a lower-status bitch is pregnant, it is advisable for her to have a place where she can be on her own if she is being harassed. Be especially careful not to leave the pregnant bitch in a confined space, such as the car, with others, if you expect friction. Similarly with dogs that you meet on walks: most will defer to a pregnant bitch, but occasionally one may show aggression. Take no risks, and make a mental note of troublemakers so that you can steer clear of them.

THE WHELPING AREA
Now is the time to get the whelping area ready, so that your bitch will be fully accustomed to it before she gives birth. The ideal is a room with an easy-clean floor, an openable window high up, electricity and water. There is nothing wrong with a similarly-equipped shed or kennel, though you may prefer to have the puppies in the house for the first three weeks, to keep a better eye on them. There should be easy access for the bitch, who will need to be able to get away from her puppies when she wants to. Her water bowl should be inside a box so that tiny pups cannot fall in it and drown, and there should be no projections, cables, pipes or holes within puppy reach, and no painted areas to chew. A baby-gate is safer than a door that swings open, as puppies have a knack of getting trapped behind doors, but the bars of the gate should be blocked off with hardboard or similar so that bits of puppy cannot get caught between them. This room is for your bitch alone: other dogs should not have access to it, and nor should people except for family. Feed your bitch in there, and if you can, get her to sleep there as well. If she customarily sleeps with you and is not inclined to give up, put her in the puppy room with a bone or some treats when she comes back from her walks. She needs to feel completely at home there.

THE WHELPING BOX
You can buy disposable whelping boxes for one use only, or you can make one up to use again when need be. The whelping box should be long enough for your bitch to lie at full stretch and still have plenty of space, should not be coated with any toxic substance, have sides of sufficient height that puppies cannot climb over them but the bitch can, and have a sliding or removable access door. It should be raised slightly above floor level, but not so much that a tiny puppy could cram itself underneath. Bitch rails are a useful extra to stop the bitch from lying on her puppies – some bitches are very clumsy about this and others never do. Bitch rails go all around the inside of the whelping box at newborn puppy height above the floor, and a similar width from the sides of the box. Other breeders of your type of dog, or your vet, will be able to help you with the dimensions and also let you know roughly what size litters that your breed tends to have.

BEDDING
Bedding for a whelping box needs to be plentiful, safe, and easily changed. Straw and hay are not suitable, as both harbour parasites, are messy to deal with, and have sharp bits that are not good for new puppies. Shavings are messy too, but more importantly, can block tiny mouths and noses, sometimes with tragic results. Sheets and blankets that can be washed are good, but you will need to be careful about newborns getting

Vet-bed

trapped in the cloth folds. By far the best that I know is the fleece bedding called Vet-Bed, which is thick, warm, safe, and washes and dries easily. Under this, I place a very thick lining of newspaper. You will be going through a lot of newspaper, and I suggest you start saving it as soon as you have the bitch mated. You don't want the fleece bedding to cover the whole of the whelping box, as puppies will endeavour to be clean and crawl off their bedding to empty themselves on the newspaper. I have seen tiny whelps do this that don't even have their eyes open.

Don't put the fleece bedding down until the pups are born, for birth is a messy business, and you would be better advised to have a thick layer of newspaper topped by old towels and sheets that are expendable. If you want your bitch to sleep in her whelping area, her own bedding will make it more welcoming for her, but this will need to be removed once she goes into labour if you don't want it ruined.

Now the whelping area is ready, the bitch is ready, and the nervous owner must wait for her to go into labour. Let us hope that she accepts her whelping place and does not insist on having her puppies elsewhere. She may try to dig an earth in the garden, or show every intention of producing on your bed. She might even want to have her puppies on your lap – or else she will want to go feral and have them somewhere dark and secret. The last few days of the pregnancy can be a battle of wills between domestic convenience and primitive instinct. Try to be flexible – as long as where she has them is safe and reasonably clean, everything else can be worked around. Contented bitches have easier confinements.

LABOUR

Very often, the first signs of labour are the bitch trying to rearrange her accommodation, digging with frantic strength, tearing at the floor and the newspaper. This does not always happen, but is a useful marker when it does. This can start a day or two before labour, but most usually the first stage of labour will follow in a matter of hours. Don't let her have the run of the house once she starts nesting, or you may find the sofa torn apart! Gently return her to her whelping area, and stay with her if you possibly can. This is a time of strong, primitive needs, and you are best to be tactful with her.

There is usually a marked temperature drop at this time. Some bitches refuse food just before they go into labour, or vomit during the preliminary stages. This is all quite normal. Once she has organised her bed and emptied her body of surplus waste, she will go into recognisable labour. She will pant, arch her back, and demonstrate clear contractions which ripple the length of her body. Eventually, she will push out a bag of jelly, which will moisten her birth canal ready for the pups.

These will arrive one at a time, often with quite long gaps between. The first pup is often the biggest, and sometimes causes problems, but most normal-shaped dogs will pop out puppies with very little fuss. The pup comes wrapped in its own membranous bag, and with its own individual placenta. The bitch will bite through the bag and the umbilical cord, and devour it – often with such speed that she looks as if she is going to eat the whole puppy! She eats the birth tissue partly as an instinctive procedure to keep the 'lair' clean and free from smells that might attract predators. Nature in her infinite economy also ensures that nutrients important to the bitch are contained in the birth debris, and also that it has a laxative effect. Some people try to stop the bitch eating all the wrapping because of this, but think a moment – this is being done for the owner's convenience and not the bitch's welfare. Even a normal labour involves a fair bit of bruising, and a softening effect on bowel contents is a great help to the bitch just after she has given birth.

There is normally no need for the owner to interfere while the bitch is giving birth. Sometimes a bitch will be a bit slow to unwrap the puppy, in which case the bag can be carefully broken open with fingers,and the puppy's head exposed, after which instinct will generally take over and the bitch will eat the bag and lick the puppy dry. This is the origin of the phrase 'licking into shape'. The tiny whelp will then be nudged towards the milk bar, where it should start to suckle. The suckling action helps the bitch's contractions, and in half an hour to an hour, another puppy will be on its way.

Some bitches prefer to give birth on their own, and every time you peep into the puppy room, there will be another puppy. Some will appreciate the moral support of the owner. One of my bitches wanted to give birth on my lap, and as she weighed sixty pounds when not pregnant, we compromised, with me sitting on a blanket on the floor and her draped across my legs. Don't stress the bitch while she is in labour by weighing or measuring the pups, or trying to see what sex they are. They will still be the same sex later, when the bitch has relaxed and is happier for you to touch them. Please don't invite other people over to see the birth, for this might so stress your bitch that she will hold back on her labour, or even try to eat the puppies. She only needs people she knows and trusts at this time, and as few of those as possible.

After a few puppies, there will be a natural lull in the proceedings while the rest work their way along the conveyor, and this is a good time to see if your bitch would like to go out and empty herself. Go with her, and make sure she does not fire out another puppy while she is there! Offer a warm drink afterwards – water with a tiny dash of milk or tea is often appreciated – and don't be appalled if she drinks it eagerly and then vomits it back a short while later. Mostly it stays down, but there are always exceptions. When everything seems to have reached a natural conclusion, give her the option of emptying herself again, and then leave her snuggled down with her babies while you pour yourself something restorative.

COMPLICATIONS

It is sensible to have warned your vet well in advance of the due date, just in case you have complications, especially if your bitch is of a breed with a proportionately larger head than back end. Otherwise, experienced breeders can deal with most birthing problems, but if you don't have one of these to hand, you will need the support of your vet. Before the puppies are due, read some of the many excellent books that are available on dog breeding. They will differ in small details, but should give you greater confidence in handling the labour. Mostly, bitches cope without incident, but sometimes they need help. Here are a few of the most usual things that can happen.

Uterine Inertia

Sometimes the bitch shows all the early labour patterns, but the contractions either don't happen, or start and then stop. Vets would rather be called too early than too late, so if she has carried full-term, her temperature has dropped, she has nested and panted and then just given up, warn the surgery and bring her in. Sometimes the motion of the car is enough to start matters off again – a lot of people have arrived at the vet's with more dogs than they had when they left! If not, there are several ways to help, from homoeopathic Caulophyllum given orally at ten-minute intervals, to an injection of the hormone oxytocin. If your bitch is of a breed or type that normally does not require a caesarian, then this is usually quite enough. The right sort of veterinary practice will let you stay with your bitch, who will be much more relaxed with you present, and should start up her contractions again having had a little help.

Caesarian

Obviously, this should be avoided if at all possible, but sometimes has to be done. Some breeds almost always have to give birth by caesarian, which is a sad comment on what breeding for show has done to the natural dog. The operation itself is usually straightforward, though some bitches reject the puppies after surgery, in which case do some homework about hand-rearing well in advance. She will in any case be very uncomfortable afterwards, and suckling may be too much for her. Ideally, a bitch that has had to have a caesarian should not be bred from again.

Foul Discharge

If, instead of the lubricating bag of fluid and jelly that precedes the puppies, your bitch produces a green, black and/or foul-smelling discharge, she needs veterinary attention at once.

Breech Presentation

Depending on the shape of the adult dog, breech presentation (rear end first) can be no problem at all, or can require human intervention. Bullet-shaped dogs such as sighthounds can push out puppies that present themselves conventionally (head between forepaws) or most other ways, without complications, but less aerodynamic puppies can get stuck. Extracting them is really a matter for experienced assistance, but if you have to cope yourself with a puppy half out, ease it downwards between the bitch's legs as gently as you can, without twisting, and in time with the bitch's contractions. Don't pull the puppy backwards, as the bitch's vagina opens downwards and the puppy should be brought down to follow the natural angle.

Retained Puppy

It is wise to have the bitch examined by your vet a day or two after she has given birth, to make sure that neither a dead puppy nor any placenta is retained inside her. Of course she is not going anywhere without her puppies, nor do you want her in a veterinary waiting room with infections flying about. Most vets will arrange for you to bring the bitch directly from the car to the surgery, and the puppies can wait in a big cardboard box. Most vets will like to check the whelps, too, and make sure that they have no deformities such as club foot or cleft palate You can have a home visit, but of course if anything has to be done, you need to be at the surgery in any case. It is best to have all this discussed before the bitch goes into labour.

Sometimes you are sure that all is well, and then the bitch confounds you by producing a dead puppy or other debris several days after the others. This requires veterinary attention as soon as possible, because you do not want her to develop an infection.

AFTERCARE

Homoeopathic Arnica 30c will go a long way towards helping your bitch get over the excesses of labour, and it helps the puppies too, who access it through her milk. For the first twenty-four hours after giving birth, your bitch will not want to leave her puppies even to empty herself, but she must be persuaded to do this. Feed her to appetite now and until the puppies are weaned – you will be astonished at how much food she will need while suckling. A good guide is the normal pre-pregnancy diet (N) times bitch plus pups divided by 2: $\frac{N \times (bitch+pups)}{2}$ divided into four feeds per day.

However, if she seems to want more food, I'd be inclined to feed ad-lib, unless she is a naturally greedy dog.

WEEK ONE

For the first few days, she will be reluctant to leave her whelps, and will spend her time suckling and cleaning them. They cannot eliminate waste without stimulus from her tongue, and she will then eat the waste, which is normal and natural. Just don't let her lick your face. All that you have to do during this spell is feed and water her, make sure that she goes out and empties herself, and keep an eye open for anyone being off-colour. Normal whelps squeak and mumble comfortably, but a little one that has a problem will produce an astonishingly loud yell. Watch out for puppies being trapped in folds of bedding, or that have crawled to the edge of the box and are getting cold. Puppies are great time-wasters, though in truth, time spent watching them is useful. Once you have a picture of how they look when normal, you will quickly pick up any signs of them being off-colour. New puppies that become ill, often through infection, need veterinary attention pretty quickly, because they don't have much in the way of inner resource to heal themselves. They can go from bright and lively to very poorly in a matter of hours. This does not often happen, but needs a fast response if it does. Puppies that become lethargic, look dull-coated or 'flat' instead of round, or that whinge querulously for no reason that you can see, need help. Puppies that don't suckle vigorously, pumping their tiny forepaws against the breast, or who get knocked off the teat by more lively whelps and don't strive to reconnect, are weak and would benefit from assistance. First have your vet check them, and if the only problem is that they are not as strong as the others, sometimes monitoring the milk bar and helping them onto a teat to suck until they are full, will be enough. Be sure that Mum cleans them up afterwards, and stimulates them to empty themselves by licking their ends. If she won't, then you will have to use the corner of a soft damp cloth to mimic the stroking of her tongue. Your vet will show you how. In extreme cases, you may have to top-up the pup with milk substitute; if this is so, try to let the pup get some natural milk as well, for it is better than the best alternative, and full of maternal antibodies.

REJECTS

Sometimes, a bitch will reject a particular pup. Bitches can be quite forceful about this, refusing to feed that whelp, picking it up and carrying it away from the nest, or even (as one of mine did) pushing it into your hands. My reaction to this nowadays is to respect her decision: there is usually something wrong with rejected pups, and they either die despite your best efforts, or live and prove later to have something badly wrong with them. I used to try and save them, but it proved a wrong decision. However, many breeders will go to enormous lengths to rear every pup. All I can advise is that if a pup is continually being pushed out by the bitch, have the little one checked for obvious deformities and then take your own decision whether you try to save it or have it put down. If you take the save-it option, don't berate yourself if the little thing quits and dies on you. Animals are pragmatic about this sort of thing, so try not to let your natural human attitude cloud your vision. Celebrate the healthy puppies, and don't get upset about the one that didn't make it. The bitch won't, and neither will the other whelps.

PUPPY-PROUD

Some bitches can get very protective about their litter – it's known as being 'puppy-proud'. She should be respected, and not have to challenge people who want to come and see her pups. Usually, after a couple of weeks she will be much more relaxed about the whole issue, but if she is forced to strike a defensive attitude in the early days, she may kill and even eat her pups to 'protect' them, and she is certainly odds-on to bite a human that she doesn't want near her babies. This does not mean that her temperament is suspect, or that she would bite in any other circumstances. It must be understood that a bitch with puppies has every right to be protective, just like any other mother. It is up to the humans never to put her in a position when she feels threatened. People will understandably want to see the puppies, especially if they have ordered one, but they will have to be patient and wait until this first phase is over. In any case, unless they are your puppies, in which case they are the most marvellous, fascinating puppies ever born, tiny baby whelps are rather boring. They look like guinea-pigs with their snub noses (the flattened face is so that they can suckle) and they mostly just eat and sleep. They have quite well-developed forearms and tiny weak hindlegs, but they can pull themselves along and are surprisingly mobile – which is why there must be nothing in their world that they can crawl behind or under, and get stuck.

THE PUPPY ROOM

Week-olds should be picked up as little as possible, for their bones are soft and their joints are weak. If the bitch is amenable, you, her owner, will be able to stroke the puppies gently, but if she is worried, then leave this introduction for another day. Some bitches, far from being puppy-proud, are happy simply to attend to their pups' basic needs and then resume their position as family dog. That's fine: she does not need to be in there with them all the time, as long as they are being fed and washed. The puppy room should be warm but not stuffy, and a heat-lamp can be used if they have been born during a cold spell. This should be suspended sufficiently high that the bitch cannot touch it, and preferably be of a type that emits heat but not light, for puppy dens are much more comfortable for bitch and pups if in semi-darkness. Though the whelps' eyes and ears are sealed, they can still tell light from dark, and darkness is what they prefer. If you have a summer litter, see that the room is well ventilated, and don't forget that summer nights can get chilly. Suspend some flypapers high up, to dissuade insect life. Air in the puppy room should not be too dry, and you can maintain humidity with a bowl of water near the puppy box, but safely contained so that the pups cannot gain access to it. You will be surprised at how readily this evaporates and needs refreshing. Summer or Winter, a well-wrapped microwaveable hot water bottle, or a stone one if you can find one, is a godsend, and very comforting to the little ones when Mum is out.

BITCH CARE

As well as being rather sore after the birth, and very involved with her whelps, the bitch will be cleansing through her vulva, and the resulting discharge may last for some time. As long as it looks healthy – it can vary in colour from dark red to brown, but must not be black or smell foul – don't worry, but do monitor it for changes. Keeping the fur trimmed around her back end is helpful, and a few drops of Bach Crab Apple in her drinking water every time it is changed will help her with internal cleansing.

MILK

Her milk should come down with or immediately after the birth, and the first milk – the colostrum – is full of antibodies for the pups. It is very important that they get this first milk, but if there has been some mishap and they do not, your vet can supply you with a suitable substitute. Some bitches produce a terrific amount of milk, and you will notice that the most desirable teats for the puppies are the ones at the back, between the hindlegs. The biggest, strongest puppies will gravitate to these, leaving

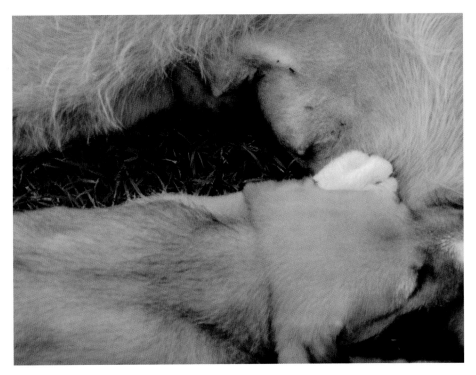

Sore nipples

the others to forage amongst the less well-loaded options nearer the front. If you have a puppy which is a little smaller than the others, but still vigorous, you might like to gently interfere with the pecking order by latching it onto one of the five-star nipples while the big ones are sleeping. Some small puppies are quite able to hold their own, however, and take their turn with the others.

MASTITIS
Inevitably, nipples will get sore and the surrounding tissue scratched with tiny nails. Pups will also suck on the wrong part of the breast, leaving sore red marks. A bitch rearing a large litter can get quite some punishment at the milk bar. Keep a close eye on her to see that she does not develop mastitis, which will cause her pain and make her reluctant to allow her pups to feed. This will show as a hardening and purpling of the breast tissue on the affected area, and will mean that no milk is obtainable from that teat. Caught early, relief can be obtained by applying a warm compress, but once the condition has developed, veterinary intervention is necessary. Should the bitch need to go onto antibiotics, these will be passed to the pups through the milk, and may cause tummy upsets.

ECLAMPSIA
The most dangerous condition to be aware of while the bitch is suckling is eclampsia, also known as 'milk fever'. This is a metabolic disturbance of the mineral balance

within the bitch while she is producing milk. It especially concerns calcium, but is not simply a lack of calcium, rather an inability within the bitch to access it in sufficient quantities, and in proportion with other important minerals. Because of this, it is important to realise that simply feeding extra calcium will not help prevent the condition, and can in fact do more harm than good. Any bitch can develop milk fever, whether she has a large litter or a small one. Symptoms can start with an early disinterest in the pups, and progress to trembling, whining and staggering, and once she displays the typical stiff-legged, tottering gait, you have very little time in which to save her. This is a veterinary emergency, so do not delay. Eclampsia responds quickly to an injection of calcium borogluconate, but the bitch will have to be carefully monitored until the pups have been weaned, in case she shows a relapse. Anecdotal evidence suggests that a diet which includes plenty of raw meaty bones will go a long way to maintaining the correct balance of minerals within the bitch.

METRITIS

This is the last of the 'three Ms' – Mastitis, Milk Fever and Metritis – that you have to watch for with your bitch. It refers to infection within the womb, caused by a dead puppy or retained placenta or bits of either. The bitch will look decidedly off-colour, be feverish, thirsty but not hungry, and very lacklustre, often not even all that interested in her puppies. The vaginal discharge may smell foul, and the bitch might vomit. Diarrhoea is also a symptom, but loose bowels in an otherwise bright and maternal bitch simply means that she is cleansing from eating the afterbirths and then the puppy waste, so it can be something of a red herring. If you suspect metritis, your bitch needs veterinary help; it is usually easily cleared, but she can't deal with it on her own.

HAND-REARING

If you have been left with a litter of puppies to hand-rear, you will be embarking on an endurance test, though one which is immensely rewarding. At first, the pups will need to be fed every two hours, and every time they are fed, their tummies and ends will need to be stroked with a warm damp cloth to stimulate them into emptying themselves. They will then need to be wiped clean of all the milk that they have poured down themselves instead of drinking it, and put back to bed clean and dry. If you have the use of a maternal dog or even a cat that will help with this by licking the whelps dry, let her – occasionally 'him' – assist, for they will do the job better than you. Otherwise, it is something of an exercise in perpetual motion. Your vet will have the right equipment and milk replacement for you, but the caring is all yours. Wrap the mite in a towel to feed, and hold slightly upright so that it does not choke. Do not overfeed. Everything that you use must be kept very clean, and the puppy box itself will have to be kept warmer than normal, because there is no bitch to snuggle up with. Dry heat is not good, though, and you will need to ensure that the air has sufficient humidity. This is easily achieved with a damp towel in the whelping box, and a bowl of water in the room. Prepare to explore the furthest reaches of exhaustion.

By the second week, they will have gone on to four-hourly feeds, and you will at last be able to get some sleep. They can eliminate waste on their own, too, so you will have to work extra hard to keep them clean. Take courage – hand-reared whelps are usually very bright and forward, and likely to wean early. By the end of week three, they will be eating solids, and able to clean food off each other. It is very hard to part with a litter that you have fought so hard to save, though – nobody else ever seems quite good enough to have them.

WEEK TWO

Between ten and fourteen days, the puppies' eyes will start to open. At first, there will be just a glint between the lids, at times a bigger gap than others, or one eye will open at a time, or you will look in on the litter and someone will be there looking back at you. At first, the eyes are milky blue and do not focus well. It is important for the puppy room to be only dimly lit, because the eyes can be damaged by bright light. After all, the pups of wild canids would still be in a dark den at this time. At the same time as the eyes are opening, ears will be as well, and the puppies will be hearing you as well as smelling you. They will have more strength in their hindlegs, and will be travelling about the whelping box quite easily at a smart crawl. If you put your hands in, they will shuffle towards you to be caressed. You will have become used to a hubbub of chatter from the puppy room, and, just as with small children, will be sharply distracted if this hum changes from contented to indignant or frightened. The bitch should be more relaxed about the puppies now, and probably asking to come for walks with you. If she wants to go, take her, for the walk will do her good and refresh her before another bout of motherhood. However, be mindful of bringing infections back to the litter: try to take her to out-of-the-way places that don't see too many dogs, and walk at off-peak times. Be careful about other dogs that you meet, not just from the infection point of view but because some bitches can get very feisty when they have pups at home, especially with male dogs which, in the wild, might be a danger to the litter.

By the end of the second week, the pups' nails may need to be cut, if they have developed sharp ends which are doing damage to the bitch's teats. This job is much easier with two people than one, as the little ones don't half wriggle, and their piercing screams of indignation will bring the bitch running. All you need is a pair of sharp nail scissors and someone to hold the puppy while you clip away. Keep a towel round the nether end of the pup as it will probably wee on you. The nails show clearly where to cut as the tips are very thin and hooked. It doesn't take long to do this, and it will save the bitch from a lot of pain.

WEEK THREE

There is a lot more strength in the legs, and the little ones will be beginning to toddle, albeit with the odd unscheduled flop. Eyes and ears work much better, and the pups will be curious about everything. Now the milk teeth come, but before they do, you will see that the muzzles have changed shape from the very snub noses of the suckling whelp to something that can fit teeth in. Milk teeth are sharp little needles, and the pups will be easing their gums on anything they can find – each other, their dam, your fingers – so see that they have a supply of safe items to chew. If the bitch is not possessive about bones, a huge bone that they cannot break bits off is ideal, but if the bitch gets awkward about bones, don't take the risk of her snapping at a puppy.

Just three weeks old

Carrots, apples and cabbage ends make good chews, but should be replaced when they start to get shabby. It does not matter if bits get broken off and eaten, for the little ones are ready to wean now.

WEANING

This can be as easy or difficult as you like to make it. Some books go through a great process of weaning, with scraped beef and warm milk, but the truth is that you never see an adult dog that isn't weaned, and if you give the pups the chance, they are self-weaning. The natural process is for the bitch to regurgitate her own food for them, and some bitches retain a strong instinct for doing this. The food is presented warm, partly digested, and smelling nicely of mother dog. It is a queasy process for humans to see, and we don't really like it, but if your bitch is one that wants to regurgitate, let her, for this is only going to happen for a couple of weeks at most. However, it is important that she doesn't give all her food to the pups, as she will still be suckling and needing a lot of food to maintain her own condition, so feed her away from the pups and don't let her back in for an hour or more, when her food should be too far down to bring up again (there will always be a bitch that still manages to, though!).

More conventional weaning is to present the pups with a shallow pan of slop four times a day, and let them fill any corners by topping up with bitch milk. This works well. But what is in the slop? Raw mince is ideal, with a little meat gravy (not from a commercial gravy mix, please, as it will be full of salt and chemicals: the juices from cooked meat or a boiled chicken broth will be excellent) and I add a small amount of live plain yoghurt or occasionally a beaten raw egg. Don't add milk, though – the only milk that is good for puppies is in the bitch. They do not need extra milk when being weaned. The pups will crawl through it, plaster themselves in it, in fact do everything except eat it, but don't worry, for in a matter of days they will be eating properly. They will still want a top-up from Mum, though, so time your feeding before she has a chance to suckle them. This way, the bitch will dry off slowly and naturally. She may carry on feeding for weeks – I had one that chose to feed into the twelfth week – or she may quit cold once the needle teeth get too much for her. Let her choose her own schedule, and it will all happen easily.

QUALITY OF FOOD

It is a false economy, though one often practised, to feed puppies on cheap rubbish. I have been horrified at some of the trash people feed puppies on, from the cheapest possible commercial food to the catholic contents of bent tins and old sandwiches thrown out by the local supermarket. Inferior food means inferior pups, and to keep them short of good food at a time of rapid growth, when their adult teeth are forming and their limbs are developing, is close on criminal. If you can't feed them, don't breed them. They never make up the shortcomings of a poor early diet: conversely, giving them the best possible nutritional start in life will result not only in good strong pups, but long-lived and healthy dogs.

Weaning

SOLID FOOD

As soon as the pups have figured out how to cope with their dish of slop, you can start them on more robust fare. Chicken wings are ideal – just watch those miniature wolves shake and growl over a chicken wing – and chunks of breast of lamb, with the soft bones and the fat left on. Still feed the mince, but start to mix pulverised vegetables in as well. You may need to feed the bitch separately, and keep her away while the pups eat, or she may be one of those very maternal ones that do not think about eating until the pups are stuffed full.

Once solids are going in, what comes out is more solid also, and most bitches will be reluctant to clear up after the pups now – which means more work for you. The shortest interval of time known to Man is between a pup emptying itself and dancing in the result. Do try to keep the pups as clean as possible: they will do their bit by struggling as far away from the nest as they can in order to empty themselves. Given the chance, pups are self-housetraining as well.

WORMING

Now the puppies have to be wormed. Ask your vet for a suitable wormer, and get it in liquid form, along with some syringes for giving it. Don't get an over-the-counter wormer from a pet shop because these aren't man enough for the job, as many a new puppy owner has discovered. Worm the bitch as well, because she has been clearing up after the puppies. Buy your wormer in bulk, because you will be worming at two-week intervals until the puppies leave home. Syringe the exact dose into each puppy and prepare for some gruesome results. If you are eating as you read this, please stop now.

Puppy digestions are too weak to kill the worms, and the result is that they will expel knots of live worms. These must be cleared up as soon as they arrive, and burned. No matter how well you have taken care of your bitch and pups, there will be worms, and the reason for such frequent worming is that there will be a new lot maturing even as the current supply is ejected. Worming is quite an assault on the immature puppy system, and it is best to time your worming so that it is a week away from any other treatment, for instance vaccinations or flea treatment. If the puppies are poorly for one reason or another, do not worm until they have picked up again. Leave intervals long rather than short, but do worm diligently for there is no point spending money on puppy food and feeding worms as well.

WEEK FOUR

They may need their nails cutting again, and if you thought they wriggled and squawked last time, you will be impressed at how much more they can object to what you are doing. Four-week-olds are utterly enchanting: they are thrilled to see you, wagging their tails madly, bomb you and each other in hectic play, and are ready for as many new experiences as you can give them. Now is the time to introduce well-behaved children and adults, having insisted that hands and shoes are disinfected before and after puppy handling. The pups will still have worms, despite your best efforts, so stringent hygiene precautions should be observed. Sharp needle teeth will test you, so equip the pups with plenty of things that they are allowed to chew, and redirect the little mouths from fingers to vegetable pieces or bones. If you are a quiet sort of person, as I am, you will have to make a special effort to acclimatise the pups to domestic noise: a radio, television, washing machines, car noises and so on. The more experiences that they have now, the better they will be equipped for the outside world. Don't let people pick puppies up, but instead have the people sit where the puppies can reach them. It is the easiest thing in the world for a pup to be dropped, with awful results, but if they are not picked up in the first place, that cannot happen.

SEPARATION

If you have chosen a puppy to keep, this is a good time to start separating her from the litter so that she can bond with you. This should not be for too long at a time, but is a most pleasurable experience for both of you as she learns to toddle after you, help you around the house and in the garden, and best of all, go to sleep on your lap. Put a soft puppy collar on her while she is with you, to accustom her to the feel, but be sure to take it off when you return her to the others, or they will catch hold of it and pull, which might cause harm. Extend the time of separation as the puppy gets older, until she is spending most of her time with you, but remember puppies need to play with other puppies, and she is better off for being with them when you are busy. When you return your pup to the puppy nursery, be aware that she may have undergone a status change while being out, and wait with her until the group accepts her again.

FIVE TO TWELVE WEEKS

Between now and when the puppies leave home, they will be getting bigger, more wilful, more destructive and more enchanting. Personalities will be well developed, and the more dominant puppies will be making life difficult for the more retiring ones:

Managing a raw meaty bone at five weeks

Nails may need cutting again

infant squabbles will be frequent, and there will be a lot of noise. Mother dog will be spending less and less time with them, and may have handed over to you completely, while you are wondering what on earth possessed you to breed a litter of puppies. Now is the time for people to choose their pup, and for you to prepare them for their next home.

It is rather strange that, legally, pups may not change homes to another private home before eight weeks old, but they can go to a pet shop or dealer at five weeks. It is a law that few know and is therefore often flouted: personally I cannot see that going from one loving, experienced home to another is in any way inferior to ending up in a pet shop window, but then the law and justice are not always one and the same. Most people like to take a pup at eight weeks old, and some prefer to wait until she has had her vaccinations, which could be twelve to sixteen weeks depending on what your vet's policies and your own beliefs are. These are critical development weeks for puppies, however, and the earlier, within reason, that the pup moves home, the easier it is on all of you. Pups go through quite a fearful stage between twelve and sixteen weeks, but are bold and outgoing at eight weeks. If you keep your pups for twelve weeks, no matter how wonderful they are, you will be exhausted by the constant squabbling and limitless energy, the huge appetites and endless supply of mess to clear up. This is Nature's way of helping you to part with them!

THE BITCH

While the pups are growing apace, the demands on the bitch will be high. Some bitches put so much into their milk that they lose condition dramatically; my farmer friend calls it 'milking off her back'. No matter how well you feed and care for your

ABOVE:
Separated from litter and learning to interact with other dogs

RIGHT:
Puppy topping up with milk

Seven weeks old

bitch, a few will look like scarecrows by the time the pups are ready to leave. Do make sure that she is getting her full rations, as much as she is willing to eat, and also see that she can get away from her babies when she wants. A bitch will appreciate a vantage point near but not in with the monsters. Encourage her to come on longer walks and take an interest in non-domestic matters. Some bitches regain their figures more easily than others, but don't fret if yours is one that takes a while. A few bitches will lose a lot of coat, too, but this is normal and the coat will grow back. The same thing happens with most mothers, including human ones, and is hormonal.

PSYCHOLOGY TESTING
This became very popular in the 1990s, and was a series of 'tests' that people were supposed to put a litter of puppies through to ascertain their different levels of dominance and trainability. The puppy would have to undergo such treatment as being turned onto her back and gently held to see if she struggled or growled. Believe me, if anyone tried that with any pups I'd bred, they would be stopped at once! Imagine how traumatised a sensitive puppy would get if every time it met new people they did things like that to her, and a bold pup would be getting distinctly more bolshie each time. Any breeder worth their salt knows their puppies' personalities inside out and will be only too pleased to describe each one to the prospective new

owners (I am afraid I don't know any officially sanctioned tests for determining the dominance and trainability of would-be puppy owners). If the breeder doesn't know one pup from another in personality terms, you may be sure that not a lot of time has been spent with the litter. I've heard comments such as 'They're all the same at that age', but they are not, and it surprises me that anyone who has had a bunch of pups around for eight weeks hasn't learned anything about them. You and I of course spend far too much time just observing the interaction between our pups, while our other commitments go to rack and ruin.

HALFWAY HOUSE

If you do not live too far apart, and you know the prospective owner well, a puppy can spend a short time at her new home every day for the week prior to leaving home for good. This means that the change of homes does not come as such a shock to her, and increases her chances of settling into her new home straight away. I have done this from both sides, as a breeder letting a puppy go out for afternoons, and when buying a puppy in. It certainly works. However, I would not advise you to let a stranger do this as the most plausible people can turn out to be criminals, and you risk seeing neither your puppy nor the purchase price again. Make it very clear if you do agree to this that any injuries or illnesses are the responsibility of the new owner, and do not hesitate to refuse if there are infections about that might be brought back to the rest of the litter.

PECKING ORDER

As pups leave the litter, you will see changes in the pecking order of those remaining. If a particularly dominant pup leaves early, the shyest ones will become more assertive, but if you are left with a very dominant puppy making life difficult for a quieter sibling, think about separating them. Two pups of equal status, especially if of the same sex, will squabble constantly. Even gentle breeds will jostle for status with each other; be very careful if yours is a feisty breed, because as they get older they can harm each other. Another reason for getting them off to their new homes before they measure their age in double figures!

STARTER KIT

I send my pups off with a 'starter kit' of diet sheet, details of when they were wormed and with what, and often enough wormer for the next dose if it is due soon. If necessary, they will have had their nails trimmed, so that the new owner does not have to worry about that for a couple of weeks. Warn people that young puppies are often car-sick, so that they can take suitable precautions. The owners know that they can contact me with any queries, and I also ask that, if things don't work out, the puppy is returned to me for rehoming. This last cannot be enforced, unfortunately, but I can only do my best by asking. It is a big responsibility to bring a litter of pups into the world.

AFTERMATH

The first season that a bitch has after whelping can take you by surprise, as the six months between conception and next season date will have passed in a blur of pregnancy and puppy rearing. This post-birth season can be exceptionally prolonged and heavy, as the bitch has a good cleanse out and her hormones return to normal. Some bitches do not settle into a regular cycle for two or three seasons after giving birth, and others are straight back to their usual schedule. If your bitch has had a caesarean, please do not breed from her again. If she was an indifferent mother this time, there is no reason to suggest that a subsequent litter will change her attitude. If you are having her spayed after her litter, it is better if you wait until her cycle has stabilised if her post-breeding season was typically heavy. Motherhood may, of course, have suited her very well – but I expect that you will need at least a year to recover from the whole experience!

8 Health Care

First aid and when to see the vet

Should your dog be unlucky enough to be injured, to be seriously unwell, or even be poisoned, then your first port of call should always be the vet. However, it is often good to have some idea of first aid measures, as well as simple home remedies, to enable you to treat minor problems either before a vet is seen, or when the problem occurs out of surgery hours, is not serious enough to necessitate a call-out and you need to tide the patient over. Vets never mind being contacted at any time if you are worried, but they have lives to lead too, and their support should never be abused.

When selecting a veterinary practice to register with, many owners will simply opt for the nearest clinic, without exploring the facilities offered. Today's vets are not only becoming more technology orientated, but individuals are becoming specialised in particular fields such that there is now plenty of choice for the service you require. All owners need a primary care practice in easy reach in case of an emergency, and whilst distance is a factor, enquire also about the structure of the practice. Is it a small, one or two vet clinic where the emphasis is on personal service, but facilities may be less unless there is a system for referral onto specialists in case of need, or is the clinic a large corporate one where staff turnover is inevitably quicker, but ability to invest in equipment is often greater, with their own specialists in linked clinics? Is there open-mindedness in the practice should you wish to consult a homoeopathic vet, which is very important for the treatment of chronic cases; is there an acupuncture therapist for when your pet becomes elderly? Good vets will never mind a client seeking a referral or second opinion as they will be confident in their own abilities, and will happily direct you to a reputable practitioner, in fact they will often suggest it. To my mind there is nothing worse in today's medical world than a clinician who believes he/she can do it all when there is so much specialist help out there in times of trouble. The service you want will be down to your own preferences, but it is well worth looking into what is available.

Some general points to remember are:
1　Learn what is normal for your dog through a routine of checking her over regularly.
2　Keep your vet's number easily to hand, ideally engraved on a tag fixed to your dog's collar as that way it is always with her.
3　Always phone the vet before dashing to the surgery to ensure he or she is ready for you, and the vet may also be able to give some life-saving advice before you set out.
4　Learn to restrain your dog so she understands the concept before a problem occurs, and ensure you and any helpers do not get bitten.

5   Never offer treats to calm a dog as an anaesthetic may be needed.

6   Rescue Remedy and Arnica are worth carrying everywhere to aid treatment of shock (owner and dog!) and bruising.

RESTRAINT AND NURSING

It may seem that your dog is so loving that you cannot envisage ever having to restrain her, but a dog that has been bitten, is injured or is even just ill can change in temperament due to the pain. Some simple rules that are easy to remember and practice are worth knowing: a dog that is used to being held still by your grabbing a bit of the neck's scruff will not be frightened if a tighter grip is needed for restraint – restraint this way is best by taking hold of both sides of the neck in a larger dog. Always face the dog away from you so she cannot bite at your arms and face. A simple muzzle can be created from a strip of bandage, a tie, stocking, or a lead, and tied over the muzzle, crossed back underneath and passed back around the head to be tied. Legs are an issue as a scrabbling dog is hard to hold so wrap a dog in pain into a blanket or coat.

When nursing a dog the rules to remember are that a good nurse doesn't fuss, and he or she does what is needed, then allows the patient to rest. Again simple rules apply:

1   Many homes are draughty at ground level so make sure the patient is not sleeping in a draught

2   Wrap hot water bottles well, inside a towel in turn inside a pillow case is often good as it avoids burns from exposed bottles.

3   Clean fresh water should be to hand, and offered to the patient.

4   Noise and bright lights upset patients.

5   Bedding should be clean and replaced immediately if soiled.

6   If not moving then patients should be encouraged to turn over every few hours to help prevent further problems.

7   Clean eyes and nose with salt water if discharges build up.

8   Follow any veterinary instructions to the letter.

9   Lastly, if in doubt ask for help.

A BASIC FIRST AID KIT

Many of the better first aid kits designed for human use can be a good place to start when putting together a kit for your dog. Often they are combined by owners for both purposes. Portability is a key part of design, as there is little use having the best kit at home, but not in the car when it's needed.

BASIC ITEMS:

At least two strong soft rolled bandages (one for a muzzle, one for the injury)

Crepe knit bandage for fixing dressings

Adhesive rolled plaster (you cannot fix ordinary plasters to hair so you need a type to wrap around)

Curved blunt-ended scissors

Cotton wool

Lint pads

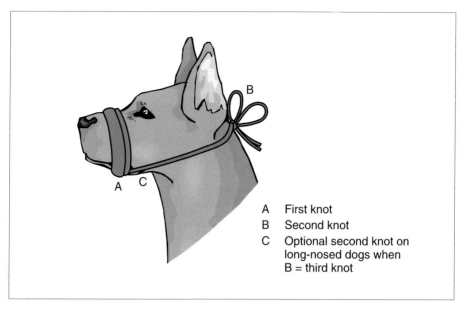

A   First knot
B   Second knot
C   Optional second knot on
      long-nosed dogs when
      B = third knot

A simple bandage muzzle

Vet-wrap (a quick and easy bandaging system obtainable from pet shops and
    saddleries)
A syringe can be very useful to wash flush water into wounds when cleaning
Alternatively spray cans of saline are available from chemists and are useful as a
    source of sterile wash solution
Tweezers for ticks and thorns
Washing soda (to use to induce vomiting if poisoned – see poisoning section)
Hypercal cream, a mix of Calendula and Hypericum to aid healing of wounds and
    reduce pain
Bach Rescue Remedy to treat shock and to calm the patient and owner (four
    drops each)
Arnica tablets for the pain of bruising, and they are also said to help stop bleeding
A blanket to wrap the dog in if needed, or to use as a stretcher
Disinfectant such as TCP or Tea Tree oil*

Also of use are proprietary first aid kits of homoeopathic remedies, sold now by many
pharmacies. Whilst packaged for humans, the indications are the same for dogs and
thus these can be useful to keep to hand to help with many of the treatments outlined
below.

Aromatherapy oils should not be used on pregnant or lactating bitches, puppies
under six months old, or very old dogs.

*Please note that homoeopathic remedies should be kept separately from strong-smelling substances such
as disinfectant or aromatherapy oils.

FIRST AID A–Z

In this section a variety of common problems are flagged up, and a range of possible treatment choices that are readily available are detailed. When considering home treatment remember the following simple rules:

1   It is better to only try one thing at a time to avoid confusion over what is actually happening, although mixing an external application with an oral tablet is OK.
2   Watch closely for results as often minor problems such as vomiting will clear quickly with well chosen homoeopathic remedies and the vet may not be needed at all.
3   Do not overdose. This is very important.
4   Lastly, if in doubt, remember it is often better to do nothing rather than make things worse.

For all homoeopathic remedies, the treatments mentioned are easily available tablets, given by mouth, unless specified. It is also possible to obtain homoeopathic remedies in tincture form, in a spray or dropper bottle. Tablets must not be touched by the fingers and are given most easily by crushing between the backs of two sterilised teaspoons and then tipping the powder in the mouth. Tinctures are either dripped on the dog's nose or sprayed into her mouth. Bach Flower Remedies may be obtained from health stores or homoeopathic pharmacies, and are liquid, given by mouth unless specified. Herbs and Aromatherapy treatments are administered in a variety of ways and these are mentioned in each section as applicable.

ABSCESS

An abscess is a collection of pus resulting from the body attempting to wall off an infection. The causes can be many; often blackthorn spikes or splinters are the culprits and should be removed if possible. At first an abscess will appear as a hot swelling with a reddened area of skin over it. With time, it will mature by the skin covering weakening until it bursts, often discharging plenty of pus everywhere, or so it seems.

Simple Home Treatments
An abscess should be gently poulticed (see Wounds) or bathed in warm salt water (made using Sea salt, or alternatively Epsom salts, at a rate of four teaspoons to a pint of water) until the abscess bursts and drains. The area can then be washed out with warm water, to which a little hydrogen peroxide has been added – this will make it bubble and foam – but do not use the hydrogen peroxide around the eye or ear.

Herbs
Poultices of comfrey, marshmallow root, plantain and chickweed can be made up by grinding the herbs, either together or separately depending on what is available, and strapping this as a compress to the abscess to draw the infection.

Honey is also useful in a poultice, albeit messy to use. The dog will benefit from licking up the excess honey left on its body after the poultice has been removed.

Homoeopathy

Apis mel 6c is an especially good remedy in dogs for relief of the pain caused by the early red and hot swelling, dose hourly for four doses, then as needed. Some early abscesses will be aborted via this and no further remedy will be needed.

Hepar sulph 6c can be given three times daily if the area is very painful to touch and the infection needs to be encouraged to discharge. Can be given with Apis.

Hepar sulph 30c is useful once the pus has discharged in assisting with clearing up the infection, given three times daily.

Silica 6c helps clear up wounds where they have burst, but the pus fails to come away properly, often given with the Hepar sulph 30c.

Aromatherapy

German chamomile and lavender oils can be used externally to draw infection by adding to any poultice.

A single application of diluted tea tree oil is often sufficient to remedy an abscess.

Bach Flower Remedies

Rescue Remedy for the pet that is very distressed is calming and aids settling.

Crab Apple will support the cleansing of the abscess and expulsion of any foreign material.

When to call the vet

An abscess should mature within twenty-four hours and burst, healing rapidly after. If this doesn't happen then your vet should be consulted. Abscesses that recur can indicate an underlying problem, or if the abscess is by the anus it may be a problem with the anal gland. In both these instances a vet should be consulted.

ACCIDENTS

Despite all precautions possible, accidents can still happen. Most will be minor and a learning experience, but if more severe and you don't know what to do the first rule is to do nothing except keep the dog still and warm whilst waiting for help, and give Rescue Remedy and Arnica 30c in alternation every fifteen minutes. If you have to move her then improvise a stretcher with blankets, boards etc. If there is a lot of bleeding try to stop it (see Bleeding) and if she is hysterical then apply a muzzle (see Restraint).

Herbs

Chamomile, skullcap and oats can all be used to make a calming tea that can be offered to dogs every few hours. They will often drink this enthusiastically as dogs, like many animals except Man, have not lost the ability to know which herbs are good for them, and when they are needed.

Homoeopathy

Aconite 30c is a must for all shock situations, give two doses ten minutes apart then move on to give Arnica

Arnica, Arnica, Arnica. This remedy in whatever strength you have it is so useful for reducing pain and bruising, and it is also said to prevent minor haemorrhages. Dose every fifteen minutes for four doses then hourly for four hours. Certainly horse riders swear by it for falls, and many sportsmen now take it routinely for competition. More people are converted to homoeopathy each year by this remedy than any other. Arnica is also available as a cream for bruising, but this must not be put on wounds as it slows healing.

Carbo veg 30c, known as the homoeopathic 'corpse reviver' should be given to collapsed cases every twenty minutes for three doses.

Aromatherapy

Eucalyptus, lavender or tea tree are all useful remedies when diluted and applied externally to bruises for pain relief and healing, but only lavender should be applied to areas where the skin is broken. Tea tree and eucalyptus are exceptionally strong and one or two drops of either in water will suffice.

Peppermint oil is said to aid recovery from shock and to calm nerve pain. Hold the open bottle under the patient's nose.

Birch oil, dropped into a little hot water in a glass, and placed in the room helps ease dogs in pain.

Bach Flower Remedies

Rescue Remedy: like Arnica, this is a must for any first aid situation, given neat as a few drops per dose to alleviate shock and at the same intervals as the Arnica. Again, this combination of five Flower Remedies converts many people to holistic therapy each year as it is so successful and reliable a treatment.

Sweet Chestnut will help calm an inconsolable patient. Dose twice in ten minutes.
Rock Rose will calm terrified patients. Dose twice in ten minutes.

When to consult your vet

It is always worth getting a professional opinion after any accident, and in more severe cases the need to get to the vet will be obvious.

ALLERGIES AND STINGS

Contact with chemical irritants, insects and plants that sting, or more unusual things like toads can set off reactions in dogs. Toad poison can cause mild fit-like episodes and drooling, but most irritants will just result in rashes or mild swellings that can often be quite painful. If affecting the face the whole head can swell up, more typically with wasp and bee stings.

Simple Home Treatments

Witch hazel diluted at one in fifty is a great reliever of minor external irritations. It can even be made up in a small spray container and sprayed onto rashes and sores to give immediate short-term relief. Many people commonly carry Piriton tablets now, and they can be used in dogs quite safely. I suggest a dose of one tablet per Labrador and scaling up and down according to body weight. The patient may get a little sleepy but this usually passes quite quickly. For stings, alkalis (like vinegar) diluted in water and applied to the sting will relieve the pain, but you have to watch that you don't get bitten at first when applying it.

Vitamin E and fish oils have an anti-inflammatory effect on dogs who have a tendency to allergies, and can be given to dogs in similar doses to humans, but scale down to their body weight.

Herbs

Chamomile and yarrow as a tea will help sooth an allergic reaction, give up to four times daily. Echinacea and elderflower are also good herbs for calming the over-response of the immune system and are both often readily available.

When the eyes are sore some chamomile and eyebright as a diluted infusion can be a very useful relieving eyewash, applied as often as needed.

Homoeopathy

Apis mel 6c can be given hourly for any skin rash, and is especially good for swellings around the eyes and ears, a must for bee and wasp stings.

Caladium 30c is good for mosquito bites, given two or three times daily as needed. Ledum pal 6c is good for puncture wounds, including dog bites, horsefly bites and wasp stings. Dose as often as needed for relief.

Urtica urens 6c is good for hives (nettle rash) given hourly for four doses

Ledum, Pyrethrum and Rumex can all be bought as lotions and combined with Hypericum and Calendula to make up an anti-sting lotion, which is then applied by diluting and holding on with a damp cloth.

For severe reactions to stings a lotion made from Arnica, Calendula and Urtica (ACU Lotion) can be applied to soothe and reduce inflammation. Best applied by putting a few drops onto a cold flannel and holding on, allowing your hands heat to warm the wound over a few minutes.

Aromatherapy

Lavender, mixed into a massage oil, ideally organic olive oil, can be rubbed into the areas of skin affected for relief. It can be applied neat onto stings.

Bach Flower Remedies

Rescue Remedy cream can be applied to any skin reaction, and is especially useful if the skin has broken and many of the other options are not possible.

A combination of Agrimony, Beech, Cherry Plum, Crab Apple and Walnut can be given as a few drops by mouth, but also diluted in a spray bottle and squirted onto the affected area a few times daily.

When to consult your vet
The vast majority of acute allergic reactions will pass in an hour or two, but if the face is affected, or the problem persists then you must consult your vet before more serious problems occur. Some dogs will tend to suffer allergic responses quite often, in a similar way to humans, and for these it is a good idea to consult a holistic vet for a longer term solution.

ANAL GLANDS
The cause of many a trip to the vets, these little, marble sized glands that sit either

side of the anus are an evolutionary remnant gland that dogs have not yet learned to delete from their genetic make-up. Modern processed diets can result in a stool that is not firm enough to massage clean these glands as the dog defecates, and the situation is often made worse by the shapes that man has bred into dogs in the pursuit of 'perfect' breed types. If not emptied properly the glands fill up with a thick, foul-smelling liquid that can become infected and cause problems. Early warning signs of problems are when the dog rubs her bottom along the floor/new carpet in an attempt to express the glands, and follows this with licking around the anus. It is wise then to get them checked before problems occur.

Simple Home Treatments
If a persistent problem ask your vet to show you how to empty these glands yourself. Whilst quite foul smelling, routine emptying can prevent problems recurring. Look at the diet also, and consider changing to a bones and raw food (BARF) diet to achieve a better stool. If infection occurs loads of live yoghurt added to the diet will help colour the stool so that a dose of 'friendly' bacteria will reach the gland as each stool is passed, and this should always be given after any antibiotics are prescribed in any case. A warm compress made from a mix of Epsom salts and water, soaked into a flannel and held onto the dog's bottom for ten minutes twice a day gives great relief, often causing the glands to express naturally.

Herbs
Dandelion root, golden seal and yarrow made into a tea and either offered to the patient, or added to the food twice a day can help with irritation and pain, as well as improving circulation in the area. Topical application of a fresh cabbage leaf can give relief.

Homoeopathy
Apis mel 6c is good for relief of pain when the area around the anus is red and swollen, given hourly for four hours.

Hepar sulph 6c is useful to encourage blocked glands to discharge, give three times daily.

Merc cor 30c will help healing when the pus from the glands is bloody, black and thin in constituency, dose three times daily.

Natrum mur 30c helps the distressed dog that is producing a green, often fluorescent, discharge, dose three times daily.

Silica 6c daily for a few weeks will often help a dog that has suffered recurrent problems, and when the openings of the glands have become scarred and closed.

When to consult your vet
In any case where the patient is distressed the local vet, and in all recurrent cases a Holistic vet, should be consulted to work out a solution. When visiting the vet, always ask to see the discharge from the glands as this can be a guide to remedies needed.

Antibiotics
These may seem an odd addition to a first aid section, but I include these here to

make a few points that can stop the development of long-term problems from their use. Firstly, if your vet has prescribed antibiotics you must use them at the advised dose and for the time specified. This is important to prevent resistant bacteria building up and causing problems further down the line. Secondly, dogs have quite short intestines, and they need 'friendly' bacteria to aid the digestive process. Most antibiotics will kill off these 'friends' as the drugs are not discriminatory, and so you will need to put some back after the medication has finished to restore a healthy gut, and also to prevent any 'nasty' bacteria establishing. Many a chronic diarrhoea and bowel problem has been the result of neglecting these simple rules, and it is much harder to correct the problem months, or even years, later.

ANXIETY

Defined as a state of uneasiness or apprehension accompanied by tension that may, or may not have an obvious cause. Often a result of us owners failing to recognise the wolf in our companions, neglected anxiety states are a major cause of long term health problems through stress effects on the immune system. Behavioural problems as a result of inappropriate adopting of avoidance techniques like disembowelling sofas and unearthing houseplants are a sign indicating this problem. If spotted early and treated, with medicines as described below as well as changing our lifestyles to allow normal canine behaviour, a lot of expense and grief can be avoided.

Simple Home Treatments

DAPs (Dog Appeasement Pheromones) that have been mentioned in preceding chapters can be bought from your vet to calm a stressed pet on a longer term basis for treatment of some problems, but the most important thing is to sit down and think out the problem, and set about changing your life to get around whatever it may be.

Herbs

Catnip, chamomile, hops, passiflora, skullcap, and valerian are all herbs that have been used with success to calm stressed dogs. Often these can be obtained from herbal suppliers in various mixes, and easily given as a tablet, or added to the food. Of especial use I find is an Indian herbal formula of asparagus, ocimum, phyllanthus and Withania marketed by specialist importers Global Herbs Ltd.

St John's Wort (Hypericum) is often used for depression and anxiety in humans, and there is some indication it can be used for the chronically anxious case with dogs too.

Homoeopathy

Aconite 30c, the remedy for an acute shock. Argentum nitricum 30c is a remedy par excellence for the dog that gets diarrhoea with anxiety. Often they have other issues as well, such as fear of the dark, fear of approach and so on.

Gelsemium 30c for the 'frightened rabbit' syndrome, where a stress creates paralysis and inability to move.

Ignatia 30c for anxiety related to separation, grief and loss, as well as change in environment. Timidity and hysteria characterise this remedy.

Natrum mur 30c for the dog that has developed odd behaviour traits from the stress. We all remember the polar bears that pace up and down all day in the zoos as a response to stress. These are the Natrum mur cases. They will also have odd obsessions such as watching birds in the sky, snapping at flies, and a tendency to hide in the dark.

Proteus 30c is a very useful remedy for the rescued dog, with intermittent stool problems, often a poor skin, and a history of recent separation from her owner.
Sulphur 30c for dogs who have developed a fear of approach after a trauma.
For all the above dose twice, an hour apart.

Aromatherapy

Lavender, Vetivert and Rose oils: adding two or three drops of each, or all, to a cup of hot water will create a gentle aroma perfusing the room to calm a stressed pet.

Neroli and Frankincense oils can be used in a similar way for pets who suffer separation anxiety problems on a longer term basis.

Bach Flower Remedies

There are almost too many of these useful here to describe in depth, and I would recommend anyone with a dog that has developed behavioural problems to read one of the many books on these for guidance. Most problems can be resolved with these so long as changes are made to remove the cause as well. A selection include: Agrimony for fear of being left alone (often given with Mimulus). Mimulus for fear and apprehension relating to known events. Oat for the odd behaviours such as pacing and rocking. Red Chestnut, for fear and anxiety about others, such as other pets and the human family. Rock rose for extreme anxiety and panic. White Chestnut, for the persistent thoughts that go round and round in the head. Hard to see in dogs but many anxiety states will be helped by this so dogs must dwell on things.

Reiki can be particularly helpful for anxiety cases.

When to consult your vet

Basically when none of the above has worked, and you have been unable to determine the problem, it is time to call in the professionals. Your vet will have a list of local behaviour therapists, and be able to recommend one, or more often now your vet may also have an interest in this field. Vets may also prescribe some drugs for more severe problems, but these have to be a last resort.

ARTHRITIS

As a term we tend to think of arthritis as a longer-term problem of age, but some modern dog breeds can develop problems as growing puppies, and injuries can happen at any time. Any joint inflammation is technically an 'arthritis', and early effective treatment can prevent damage to the delicate cartilages in a joint and thus also reduce the chances of developing age-related arthritis.

Simple Home Treatments

For most joint problems there are simple supplements available from the health store that can be of great help in longer term cases. Glucosamine, combined with chondroitin sulphate, can be easily obtained and given to great effect. A simple guide is to take a 500mg tablet as a daily dose for a 35kg Labrador and scale up and down accordingly.

Another useful tip is to massage the acupuncture point that is known as the 'Aspirin point'. This is BL60, and is to be found on the top of the ankle joint on the outer side. Massaging for sixty seconds a side twice a day can bring great relief.

Cider vinegar, honey and corn or olive oil , mixed together in equal portions and given at a rate of one teaspoon twice daily in the food is a great and easily available remedy that helps many mild cases.

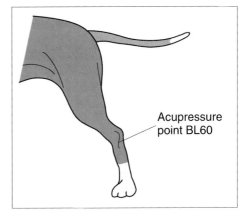

Acupressure point BL60

Acupressure 'Aspirin Point' BL60

Herbs
My favourite herbs here are two Indian, or Ayurvedic remedies, boswellia and turmeric. The former is the number one arthritis treatment in India, and outsells more conventional painkillers. Mixed together they are a powerful formulation, but if you have nothing else, you will often have turmeric as a herb in the kitchen, and you can add a little powder (typically one quarter teaspoon for a Labrador) to your dog's food (but don't panic if the stool goes orange for a while).

Homoeopathy
Rhus tox, Ruta grav and Arnica in 30c are the main remedies for joint pain, and they are often combined and given together, up to three times daily. This is often sold as Homoeopathic 'injury remedy'.

Calc phos 30c should be given daily to all puppies with growing problems to promote healthy bone and cartilage formation.

Aromatherapy
Chamomile, Eucalyptus, Ginger, Juniper and Lavender are all said to provide relief, a few drops being added to a massage oil and worked into a sore joint. If the arthritis is active and the joint is warm, cool with Eucalyptus and/or Juniper: if cold and aching, warm with Ginger; Lavender and Chamomile are always appropriate. Vegetable gel for Aromatherapy use is often easier to use with heavy-coated dogs than massage oil.

When to consult your vet
In all cases it is especially important to consult a Holistic vet as the causes and potential treatments for best outcome must be found as soon as possible. Treatment with painkillers (often called anti-inflammatory drugs) just masks a problem and is not a solution in the majority of cases. Young dogs especially need assessment as they may develop a condition known as OCD (Osteochondrosis dessicans) that is

potentially serious if left. It is worth noting however, that breeders whose dogs used to suffer this problems but then changed to a bones and raw food diet for their puppies have reported the problem disappearing – convinced yet?

BANDAGING

Most dogs have a desire to lick their wounds, and will try and chew off bandages and dressings unless they realise it is hopeless. Unfortunately some dogs will get so distressed by bandages they will actually cause further injuries by tearing frantically at dressings so care is needed to ensure this cannot happen. Vets will therefore often bandage right around the limb or body, even if it is only a small area that needs dressing. A good bandage will be firm and wide, but not too tight that it cuts off the circulation, and will be typically covered in Elastoplast to protect it from biting. Plastic collars to prevent chewing may be needed as well for persistent offenders. It is interesting that vets do not receive much instruction on this when training compared to veterinary nurses, who have made the bandaging of animals an art form of its own, and are often the best source of advice.

Simple rules to remember at home are: cover the wound with lint, or similar, dressing to ensure the bandage doesn't stick to the skin, then apply a thin layer of rolled gauze bandage, a layer of cotton wool is placed around that and a further layer of bandage applied around this before an Elastoplast or Vet-Wrap outer is applied. The resulting dressing should be firm, but not too tight that it acts like a tourniquet and cuts off the blood supply (with obvious devastating consequences if not spotted in time).

BITES

Despite the best socialisation classes and early puppy training, some dogs seem to be prone to getting into scraps, even if it is not always their fault. Bite wounds can be very painful, often some time after the initial bite as the swelling develops. However they are best left open and bathed rather than covered up. Covering can seal infection in and lead to an abscess forming, or worse, septicaemia. Obviously if bleeding a lot to start with the follow the rules for bleeding (see Bleeding), and also follow the rules for wound care (see Wounds).

Simple Home Treatments

Clean the bite with witch hazel diluted one in forty. This is a level at which it will not sting and upset the patient, yet is strong enough to be mildly disinfectant. If you do not have Witch Hazel to hand then salt water at a rate of two teaspoons to a pint of water is a good second best.

Herbs

Marshmallow made as a tea, to which is added some Arnica tincture can be soaked into a flannel and applied as a warm compress to relieve bruising and swelling once the wound has been cleaned. Calendula (marigold) can also be made as an infusion and dabbed on at regular intervals to cleanse and promote healing.

Homoeopathy

Arnica 30c should be given to all patients to relieve the pain and swelling of the bruise; alternatively 'Injury Remedy' can be used. Dose hourly for four doses then as needed.

Ledum pal 6c is a major remedy for dog bites, which tend to become swollen and inflamed. Dose hourly for four hours, and then three times daily.

Vipera 30c can be given along with Ledum for snakebites.

Aromatherapy
Tea tree or Lavender oil diluted in water can be applied around the wound for pain relief and cleansing.

Bach Flower Remedies
Rescue Remedy drops and cream, the former to calm the patient, the latter to put on the wound to cleanse and promote healing.

When to consult your vet
Many bites do not need more than cleaning and the care as described above, but those near the eye, ear or anal area should be checked by a vet for other complications. Any case where pus starts to form may need antibiotics (one never knows how clean the teeth of the biter were), and any case where the patient becomes quiet and withdrawn should be checked over. Snakebite cases should always have veterinary attention.

BLEEDING
Rule One – don't panic. A little blood goes a long way, and especially if the dog is wet it can seem that there is a vast amount of blood everywhere. If there was that much you probably couldn't do much about things anyway, which is generally not the case. In a panic situation it is hard to know where best to bandage so the best rule is to first restrain the dog so she cannot hurt you. Then apply firm pressure to the wound area using a handkerchief, torn shirt or even a pack of tissues. Once this is achieved either use bandages or torn cloth to bind the area firmly, then wrap the patient in a blanket and get her to the vet.

Bandaging leg wounds is straightforward as you can simply wrap around a leg. Tails are more difficult as you often have to wrap the whole tail, and even then it can be hard to keep a dressing on. Body injuries are best wrapped in a criss-cross fashion around the whole body. Eye injury is hard to bandage and it is probably best just to hold a pad against the eye, whilst ears can be bandaged by folding up over the head and bandaging around the whole head, again easier in a criss-cross pattern. Noses and bums are impossible to bandage so here the rules of restraint and warmth apply (ie wrapping in a blanket) whilst getting to the vet.

We're beginning to see here the importance of that blanket in the first aid kit. Combining as a stretcher, restraining method and warmth provider, they are so useful to carry in the car.

Remedies to carry always are Arnica and Rescue Remedy, and both should be given to all cases that are bleeding every fifteen minutes, whilst heading to the vet.

BURNS
The most common burns affecting dogs involve the pads through walking on hot ash,

or the back of the head as a result of spilling hot water or food as she gets under your feet at the wrong time. Aside from the initial pain, symptoms may take some time (even days) to show, as fur can be not only protective, but also hides problems from view. Treatment of severe burns is really a matter for the vet, but minor burns can be treated safely at home.

Herbs
Aloe vera is an excellent remedy for all burns, and every vet practice and home should grow a plant. If you have a plant, break off a leaf and squeeze out the gel-like liquid onto the burn. If you only have it as a commercial ointment or liquid that will suffice, and you can literally plaster the area with it if you've enough.

Comfrey, marigold and St John's Wort can all be made as an infusion and the burn bathed four times a day or more. Comfrey promotes healing, marigold does too and St John's Wort relieves the pain. Urtica urens (nettles) can be made also as an infusion and washed onto the wound for pain relief.

Homoeopathy
Cantharis 6c, dosed three times daily will help relieve the pains where there is blistering. Causticum 30c twice a day is said to help severe burns heal quickly.

Kali bich 30c twice daily should be given later to help with the skin itching that occurs as a burn heals.

Urtica urens 6c three times daily for mild burns to relieve the pain and aid healing. A lotion of Arnica, Calendula and Urtica can be applied as soon as possible to the area burnt to soothe and promote healing, and as an ointment is excellent at promoting healing if the wounds blister.

Aromatherapy
Lavender oil applied neat or slightly diluted with water will soothe and prevent infections: it is also said to promote tissue repair. The fragrance calms the patient and avoids panic happening.

Bach Flower Remedies
Rescue Remedy again as a cream onto the burn, and internally as drops to calm the patient.

When to consult your vet
In any case where the eye is affected, and in anything other than very mild cases.

CLAWS
Just like your nails, claws can be broken and torn. Amazingly, if this happens during play or walking the first thing noticed may be the blood all over the car on the way home. The pain tends to come later when the adrenaline rush has worn off. However, the majority of nail injuries are immediately painful, with the dog unable to put the paw down, or limping badly. If the affected nail is broken and loose you can grip the broken bit firmly and tug it off sharply, but beware, the pain can cause the mildest dog to bite so if in doubt, ask the experts. Cracked or firmly held fragments may need

an anaesthetic to remove. In all cases where there is bleeding, apply firm pressure with a pad for a few minutes until bleeding stops. Remember prevention is better than cure, and well trimmed nails are less likely to tear than overgrown ones, and it is as well to get a puppy used to nail clipping to enable this.

Simple Home Treatments
Healthy nails can be encouraged by adding Omega-3 fatty acids such as fish oils to the diet. I especially like halibut oil, and the knock-on benefits of this can be seen in energised and gleaming dogs. It's a sad fact that there can never be enough Omega-3 in processed foods, and this is a cause of poor nails in some dogs.

Herbs
Calendula and St John's Wort tincture can be used as a rinse on nail injuries. This reduces swelling and helps to prevent infection. If removal of the nail is needed, washing with this before, and after, is said to reduce bleeding.

Homoeopathy
Staphysagria 30c given twice on the day of injury helps reduce pain and also phobia about the foot being touched after an injury.

Phosphorous 30c given hourly for four hours to cases where the blood is persistently oozing will often stop the flow.

A lotion made up from Arnica, Calendula and Urtica is excellent for soaking the foot in to heal any injuries to feet and claws.

Aromatherapy
Lavender applied neat to the site of the injury once will ease pain and help prevent infection.

When to consult your Vet
When the torn nail needs to be removed, or if lameness persists for more than twenty-four hours.

CUTS AND SCRAPES – See Wounds

CYSTS – See Abscess section as the treatment is the same

DIARRHOEA
It has been said that diarrhoea always has character! Observing the colour, development and progression of a diarrhoea problem is a vital aid to diagnosis in more severe cases. However, dogs are fairly prone to mild diarrhoea and they do not need to be rushed to the vet at the first sign of anything other than a perfect stool. Diarrhoea can vary from a soft, cow-pat like stool, to watery mucous, the latter obviously being the more serious. Causes can be many: viruses, bad food (that lovely rotten rabbit crunched enthusiastically on a walk), contaminated drinking water etc. The first rule of diarrhoea is to not feed any infection, so starve the patient for twenty-four hours. Often this alone will solve the problem. Following the period of

starvation a small amount of bland non-irritant food for a couple of days is a good idea, scrambled egg with rice or mashed potato is a good standby, before introducing normal food again. Chicken and rice used to be the recommended bland diet but many dogs now are becoming sensitive to chicken, possibly as a result of the chemicals used in the poultry industry so I advise steering clear unless you have a good organic source of this meat.

Simple Home Treatments

Kaopectate oral liquids from the chemist are a good way to help most cases of diarrhoea. These contain a clay which absorbs the diarrhoea-causing bacteria and poisons in the gut. Doses generally are a teaspoon per 10Kg bodyweight hourly for four hours. If you don't have this then arrowroot, oatmeal porridge, tapioca or semolina are useful alternatives.

If the diarrhoea is very watery, rehydration of your pet can be aided by offering a mix of one pint water to one dessertspoonful of honey and a large pinch of salt. Water is carried better across the gut wall by the presence of glucose, and the glucose is aided further by the salt, similar to many of the sports drinks one sees sold today.

Also useful, once over the twenty-four hour starve, is to add some dietary fibre in the form of freshly crushed flaxseed, at a rate of half a teaspoon per 10kg body weight to each meal.

Herbs

Ginger, Peppermint and Slippery Elm. Make the first two into an infusion, and then stir in a heaped teaspoon of Slippery Elm into a cup of the tea before offering it to your dog. Chamomile tea is a good alternative to calm the gut, and is probably preferable for puppies.

Homoeopathy

Aloes 30c is indicated for the spluttery, jelly-like diarrhoea. Dose three times daily. Arsenicum alb 30c. – probably the major diarrhoea remedy in the dog. Its indication is for watery burning diarrhoea, often caused by eating bad food, and it will calm the restless and anxious patient. Dose hourly for four doses.

Colocynthis 30c may be given hourly for the dog that is hunched up with pain.

Merc sol 30c can be given for foul-smelling, watery and bloody stools with constant urging and straining. Dose three times daily.

Podophyllum 30c is for painless watery stools that gush from the rectum, and there will be the characteristic rumbling of the intestines. Dose three times daily.

Sulphur 30c is indicated for the bright yellow to orange diarrhoea that greets you at breakfast, with that foul, rotting odour. Dose 3 times daily.

Aromatherapy

Peppermint is an anti-spasmodic oil, and can be diluted in a little massage oil (or vegetable oil if nothing else is to hand) and massaged into the ear tips. Dogs get a lot of stomach pain with diarrhoea and the response to this can be quite remarkable at times.

When to consult your vet

Vets generally are taught to let most diarrhoea run its course, to starve and treat as we have discussed. However, if the diarrhoea persists for more than twenty-four hours, blood is seen in the stool, or if the patient appears obviously lethargic and unwell, then advice should be sought. It is worth noting that older dogs may become weak in their back legs with diarrhoea and so need veterinary care earlier, as do puppies who can dehydrate quickly. Diarrhoea with vomiting is also serious in the dog, and needs attention.

EARS

Man has bred many different types of ear into dog breeds, and not all have a lot of logic in their design. Folded over ears are warmer and can be more prone to infection that is at the same time hidden from view, while some breeds have narrow ear canals that hold wax and get infected, and still others have hairy ears resulting in the same problems. It is a good idea to regularly check your dog's ears, ensuring they are clean and not inflamed in any way.

Most ear problems only affect the outer part of the ear and can be simply treated at home. Remember never to poke anything into the ear like cotton-buds, as you cannot see what you are doing and may cause more harm than good.

Simple Home Treatments

If there is mild inflammation then some warm almond or olive oil poured into the ear, followed by gentle massage of the 'ice-cream cone' like ear canal that can be felt below the outer ear, will float most problems to the surface.

For dirty, waxy ears a dilute solution of white vinegar, one teaspoon to half a pint of water is a useful cleaning aid and can be syringed into the ear canal, which is then massaged and wiped clean. This will also clear many mild yeast (musty smelling) infections.

Herbs

Pau d'arco, known as Inca Gold, is a natural antibiotic that kills fungi and bacteria, and if you can get it as a mineral oil this can be used a few drops three times daily into the ear for a few days, starting at the first sign of any infection. This is probably of more use in recurrent cases as it is rarely to hand.

Homoeopathy

Belladonna 30c given hourly for four doses will relieve an acutely hot, red ear.

Ferrum phos 30c is very useful to give after the Belladonna if there is no discharge and the redness has not completely gone. Dose three times daily.

Hepar sulph 6c for any pus or creamy discharge from the ear. Dose three times daily.

Merc cor 30c for ears that produce a black, thick waxy discharge with a dark redness to the visible ear canal. Dose twice a day.

Pulsatilla 30c for thick yellow discharges; often the ear canal will surprisingly not even appear inflamed in these cases. Dose twice a day

Silica 6c for yellow or greenish discharges. These cases will often have swelling around the ear. Dose three times daily.

Aromatherapy

Lavender oil, dropped onto a warm wet flannel and held against the ear can give a lot of relief.

Bach Flower Remedies

Mimulus can help calm the patient that will not allow you to look at the ear. Rescue Remedy is useful on arrival at the vet if ears have been a recurrent problem and the patient dislikes having them examined.

Other

'Thornit' is gentle and very effective. (see Useful Addresses)

When to consult your vet

Acute distress with head shaking often indicates a foreign body, such as a grass seed, down the ear canal, and this should be removed by a vet ASAP. If the head is being held to one side the infection is deeper and may be affecting the middle part of the ear – seek professional help soon and put nothing yourself down the ear until it has been checked. Dogs can also suffer a problem known as a haematoma, where a blood vessel is broken in the earflap, which swells with blood. This needs to be drained to prevent the ear scrunching up with scar tissue at a later date.

ELECTRIC SHOCK

Puppies are notorious for chewing electric wires, and quite nasty burns can result. If you find an electrocuted dog the first rule is to stop and think as you could end up in trouble as well if not careful. Many animals urinate when shocked, and if you tread in that urine, which is a good electrical conductor, you could get a shock too. Find and switch off the electrical source first before doing anything at all. Once you are sure this has been done separate the patient from the wire and then, if not breathing, apply artificial respiration (mouth to nose, gently holding the muzzle closed) and massage the chest vigorously in-between breaths, while someone phones the vet.

Herbs

The main problem with electric shock survivors is organ failure some time after. Herbal treatments should be directed towards supporting the liver and de-toxifying the body.

Burdock, centaury, dandelion, nettle, milk thistle and cleaver can be obtained as tincture, or combined and made into a tea, giving a dessertspoon of the mix three or four times daily.

Homoeopathy

Natrum sulph 6c twice daily for ten days to support the liver.

Aromatherapy

Not appropriate in this case.

Bach Flower Remedies

Rescue Remedy should be given immediately, and hourly for at least six hours.

When to consult your Vet
Always!

EYE INJURIES

Dogs love to search under bushes and brambles for those elusive pheasants to chase, and for the lovely smells they find (wouldn't it be great to have their experiences?) and eyes can occasionally get scratched and infected; fragments of dirt, grass and bark may also get trapped under the lids. Again man has created difficulties for dogs by selective breeding for odd head shapes, where the relationship of lids, eyeballs and sockets is not as evolution determined, and so the eyes can become more exposed to injury. This is particularly seen in dogs like pugs and other short-nosed breeds. Problems show first as watery discharges and a squint, and may progress to soreness and pus-like discharges if more severe.

 Simple Home Treatments
Mild problems often respond to simple bathing of the eye in salt water (one teaspoon added to a pint of boiled water and allowed to cool before applying) or the liberal application of Optrex drops. If dirt or some other foreign body is trapped, use bathing liberally to flush the problem out.

Cold tea, made with fresh leaves and stewed for a minute, then allowed to cool is a good old-fashioned cleansing lotion for eyes. A mistake many people make is to use teabags, but these are held together with an irritant glue and should not be used.

 Herbs
Witch hazel applied very dilute (more than one in fifty) in cool boiled water soothes inflammation and bruising.

Euphrasia, also known as 'Eyebright', can be purchased as a sterile tincture, and a few drops added to an eyebath then applied to the eye. It is very soothing and antiseptic, as well as having antioxidant properties which help healing.

 Homoeopathy
Argentum nit 30c should be given if any infection starts to appear, and especially if there is any cloudiness of the cornea (the glassy part of the eye). Dose three times daily. Arnica 30c given following any injury helps prevent bruising and haemorrhage. Dose hourly for four doses.

Ledum pal 30c is given for 'poking' injuries such as a stick into the eye. Dose twice a day.

Symphytum 30c should be given three times daily to any case where the eyeball is injured to relieve pain and encourage healing.

 Aromatherapy
Chamomile and lavender oils – add one drop of each to an eyebath of cooled boiled water, and bathe the eye with cotton wool soaked in the resulting mixture three or four times daily.

 When to consult your vet
If problems persist for more than twenty-four hours, or immediately if there is any

cloudiness or obvious scratch affecting the glassy part of the eye – the cornea – and if the discharges turn coloured indicating infection.

FEMALE SYSTEM

If you decide not to spay a bitch early in her life (many are spayed after the first season if not to be bred from), then it is important for owners to know what is normal for a season (oestrus or heat period) and what is not. Bitches normally have two seasons a year, and the first will generally occur between five and eighteen months of age depending on many factors, including breed. When a bitch is on heat her vulva will swell and produce a blood-tinged pink to dark red discharge. This bleeding will occur for about a week before the attentions of a male dog will be accepted. The most important thing to remember is that the main danger period when conception is possible is after the blood has stopped, but that conception has happened at all stages and you should keep the bitch away from males for three weeks from the first sign of blood. After a season the bitch will often gain a little weight, irrespective of whether or not she has conceived, and at around nine weeks after the bleeding stopped she may show nesting behaviour, even a little mammary gland development and milk, which is known as false pregnancy.

Bitches can suffer from a number of problems relating to this cycle. The first is excessive symptoms of false pregnancy, and this is thought to indicate an increased likelihood of developing the second major problem, which is pyometra after subsequent seasons. Pyometra is a type of womb infection and will occur at some stage within the nine week period after the season, but typically sooner rather than later. The bitch will start drinking excessively, may produce a pus discharge from the vulva, and as the problem progresses will start vomiting. This condition is a medical emergency and the only solution is an emergency hysterectomy. However, the majority of bitches will not develop these problems, and prevention of these problems is not, to my mind, reason enough for spaying a bitch in the middle of her life unless indications are that they are happening.

 When to consult your vet

This section is included more because one needs to know the normal aspects, rather than any treatments. The best thing one can do if problems occur is seek professional help, and all problems are best treated sooner rather than later.

FOREIGN BODIES

For eyes and ears this has already been covered, so what we are discussing here is the swallowed item. Puppies especially are devils for swallowing bits of plastic toys, bits of rubber balls and all manner of other items. Occasionally this can persist into adulthood, and some dogs, spaniels especially it seems, will chew and swallow items such as stones, clothing etc. So if you have a pup in the chewing phase, or an adult with a chewing history, it can be as well to be able to spot signs of trouble. The first sign is usually vomiting, especially vomiting back anything eaten or drunk. Then, as the problem persists, tenderness around the abdomen can occur, and the patient becomes quiet and withdrawn. Thinking around the subject may reveal a missing sock, underwear, plastic toy etc, and it is as well to consult a vet as soon as practical. These cases can present a diagnostic challenge, especially if the item swallowed will not show on an X-ray. Often they will need surgery to remove the offending item so the guidance below is really preparatory for this.

Homoeopathy
Arnica 30c should be given before going to the vet, to ease the bruising of any possible surgery, and for the relief of pain. Continue the treatment three times daily post operatively at home.

Carbo veg 30c, dose every fifteen minutes whilst on the way to the vet, for any animal that has collapsed, has blue mucous membranes, and/or is cold to touch.

Colocynthis 30c can be given hourly for the relief of gut cramps, and dogs that need this will be restless and walk around with a hunched back, and often also a bloated abdomen.

Aromatherapy
Lavender oil massaged into the ear tips can bring great pain relief.

Bach Flower Remedies
Rescue Remedy if the patient is collapsed. Dose every fifteen minutes for four doses.

When to consult your vet
Always if you believe your dog/pup has swallowed an item.

FRACTURES
Broken bones are usually pretty obvious to almost any observer, and they necessitate a trip to the vet to define the problem and how it may be resolved, often surgically. However, dogs can be surprisingly good at coping with a fracture, and the only outward sign may be an intermittent lameness, or holding a leg up. With a prop on each corner they can get around quite well on three legs. Obviously pain on examination will be revealed. Fractures are not necessarily an emergency, apart from relief of pain, as many surgeons will prefer to wait for swelling to subside before operating. Do not try to splint or immobilise the problem yourself, as this can do more harm than good. Carry the dog to the car, if necessary wrapped in the ever-present blanket, and have the case assessed as soon as possible by a professional. Once fixed, there are remedies to aid healing and pain and these are detailed below, along with those to give immediately the problem is identified.

Herbs
Comfrey (also know as 'knit well' or 'knitbone') and horsetail are both reputed to aid faster healing of bones, and comfrey is also said to reduce pain as the bone heals. The leaves of both can be made into a tea and applied locally around a break unless it has been put in a plaster cast.

Comfrey root can be made into a decoction (different from a tea/infusion as this involves simmering for 10 minutes and then straining off the healing liquid) and taken as a drink, one teaspoon three times daily until the fracture is healed.

Homoeopathy

Arnica 30c may be given initially for shock and bruising. It is often used by some consultant orthopaedic surgeons pre-and post-operatively to reduce swelling and bruising, making the operation easier.

Calc phos 30c is useful given daily to young pups that suffer fractures, often known as 'greenstick' as they don't fully break, to speed the healing. It is also indicated in all cases where a growth plate has been damaged to restore its development potential.

Eupatorium perforatum 6c can be given twice daily where there is aching pain in bones. It is hard to assess this without speaking 'dog', but I tend to give it to those that grumble and cannot settle after surgery.

Hypericum 30c can be given as often as is needed if nerves have been damaged and the pain is severe. It is especially useful for crushed toes and for fractures of the upper arm.

Symphytum 6c is the homoeopathic comfrey, and can be given daily whilst the fracture heals.

Bach Flower Remedies

Rescue Remedy should be given initially for the shock. Walnut can be given three times daily to settle patients that find the immobility hard to deal with.

When to consult the vet

Always.

HEAT STROKE

Unfortunately, despite all the warnings about, dogs do still get left in hot cars, and this is the commonest cause of heat stroke. Dogs cannot sweat over their bodies, and so they lose heat by panting and through the pads. When this simple system of heat control is overcome, then the dogs will rapidly heat up, become lethargic and may even collapse. Short-nosed and dark coloured dogs are more prone.

Simple Home Treatments

First aid is to get the animal into shade, and either apply ice packs to the body, place the dog in a cool bath, or ideally run a cold hose over the dog.

A glass of cold water with a teaspoon of salt added can help a lot if your dog will accept it.

Herbs

Chickweed, nettle and peppermint are a cooling combination and a cold infusion can be bathed over the patient as they recover (although there is rarely time to get this ready unless there are many hands available).

Homoeopathy

Belladonna 30c given every five minutes for four doses, then every half hour for two hours is very useful. This is the primary remedy for heatstroke.

Aromatherapy
Lavender and peppermint oils can be added to a cooling bath.

 When to consult the vet
You will need to contact the vet as this can be rapidly fatal, and intravenous fluids may be needed. Overheating, unless due to an obvious cause such as being left in hot car, can be an indication that other problems exist in the patient and so all cases should be taken immediately to the vet for a check over and further treatment as required.

KENNEL COUGH
A common problem each year, kennel cough is caused by a number of bacterial and viral infections that spread rapidly from dog to dog. It is usually self-limiting and will pass in a couple of weeks. There are vaccines that can be given for two of the causative organisms, but it seem these are never the ones involved, and some feel that dogs vaccinated for kennel cough get the other forms much more seriously. This is probably because any vaccine, although it may provide some specific protection, can also compromise the immune system.

 Simple Home Treatments
Natural cough syrups available from most health stores are all right to use in dogs, just give at a child's dose for most animals.

Honey and lemon juice has been used for years to soothe sore throats and coughs. Two tablespoons of honey mixed with a teaspoon of lemon juice in half a cup of water is a very palatable mix that can be given often throughout the day.

Vitamin C at 250mg per day to a 15kg dog (scale up and down) can be given for its antiviral properties, but beware, it can cause diarrhoea in some dogs.

 Herbs
Echinacea and Goldenseal herbs have immune stimulating properties and both can be given to strengthen the immune system. In general the liquid extracts available commercially from health shops or your holistic vet are best.

Mullein is also often available and can be given, especially if the cough sounds congestive.

 Homoeopathy
Kennel cough nosode 30c can be obtained from a good homoeopathic pharmacy and given twice daily to affected dogs with great success, and may be combined with other remedies that may be indicated as well. The nosode is also a useful preventative and many kennels now give it routinely to all dogs in their care weekly to prevent the problem occurring; give it to your dog if she has been in contact with the illness.

Bryonia 30c can be given three times daily to cases where the hard dry cough is set off by any movement.

Drosera 30c can be given to alleviate the spasmodic and incessant cough that has accompanying retching. Dose three times a day.

Veratrum alb 30c twice daily for the continuous violent barking cough.

Aromatherapy
Eucalyptus and Cypress oils dropped into a glass of hot water will perfuse the room and alleviate the cough.

When to consult your vet
Most dogs will suffer the cough with a degree of resignation, but if they become withdrawn, lethargic or develop a temperature then professional help should be sought.

LAMENESS
Whilst arthritis has been partially covered in earlier section – see Arthritis, Claws, and Cysts – lameness can be caused by almost anything that stresses the locomotor system. Landing awkwardly, twisting the foot in a rabbit hole, tearing a nail, cuts to the pad etc. are all possible causes. If the exact problem is not easily defined then some simple remedies can help speed recovery.

Simple Home Treatments
Just like humans, one can use heat and cold to affect the pain. Ice packs using frozen peas, or similar, can be applied to inflamed joints and muscles in the early days after a lameness occurs to reduce swelling. If problems last more than a couple of days heat becomes more appropriate and wheat-filled bags that can be heated in the microwave are useful as they mould to the limb, or alternatively a hot water bottle wrapped in a towel can be applied as often as is needed for relief.

Herbs
As with arthritis my favourite herbs here are the two Indian, or Ayurvedic remedies, Boswellia and Turmeric (see Arthritis for doses).

Celery seed, Meadowsweet and White Willow are also herbs that can be combined in an infusion to reduce pain and inflammation, as well as to eliminate toxins released from damaged tissue.

Devil's Claw Root can be made as a decoction and given as a drink. This is becoming a popular remedy for pain relief and so is often also available over the counter in a ready to use liquid or tablet form.

Homoeopathy
Rhus tox, Ruta grav and Arnica 30c ('Injury Remedy'): this has proven a particularly useful combination of remedies for dogs suffering arthritis, tendon, ligament and muscle problems, including chronic back pain. Although Homoeopathy traditionally adopts a 'one-remedy' approach, there are cases where exact definition of the symptoms is not possible, particularly as we cannot talk to our patients. From time to time good synergistic combinations of remedies are discovered and this is one. Dose twice daily.

Aromatherapy
Lavender, Juniper and Pine can be added to warm water and applied as a compress to inflamed areas.

Eucalyptus, Lavender, Marjoram and Rosemary can be added to massage oils and rubbed into painful areas for relief.

When to consult your vet
Most lameness is temporary and should gradually get better. However, a lameness that persists beyond 3 days without improving generally merits attention.

OWNERS
The commonest cause of disaster is panic: remember ninety per cent of things we worry about never happen. If an accident or problem occurs, take a deep breath and help yourself to four drops of Rescue Remedy to calm the nerves. If feeling weak and shaky some Homoeopathic Aconite from the first aid kit will settle your fears and then you can make the decisions needed. You'll do your pet no favours if you cannot drive properly and have an accident, or you cannot deal rationally with the problem presented. If an emergency, do remember to call the vet before setting out as s/he may not be at the surgery ready to receive the patient otherwise, and on arrival remember s/he has been trained to treat problems and needs space to do so. The patient will come first in a life-threatening situation and the vet may not be able to attend to the owner's concerns until later.

POISONING
Unfortunately an all too common event as dogs do seem to love baited food left around for rats and squirrels; additionally they seem to crave slug bait. If your dog does come into contact with these then veterinary attention is certainly needed, and if you have to use poisons, then make sure there is no way that your pet can access them.

Simple Home Treatments
Your first aid kit (as designed above) will include some washing soda crystals. These are an effective emetic, which means they will make your dog vomit if you place a few crystals on the very back of the tongue. As most poisons are rapidly absorbed from the gut, and certainly quicker than you could get to the vet, it is important to make your pet vomit immediately if she has eaten any poison. Then seek professional advice. Remember to always keep some of the vomit, as most poisons are colour coded, and your vet will be able to identify the class of the drug from that. If you don't have washing soda, a solution of mustard powder can also work in many cases.

Herbs
In cases showing nervous symptoms, skullcap and valerian can calm your pet without masking important signs for the vet.

Homoeopathy
Arsenicum album 30c is the major remedy for poisoning, and should be given three times daily for a few days to all cases, even if they look OK afterwards.

When to consult your vet
Always, and if there are any chronic symptoms left over then seek the advice also of a holistic vet as there is much they can do to help.

ROAD TRAFFIC ACCIDENTS – See Bleeding, Wounds, and Shock sections

SNAKEBITES – see Bites

STINGS – see Allergies and Stings

TEETH

In general, dogs fed on a good diet will have healthy teeth and gums throughout most, if not all, of their life. However, tartar from poor diets, or caused by health problems, can form on teeth leading to gum erosion and decay. This affects binding of teeth into the bony jaw and they may become loose. A dog's jaw action is very strong and so loose teeth can become dislodged and can even fall out. A loose tooth can be painful and should be pulled out if possible, by grasping firmly and giving a quick tug, or by the vet under anaesthetic. Abscesses may also form, and these often present as swelling just in front of, and below, the eye (see Abscess section for remedies). As always, prevention of problems is better than cure and teeth should always be part of the vet's annual health check, so problems can be headed off before they occur. It is always a good idea to get your pet to allow regular examination of the teeth from an early age, and even to allow brushing if you have elected to go for a processed diet. Do not use human toothpaste as this is bad for dogs – special dog toothpastes can be bought from the pet shop.

Sometimes even healthy teeth can become damaged, and slices of enamel can shear off as a result of chewing stones and other hard objects. So long as only the enamel is affected a problem may not occur, but if you can see the underlying dentine then pain can be an issue and treatment is needed.

Herbs

Chamomile tea is a useful wash for sore or injured gums, and if drunk as well calms and soothes the distressed patient.

Homoeopathy

Chamomilla 30c is useful for puppies with teething pain, especially if the pup has started chewing anything and everything. Dose twice daily.

Ulmus fulva 6c four times daily is said to ease gum pain and inflammation.

Fragaria 6c helps with problems created by tartar, given especially after dental work at the vet's. Dose daily for one week a month to prevent tartar in susceptible cases with gum recession.

Hepar sulph 30c is useful if abscess formation occurs around a tooth. Dose twice daily.

Merc viv 30c is useful for relieving gingivitis problems: dose twice daily for a few days as needed.

Aromatherapy

Oil of clove, diluted a few drops into a teaspoon of olive oil and then mixed with baking soda into a paste is a useful topical application to gum and tooth injuries.

Bach Flower Remedies

Walnut and Vervain are two remedies that can be given together and ease the distress of dental pain. Dose a few drops neat, three times daily.

Rescue Remedy, as ever, is a good standby if nothing else is available.

 When to consult your vet
This has been covered above.

THUNDER, LIGHTNING AND FIREWORKS
Many dogs will suffer fear of these events. Often it may be specific to one type, but in most cases all will be feared. Tranquillisers have commonly been used, but these do not allow adaptation to the fear, and so are not a cure long term.

 Simple Home Treatments
Closing the curtains and creating distracting noises such as having the radio or TV on, and playing with your pet all help.

DAPs are useful in many cases, and can be switched on for stressful periods like November and New Year. Start this off a few days before events occur.

 Herbs
Skullcap and valerian can be given as a mild tranquilliser for minor cases.

 Homoeopathy
The only solution I find reliable is the homoeopathic remedy Phosphorous. Usually in a 12c potency and given hourly at first, later as needed. The great thing about this remedy is that it seems to work almost instantly, and with time the dog will often adapt to the fears and learn to cope. Many will even eventually need no treatment, or just a single dose on the evening of fireworks, or as a storm approaches.

 Bach Flower Remedies
Walnut and Mimulus; a few drops given together, neat, is a really useful mix, especially for those cases that anticipate storms coming. It can be given three or four times daily, and can also be given alongside the Phosphorous in particularly sensitive cases. Rock rose is helpful in severe cases as well.

 When to consult your vet
In severe cases tranquillisers are the only solution, and are a last resort.

TRAVEL SICKNESS
Not all dogs will travel happily in cars, and although, for some, it may be sensitivity to movement or to static electricity, more often it is a result of fear created by early experiences. Often a puppy's first trip will be to leave its home, or to go to the vet, where it is prodded, poked and injected. This fear and insecurity can last for life, and so it is a good idea to ensure the breeder has introduced the litter to cars and short journeys as soon as possible in a pup's life; they can then experience the fun of travelling with their litter mates and with their mother, thus never developing the problem. If this has not happened then playing with the pup in the car, feeding there, and lots of short journeys to fun destinations will soon adapt most. For those left with a problem the remedies described below can help.

Simple Home Treatments

Antistatic strips attached to the bumper of your car will often resolve the static sensitive pup.

Herbs

Ginger tablets from the health store are a great stabiliser of nausea, and when given fifteen minutes before a journey will help mild cases get over the problem.

Meadowsweet and peppermint tea is useful if your dog will drink it prior to travelling, and it can be taken in the car to give before the journey back to avoid vomiting then.

Homoeopathy

All the remedies listed are given fifteen minutes before, and just before each journey, stopping once there has been a few successful trips.

Argentum nit 30c, for the dog with fear of being shut in, or which gets diarrhoea with the vomiting.

Gelsemium 30c for fear that is anticipatory – i.e. the case that won't even get in the car.

Pulsatilla 30c for the case that is better for fresh air – i.e. all right if the windows are down.

Tabacum 30c for the dog who seems collapsed as soon as the car moves, and is even wobbly for a while after stopping the journey.

Cocculus 30c for the dog that vomits if it can see out of the window, but is all right if kept on the floor.

Petroleum 30c for dogs that need to keep their head up or else they are sick, and for dogs that are all right in one car, but not another – this is often worse for diesel engines.

Cocculus and Petroleum 30c in combination is a good place to start if you are unsure.

Aromatherapy

Ginger and Peppermint oils can all be dropped onto some tissue and put in the car with the dog to perfuse the car, calming anxiety and nausea.

When to consult your vet

Strong tranquillisers are possible for severe cases for long journeys, but they are not a cure. Some vets will also recommend human anti-seasickness tablets, but generally there is little medically that can be done.

VOMITING

Dogs have a great ability to vomit, usually at the most inconvenient times and in all the awkward places! This is a good thing for a scavenging species as it allows old, 'off' food eaten to be chewed twice and to get a double dose of those important stomach enzymes. However, to us it seems unpleasant and hard to comprehend that it may be 'normal'. So isolated acts of vomiting are not usually a problem, but if blood is seen, if the dog vomits a few times in a day, develops a related diarrhoea, or vomits after each meal and after drinking then attention is needed.

Simple Home Treatments

All cases should be starved for twenty-four hours and then given a bland diet (see Diarrhoea). As before, don't feed an infection.

Pectin, used in jam making, binds to irritant surfaces in the gut and can ease vomiting problems. Give one teaspoon to a Labrador and scale up and down accordingly.

Herbs

Aloe vera juice, one teaspoon three times daily for a Labrador (scale up and down), reduces nausea and pain. Make sure you use the drinking version only.

Liquorice extract, available from health stores or holistic vets, is a favourite for calming inflammation and promoting healing of the stomach walls.

Chamomile, Balm and Meadowsweet herbs combined and made into a tea is also extremely useful, and quite palatable to most dogs who will be thirsty after the loss of fluids. Peppermint tea is also a good anti-nausea therapy.

Slippery Elm tablets, or powder, made into a paste is a useful therapy for sore stomachs, and can be spooned into the dog's mouth if she won't lick it off a spoon.

Homoeopathy

Nux vom 30c is probably the most indicated homoeopathic remedy in vomiting dogs. Dose hourly for four doses then three times daily.

Arsenicum alb 30c is indicated if diarrhoea develops as well (see Diarrhoea).

Phosphorous 30c is indicated to help cases that are extremely thirsty, but vomit back water shortly after drinking. Dose hourly for four doses.

Aethusa 30c can be used for puppies upset by a change of milk, such as when offered cows' milk for the first time, as happens.

Aromatherapy

Peppermint, Melissa and Chamomile are all useful remedies here. Add a few drops to a massage oil base and rub gently into the hairless skin of the abdomen to give relief.

When to consult your vet

If blood is seen, if the dog vomits a few times in a day, develops a related diarrhoea, or vomits after each meal and after drinking, then attention is needed fairly quickly. All puppies that vomit should also be checked for worms as this is a major cause of problems in young dogs.

WOUNDS

Whilst a huge subject that could make up a chapter on its own, simple guidance can go a long way to prevention of problems and to ensure good wound healing. When skin is broken, bacteria and other organisms that inhabit our surroundings can get into the system and cause infection. Creation of wound environments that promote healing, whilst at the same time preventing infection, is the key to this subject and hence the treatments below, some of which are for the wound itself, and others to support and promote the immune system.

Simple Home Treatments

Once bleeding has being controlled or stopped (see Bleeding) then cleaning of the wound is the first priority. Simple solutions of salt water (two teaspoons to a pint of water) can be used to flush away dirt. It is often a good idea to trim away fur from the wound edges, but dip the scissors in some olive oil first so the hair sticks to the scissors rather than gets into the wound. If the wound is dirty then a poultice to draw away infection is indicated. An advantage of these is that they keep the wound moist, this keeps the skin edges supple and supports their healing across the injury, and they reduce pain by relaxing tension of the underlying tissues. Poultices are made by treating the source as detailed below, and then wrapping the result in some linen cloth, before holding onto the wound for ten to fifteen minutes three times daily.

Linseed Meal Poultice: take ground linseed and sprinkle into boiling water until a thin smooth dough is formed. Allow cooling to bearable warmth before applying.

Bread Poultice: a very effective non-irritating poultice made by pouring boiling water onto a few slices of bread, pour off the water after a few minutes and repeat twice, then mash the bread with a fork into a paste. Note: fresh wholemeal bread made with flour that does not contain soya is the only sort that should be used. Be advised that most shop bread does contain soya unless specifically stated otherwise (as in 'one hundred per cent wholewheat flour').

Carrot Poultice: boil organic carrots until they are soft, drain, and mash. Allow cooling to bearable warmth before applying.

In between poultices cover the wound with some ACU Ointment (see Homoeopathy) and keep larger wounds covered with dressings/bandages.

Herbs

Echinacea may be given to support the immune system. I prefer the liquid extract obtainable from health shops, given at the human dose, but scaled according to your dog's bodyweight. Note for most calculations a human dose is based on a 70kg female adult as they spend more on health supplements than men.

Garlic ointment can be used to cover dirty wounds, being antiseptic and antibacterial. As a general rule ointments are better than creams for open wounds as they maintain a moist environment suitable for encouraging healing.

Comfrey, marigold and marshmallow made as a tea and then applied in a compress three times daily is soothing and healing to wounds.

Astragalus root, taken internally, stimulates the immune system, and can be of use in chronically infected wounds. This is obtained from Chinese herbal medicine shops.

Homoeopathy

ACU Lotion, added one teaspoon to a pint of water, can be used to cleanse a wound initially, and also as a general cleanser for long term management of dirty, and all, wounds between dressings and treatments. It is better than salt water for the latter as the salt can be too drying.

Calendula and Hypericum ointment applied twice a day once a wound is clean rapidly promotes healing over of the wound, and has the added advantage of reducing the pain and itching of healing. Never apply this to a dirty wound as it works so fast infection can be sealed in!

Arnica 30c should be given to all cases to reduce swelling and bruising. Dose two or three times daily.

Phosphorous 30c is good for stopping oozing of fresh blood from fresh wounds. Give twice in one hour.

Staphysagria 200c is excellent for the pain and distress of stitched wounds, where the dog becomes focussed on removing the sutures. Dose twice in one day.

Hypericum 30c will relieve the pain of crushing injuries, and is useful in wounds affecting any area, but especially the toes. Dose twice daily.

Hepar sulph 6c can be given three times daily if the area is very painful to touch and the wound is dirty, with infection that needs to be encouraged to discharge. Dose three times daily.

Hepar sulph 30c is useful once the pus has discharged in assisting with clearing up any infection, given three times daily.

Silica 6c helps clear up wounds where there is infection. Often given with the Hepar sulph.

Aromatherapy

Eucalyptus, Frankincense and Lavender are all useful oils and can be dropped into a little water, then soaked into a flannel or gamgee, and applied frequently for ten to fifteen minutes a time, as a compress.

Tea tree oil can be diluted in water and used as a wash to cleanse wounds. Use only one or two drops.

Bach Flower Remedies

Star of Bethlehem will calm a dog that refuses to allow wounds to be attended to. Give a few drops before attending to the wound.

Other treatments

Large wounds do seem to respond well to Magnetic Therapy. More commonly used now by people for their own health, and so a soft flat magnet may be available. If placed over a wound, often bound into the dressing, healing seems to be quicker and less painful.

Lasers are also extremely good at getting non-healing ulcers and extensive wounds to heal, and you may know someone who has one available. For wounds one uses an adaptation of the acupuncture method known as 'circling the Dragon'. The laser light is slowly scanned around the edges of the wound twice daily to encourage the skin cells to grow across the gap and form new skin. Obviously protective eyewear should be worn and avoid shining the laser towards the dog's eyes.

When to consult your vet

Major wounds will need veterinary attention and possible stitching/bandaging. Minor injuries are often treatable at home.

Lastly, never leave an animal in distress. If you are in any doubt at all your vet is the professional trained to treat your pet so do not delay in seeking advice.

Appendix 1

FURTHER READING

Billinghurst, Dr Ian

Give Your Dog A Bone
Grow Your Pups With Bones

Available in UK from Canine Natural Cures (See Useful Addresses)

Elliot, Mark and Pinkus, Tony

Dogs and Homoeopathy, The Owner's Companion

Available from Ainsworth's Homoeopathic Pharmacy (as above)

Lawless, Julia

The Encyclopaedia of Essential Oils,

Published 1992, by Element Books Ltd., Longmead, Shaftesbury, Dorset

Levy, Juliette de Bairacli

The Illustrated Herbal Handbook,

Published 1974, Faber and Faber Ltd.,3 Queen Square,London WC1

The Complete Herbal Handbook for the Dog and Cat,
Published 1955, as above.

Appendix 2

USEFUL ADDRESSES

Please note that addresses and telephone numbers may change

Ainsworths Homoeopathic Pharmacy
36 New Cavendish Street
London W1M 7LH
0207-935-5330
www.ainsworths.com

British Association of Homoeopathic Veterinary Surgeons
Faringdon
Oxon
01367-710324
http://www.bahvs.com/vetmfhom.htm

British Holistic Veterinary Medicine Association
01273-725951
www.bhvma.com/

Canine Health Concern
Box 6943
Forfar
Angus DD8 3WG

Canine Natural Cures
49 Beaumont Road
Surrey CR8 2EJ
020-8668-8011
www.caninenaturalcures.co.uk

Country Mun
Bines Green
Partridge Green
Horsham
West Sussex RH13 8EH
01403-711305
sales@countrymun.com

Dorwest Herbs Ltd
Shipton Gorge
Bridport
Dorset DT6 4LP
01308 897272
info@dorwest.co.uk

Fragrant Earth (for Aromatherapy oils etc.)
Glastonbury
Somerset BA6 9EW
01458-831216
www.fragrant-earth.co.uk

Global Herbs Ltd
Tamarisk House
12 Kingsham Avenue
Chichester
West Susssex PO19 2AN
01243-773363
herbsvet@aol.com
globalherbs.co.uk

Natural Touch Aromatherapy
Holton House
Mayles Lane
Wickham
Hants PO17 5ND
01329-835550
sales@aromatherapyonline.uk.com

The Kennel Club
1 Clarges Street
London W1J 8AB
0870-606-6750
www.the-kennel-club.org.uk/

www.championpets.co.uk for Thornit Ear Powder
also
DW@kensmithcanine.co.uk

Lurchersearch UK for missing dogs
01422-240168/01522-821074/01598-753563
www.lurcher.org/lsuk
also
PetsearchUK
0121-743-4133
pet.searchuk.org.uk

Index